THE SABIAN SYMBOLS:

A Screen of Prophecy

THE SABIAN SYMBOLS:

A Screen of Prophecy

DIANA E. ROCHE

ASTROLOGY CLASSICS
207 VICTORY LANE, BEL AIR MD 21014

The Sabian Symbols: A Screen of Prophecy by Diana E. Roche
© 1998 by Diana E. Roche. All rights reserved. Reprinted 2010.

Information on the Sabian Assembly may be obtained through the Sabian Assembly
web site at http://www.sabian.org.

Cover design by William Roche
Front cover art: La Plume. Zodiac Calendar by Alphonse Mucha. Paris, 1896.
Background: Watermark design featuring hand-pencilled notes of the Sabian symbols
by Marc Edmund Jones. Back cover art: Moravian Teachers' Choir by Alphonse
Mucha. Prague, 1911. (Dover Publications, Inc.)

Text font: Garamond Antiqua
Astrological fonts: Astrolabe Font 1 created by Gary Christen, provided by Astrolabe,
Inc.

ISBN: 978 1 933303 34 5

Published by
Astrology Classics

The publication division of
The Astrology Center of America
207 Victory Lane, Bel Air MD 21014

On the net at www.**AstroAmerica.com**

CONTENTS

Preface

This book is the result of an endeavor to present the Sabian symbols in modern and user-friendly terms while preserving the unique philosophy of Dr. Marc Edmund Jones, the originator of the Sabian symbols and author of *The Sabian Symbols in Astrology*. It is the culmination of four years of struggling day by day with the incredible significance built into each of the symbols.

Having been a member of Marc Jones' Sabian Assembly for 25 years I have been, as he would say, saturated or grooved in his philosophy of dynamic idealism that is at the core of all of his books and the 3,002 lessons he wrote. As I worked with the Sabian symbols through the years, I gradually came to realize that nearly the entirety of his philosophy was summarized in the commentaries that accompany the descriptive images in his book. Unfortunately, the cabalistic and academic structure of his writing is difficult for many readers to understand.

My goal here is to simplify the Sabian symbols for those who are not familiar with Marc Jones' style of writing This volume is not meant to replace *The Sabian Symbols in Astrology*. Rather it is presented as a bridge to his unparalleled contribution to the field of astrological symbolism. If you enjoy this book, and would like to go deeper, I highly recommend that you read or revisit that classic and memorable work.

I have added a few extra features here such as a theme word or phrase that captures the meaning of each symbol. There is also a section called "The Daily Guide" for the astrologer who wishes to work with the Sabian symbol for the sun at sunrise. At the end of each symbol there is another section called "Stepping Stones" that contains a list of keywords to help the reader more easily comprehend the meaning of each symbol.

The original index cards, on which Marc Jones made his hand-pencilled notes, have been reproduced to scale and inserted after each degree title and keyword in the chapter on the symbols. In all but two cases (Libra 18 and Libra 19—which were reversed and corrected just after the session in which they were obtained), the notations on the index cards relating to the signs and degrees have been omitted to save space. It is my hope that the reproduction of these notes will end the controversy that has existed over the years as to whether the descriptive titles in the 1931 mimeograph version (which Marc asked not be used any more) or his 1953 book, *The Sabian Symbols in Astrology*, more accurately reflects his notes on the index cards.

I have followed Marc's lead in not using the personal pronoun "you" in the commentaries (although that word does appear in the Daily Guide section and other chapters). My experience is that it is easier and more appropriate, when applying a symbol to events or others, to read the meaning of each symbol in terms of "the individual" rather than "you." I have also retained the use of the masculine gender (when I felt gender had to be used) rather than struggle with "he" and "she" or try to gender-neutralize the text. So please feel free to "genderize" the book as you wish or feel the need to.

As you work with the Symbols you will soon begin to develop your own personal meanings. The goal of working with the Symbols is to be able to make them your own.

I would like to thank my best friend and husband Bill for designing the cover of this book, and for his incredible patience with me as I struggled through this four-year project.

Finally, I would like to express my profound admiration for Elsie Wheeler, who actualized her potential far beyond what she ever would have dreamed, and my deepest appreciation and respect for Marc Jones and his genius in interpreting the ancient wisdom of these symbolic images.

DIANA ROCHE
Berwyn, Pennsylvania

October 17, 1998

Introduction

For astrologers who work with the Sabian symbols, no description of them is necessary. For those who haven't heard of them until now, they can most easily be described as a set of 360 symbolically descriptive images or vignettes, each of which is accompanied by a keyword and commentary, or interpretation of each image.

The Sabian symbol images can easily be compared to a Rorschach image in that the user is free to make his or her own associations. Each time a symbolic image or commentary is read, the reader seems to pull out just what is required at the moment. The symbols are filters through which a meaning pertinent to a situation, moment or problem can be individually and uniquely intuited and experienced. They can also serve as a "screen of prophecy" in that they "have a rapport with cosmic order that gives them potential signature value every moment of their emergence in attention."[1] Thus, these descriptive images can be prophetic in the sense that they can trigger an inner understanding or awareness of where current events are headed and will end up unless something is done to alter their course.

The first version of the Sabian symbols was a short, typed summary of the 360 vignettes that was distributed among the Los Angeles students of the Sabian Assembly group that Marc had founded three years earlier in California. The reception was enthusiastic and a more fleshed-out mimeograph version was issued as a special astrological lesson set in 1931.[2] Marc shared this version with astrologer Dane Rudhyar and gave him permission to publish them in abridged form in his 1936 book, *The Astrology of Personality*.[3]

In 1953, Marc published his final version of *The Sabian Symbols*. He took the wording for the images from the original hand-pencilled notes he first recorded on 3" x 5" index cards after correcting punctuation and spelling, fleshing out his abbreviations, eliminating several side comments and changing several words. He also revised the keywords he had earlier assigned to the images. He then rearranged the presentation and positioned the opposite degrees side by side in his book to show the inner and outer complementation of the degree symbols. Although his pencilled notes "were never intended to be more than a sort of shorthand memorandum for the creative authorship to follow," Marc lamented that "much of the intuitive force of the initial descriptions was lost" and the requisite genius needed was not available "to get the ideas in the universal form needed for the astrological techniques."[4]

In 1973 Dane Rudhyar published his own final and expanded version of the Sabian symbols in *An Astrological Mandala*.[5] Since that time, several astrologers have written new and different versions of the Sabian symbols.

Marc Edmund Jones, the originator of the Sabian symbols and author of *The Sabian Symbols in Astrology*, had this to say about the Symbols:

> Here are speculative vignettes designed to fall into place in any possible connection of experience or potentiality, and to resist all attempts to use them as statements of direct or specific probability in any sort of mechanical fortunetelling. They have been conceived as a species of poetry, working with the symbolical notations as a catalyst for the creative inspiration and remaining forever fresh and unique in every single instance of their employment.[6]

1

The Origin and History of the Sabian Symbols

On some unrecorded date in 1925, the Sabian symbols were brought into manifestation in the span of a single day in Balboa Park, San Diego, California through the combined efforts of Marc Edmund Jones and Elsie Wheeler.

The story began in 1923 when Marc met Elsie Wheeler. Two sisters, friends of his from Los Angeles, had driven him to a little town in the back country of Orange County to meet her.[1] Elsie had a brilliant and imaginative mind but she was seriously crippled with arthritis and confined to a wheelchair. "She couldn't turn her head and could barely hold her hands."[2] But because of her determination to live independently, she was somehow managing to support herself by making and selling doll clothes. At some point, Marc erected her astrology chart and interpreted it to her in light of her highest potential—totally disregarding her handicap.

Although he suggested that with her special creativity she might develop a new kind of doll, he more correctly foresaw that she would launch something unique that would gain her national recognition.[3] At that time Elsie was afraid of anything psychic. But within a year she had become one of Marc's students, joined a spiritualist church and was making a good living as a medium. She was by her handicap, however, very limited in general world experience, and that limitation would later determine her role in bringing through the Sabian symbols, a set of 360 separate and unique images.

The Early Influence of "Charubel"

At about the same time that Marc met Elsie, he had become interested in the symbolic astrological degrees of a Welsh seer by the name of John Thomas (better known as Charubel). Thomas had obtained his degrees psychically for the basic purpose of helping him rectify the ascendants of horoscopes. Those degrees were published in Alan Leo's *Astro-*

logical Manual No. VIII in 1898 and again by Aries Press as *The Degrees of the Zodiac Symbolised* in 1943. At first, Marc thought of obtaining permission from Thomas to recast the descriptions of the symbols so they would have a more general application. Later he decided that they were too moralized for his purposes, or too "grooved in a single mood—no less objectionable than the older identification as good or bad . . . ."[4] He wanted to create a more universal set of symbols.

The Mesopotamian Connection

Elsie had mentioned several times that she wanted to do something significant. As Marc told it, "She was tired with the average run of questions that she got from her clients. Highly handicapped but happy to use the psychic thing, disappointed to find the low level on which that held her."[5] He had already obtained symbolic degrees for playing cards from an experiment with Zoe Wells, another psychic. He later commented that through his association with Wells he was "only most instinctively if at all aware of a strange genetic tie of some sort back into exceptionally early Mesopotamian or even earlier foundations of human intelligence, into which she more and more pressed me, and with a nascent scientific skepticism I did not take it all too seriously at the time and so there was much that slipped away."[6]

Then one day he had a brainstorm and decided to start fresh with the astrological symbols to see if he could get a series of pictures that would serve his purpose. He thought of working again with Zoe Wells but, as he put it, "She had too wide a vocabulary, too wide an experience of things, so what she got with the playing cards was too generalized, not specific enough." On the other hand, "Elsie Wheeler had very limited experience and so had to have a very limited picture." That was what he wanted. Elsie eagerly agreed to work with him on the project.[7]

The Plan

Marc was certain of how the work had to be done—"in one fell swoop." He later wrote:

> I had to find a place where the conditions would be proper for Elsie Wheeler, through whose consciousness the

laya center in each of the three hundred and sixty cases could get in a picture or situation with meaning in modern and common everyday life, for that one of the Brothers who had the age-old and particular saturation in the true Memphite (earlier Egyptian) schematism from which the zodiac was derived originally, and myself, supplying the especially refined cabalistic training needed for the critical interpretation or rationalization of the relationships at the threshold of a new or atomic age, and so I located a section of Balboa Park, in San Diego, California, where a park lane with little traffic was within feet through a fringe of trees of one of the city's busiest intersections. The whole task had to be completed without any breaking in of any other living entity or the intrusion of any sort of life situation, but here we could sit in a parked car attracting no attention, and yet we were meeting the requirement of natural law itself that this highest of spiritual tasks be framed in a milieu of the most complete possible intensity or turmoil of normal human living or business and personal affairs in the broadest possible intermeshing or superficial conflict.[8]

The Event

Elsie had to be carried and no others could be present, so Marc picked up Elsie and, alone in his car, they drove to Balboa Park. Some time prior to that day, Marc had carefully prepared 360 white, unlined, 3" x 5" index cards for the session by writing one of the astrological degrees on each of the cards. Because he realized there could be interruptions he decided to break up the session into quarters. A quarter of the cards were taken at random for each session and the cards were shuffled continuously during the process. Each card was placed face down before Elsie and "she reported on the picture she saw by inward vision."[9] Neither of them knew which degree was being dealt with during the time she was describing the picture. Marc hurriedly wrote down the brief description on each card as she described the image. The first session took approximately two hours. They took a brief break and another ninety symbols were recorded. "After a drive well into the country, where there was little chance for any intrusion of alien interest, but an opportunity for a pleasant and leisurely noon dinner, the sessions were resumed at the same spot in the park and the other degrees interpreted in a similar fashion."[10]

As Marc later described it, the cards reflect, "the simple few words in which Elsie Wheeler described the picture that she saw in the fleeting seconds that she had to describe it and I had to write the notes down."[11] In his book, *The Sabian Symbols in Astrology*, Marc explained his part in the project:

> The author had three tasks in addition to the physical care of his student sensitive. These were (1) the shuffling which maintained the immediate synchronization with the source material, (2) making pencil notations of the psychic pictures with critical rejection and selection at each point of progress, and (3) sustaining the ancient mind-matrix which made the whole procedure possible. The third task had its expression, in terms of any human experience to be captured in words, through the presence and co-operation on the invisible side of life of that one of the Brothers (to use the term by which he would be identified in Theosophy) who has been concerned in every spiritistic phase of Sabian investigation.[12]

After the entire session had been completed, Marc felt that one of the symbols seemed wrong and he made a correction by having Elsie do that particular one over again. In doing so, it occurred to him that he could have cooperation from the other end, and so he asked Elsie, "Is so-and-so there?" She answered that he was. He then asked, "What is he doing?" Elsie responded, "Standing with his arms folded." Marc then said, "Ask him why he didn't correct that." and Elsie responded, "He says that is up to you." When Marc reflected on this episode later, he remarked that this was correct because he was in time and space and the Brother was not.[13]

At another time, Marc mentioned that during the session with Elsie "something destructive got in . . . 'A large disappointed audience'; 'An automobile wrecked by a train' . . . that at the time I didn't realize were the destructive sort of things that I didn't want. And with no sense that it would be possible to reestablish the connection that I had originally, I decided to leave them but describe them as inverted or destructive or negative and interpret them in the same way."[14]

The pictures or images that Elsie Wheeler saw evidently came from many sources. According to Marc, "Some were directly out of her own experience, or as she reached out to take them from other minds directly available to her. Some were beyond her range of comprehension and were impressed upon her consciousness, and so were received in distorted fashion or with an overlay of detail which had to be screened out." But his admiration and appreciation of her contribution was evident. He wrote in his book, "As events have shown, her total contribution was an exceptional achievement and this one of the author's volumes is dedicated to her memory, in the hope that it may in time become a monument to the beauty of her character and the immortal quality of her ideals."[15]

Early Work on the Sabian Symbols

After the session, Marc put the cards away in a trunk, thinking that this type of work was too far afield from the kind of scientific work in which he was interested.[16] He later commented that "when I got all through [with the project] I discovered the structure [in the Sabian symbols] and worked out all the interrelations. That was an order that I found there but was not looking for. That was gratuitous, serendipity."[17]

Because some of his students were concerned about the fact that he had said it would not be possible to reestablish the original connection, he decided to write them up as a typescript for them to use. That version expanded the description of the images and included a little story or vignette with each image. The initial response was so encouraging that he worked out the mathematical structure that he had discovered in them and put the whole thing together as a mimeographed astrological lesson series entitled *Symbolical Astrology*. He later became disenchanted with this version, however, as he felt he had done precisely what he sought to avoid—moralize the symbols in terms of the "white-Anglo-Saxon culture of [his] upbringing."[18] And he became so disenchanted with that version that he asked his students not to use it.

In preparation for a book publication of the Sabian symbols, Marc created a new version in 1948, but he felt that the original intuitive force of the initial descriptions had been lost and so he put the project aside until 1951.[19]

The Sabian Symbols in Astrology

After going back to the original, brief, pencilled descriptions and reworking the commentary and formula for two years, he published his "official" and last version of the symbols as *The Sabian Symbols in Astrology*. In his foreword, he describes the book as "the fruition, for the present lifetime of its author, of a project in astrological research which has occupied him for more than three decades."[20]

He also gave tribute in his book to Dane Rudhyar, saying he, "more than any other one person, was responsible for the initial popularization of these degree interpretations, virtually compelling the organization of the project on a scale sufficient to make publication possible."[21] It was shortly after Marc published the 1931 mimeographed version of the Sabian symbols that Rudhyar became interested in his work. Marc described their association as follows:

> The Sabian Symbols happened to fascinate Dane Rudhyar and I gave him permission to present them in the frame of, in his way today of explaining it, his different or "special social psychology and abstract philosophy" and in his abridgment they gave a redoubled indication of their validity. His *Astrology of Personality* and articles in the magazines at the time were very largely responsible for bringing my contribution out in the open or to first broad public notice. He however has never been a member of the Sabian Assembly or in any real sense a student of mine, but always has been his own man very completely, and this makes the current development all the more significant. In his new book that has just by several days come to my hand from his with a warm autograph, *An Astrological Mandala: The Cycle of Transformations and Its 360 Symbolic Phases*, he explains this later contribution of his on the dust jacket as "A reinterpretation of the Sabian symbols, presenting them as a contemporary American I CHING." In other words from a different worker in the cosmic vineyard is a variant establishment of what we identify as the screen of prophecy and one that under the circumstances is remarkable testimony to the universal Sabian depth."[22]

The Sabian symbols are a fascinating, powerful and useful set of images for the astrologer and nonastrologer alike. The images, themselves have been the subject of quite a number of new commentaries. Indeed, Marc himself wrote "the Sabian symbols are a fact and they may be examined or employed by anybody who wishes. They have entered the realm of common reality and become subject to the universal logic of man's mind."[23] What should be is.

Today

Many students of the Sabian Assembly and others are presently writing and working on various projects with the Sabian symbols. If you would like more information on the Sabian symbols or the Sabian Assembly, please write the author in care of the publisher or you can send an e-mail from the Sabian Assembly web site on the internet at http://www.sabian.org.

2

Methods and Techniques

The Sabian symbols can be used by astrologers and nonastrologers alike. Astrologers frequently use the Symbols to deepen their understanding or expand the meanings of how the planets, cusps and Arabian parts function in a particular chart. Most commonly, the symbols are used to interpret the sun, moon and ascendant in a chart, but they can also be used to interpret any degree in a chart. When reading a symbol for a particular planet it is important not to read it in isolation. Rather, the symbol should be filtered through the meaning of the specific planet involved. Thus the symbol for the degree of the sun would be interpreted in light of the individual's *purpose* in life. The Sabian keywords for the planets are:

SUN	Purpose
MOON	Feeling
MARS	Initiative
VENUS	Acquisitiveness
MERCURY	Mentality
JUPITER	Enthusiasm
SATURN	Sensitiveness
URANUS	Independence
NEPTUNE	Obligation
PLUTO	Obsession

Determining Which Degree to Use

In deciding which Sabian symbol to use it is necessary to consider both the degree and minutes of the position of a planet, cusp or Arabian part. The method used by both Marc Jones and Dane Rudhyar was to read the next higher degree if a planet had reached at least the one minute mark of a degree. "When consideration is given to moving bodies, as in astrological progressions or directions, the indication is to be seen as in full force from the crossing of any 1' point to the arrival at the threshold of the next 1'."[1] The steps to determine the correct symbol to use are as follows:

1.   If the position of a planet, cusp or part is at an even degree (for example, 26° Leo 00'), read the Sabian symbol for that degree (26 Leo).

2.   If the position of a planet, cusp or part is at least one minute over an even degree (for example 26° Leo 01' or 26° Leo 02') read the Sabian symbol for the next higher degree (27 Leo).

3.   If the position of a planet, cusp or part is over 29 degrees and 01 minute, it is read as 30 (for example, 29° Leo 01' is read as 30 Leo).

4.   There is no 0 degree of anything in the Sabian symbols. The symbols are written for degrees 1-30 of each of the twelve signs.

5.   If a planet, cusp or part is exactly at the zero degree point of a sign, and it hasn't yet reached the one minute mark, then round down to 30 of the previous sign. For example, 00° Leo 00' would be rounded down to 30 Cancer. Likewise, 00° Leo 00' 59" would be read as 30 Cancer. Round up to the first degree of the next sign if a planet is at zero degrees and at least one full minute (for example, 00° Leo 01' would be read as 1 Leo).

Transiting Planets

The Sabian symbols can also be used to interpret the degree of transiting planets. These degree readings are most dynamic when any transiting planet reaches its zodiacal place in a natal chart or is situated directly opposite its natal position (within 1 to 1-1/2 degrees of exactness), and particularly by station retrograde or direct. They also measure the critical points in history for all people collectively.

Chart Angles

The late Dane Rudhyar used a technique for looking at any astrological chart in terms of the what, whereto, how and why of our lives by using the Sabian symbol for the degrees on the angles of a chart.[2] Using this method, the ascendant, descendant, nadir and midheaven are examined in the following manner:

ASCENDANT: (What) - What is the nature and meaning of the situation?

DESCENDANT: (Whereto) - Where is this situation leading? What kind of result can be expected? What is the potential?

NADIR: (How) - How can this issue, situation or goal best be handled to successfully accomplish the goal?

MIDHEAVEN: (Why) - What is the essential goal or purpose in this current struggle or cycle of development?

New and Full Moons

The Sabian symbols can also be used for New and Full Moon interpretations. The symbol for the degree of the New Moon (inauguration) will often describe the new cycle of events, reveal the best way to start new projects, approach your goal, promote your ideas, develop your plan and identify new opportunities. The symbol for the degree of the Full Moon (culmination) will often describe how the current cycle will end or help you determine the most effective way to achieve your objective and finalize or wrap up what you started under the New Moon.

The Sabian Symbol at Sunrise

The degree of the sun at sunrise represents the "passing frame for self-realization and practical self-assertion."[3] This translates to the "flavor of the day" in terms of maximizing your potential and gaining self-understanding. The sunrise symbol reflects the objective side of things—outer events, interactions with others, etc. You may frequently find the day's events reflected in a Sabian symbol or you may find that you can understand the significance of some situation or event in terms of the symbolic meaning of the Sabian symbol for the day.

In order to determine the Sabian symbol for the day you must first calculate the astrological sign and degree for the sun at sunrise at your own geographical location. Next, look up the Sabian symbol for that degree, according to the method described above for rounding up or down, or using that exact degree if the one minute mark hasn't yet been reached (for example, for 26° Leo 00', read 26 Leo).

Because there are 365 days in a year, but only 360 symbols, there will naturally be some days in which the same symbol will rule (or hold over) for two consecutive days. Contrariwise, it will also be discovered that there are a few days in which the sun is just leaving a degree at dawn on one day, and by dawn the next day it has traveled completely through the following degree and entered the next degree. Thus one of the degrees is skipped.

The Sabian symbols that hold over for two consecutive days, and those that are skipped, are not always the same each year. Further, although most of the Sabian symbols appear on the same day each year, there is some variation from year to year. For this reason, it is necessary to calculate the symbols for your specific location for each day, every year, if you wish to work with the symbols in this manner. It should also be noted that the symbols that are skipped or hold over may not be the same at different latitudes. For example, while 8 Taurus may be the symbol that holds over for two days in Washington, DC, it may be that 7 Taurus is the symbol that holds over for two days in Miami, Florida. It is the latitude that determines the symbol for the sun at sunrise. For those who would like to use this technique, there is at least one computer program on the market that will calculate the degrees for the year and other astrological programs that will calculate a chart for sunrise.

The Sabian Symbol at Moonrise

The Sabian symbols can also be used for the time of moonrise, following the same steps to determine the degree for the sun. The symbol for moonrise reveals the "rhythm for the emotional side of the self and the momentary framework for every fresh adventure in self-discovery."[4] The moonrise symbol reflects the subjective side of things—emotions, opinions, memory and attitudes.

Chart Rectification

The Sabian method focuses primarily on the *ascendant plus the part of fortune* for chart rectification. Since the position of the part of fortune moves whenever the ascendant is moved, the astrologer using the Sabian symbols can take both degrees into account on the basis of their mutual suggestiveness.[5] The horizon at the instant of an individual's birth "becomes the ascendant of the astrological chart and so the mathematical representation of the *nascent personality*. "It is in this fashion that an individual is framed in a pattern of illimitable generalizations, derived from all human experience, for the sake of a particular and detailed psychological examination."[6] Thus the personality of the individual should be reflected by the Sabian symbol for the degree on the ascendant.

Horary Charts

The Sabian symbols can also be used very effectively when examining a horary chart, using the guidelines above.

The Astrological Formula

The astrological formula set forth in *The Sabian Symbols in Astrology*[7] is probably the feature most neglected by the casual reader of that book. Although I myself prefer to work primarily with the five-degree sets (explained in more detail below), the Sabian formula can deepen the understanding of any symbol in terms of its placement by sign and degree. I have therefore summarized the basic elements of Marc Jones' formula on the following pages:

POLARITY

POSITIVE	NEGATIVE
(Manipulating and Extensional)	*(Sustaining and Intensive)*
High potentiality out of control.	Effectiveness of impact by a catalytic rather than a direct influence.

Fire and Air		Water and Earth	
Aries	Libra	Cancer	Capricorn
Leo	Aquarius	Scorpio	Taurus
Sagittarius	Gemini	Pisces	Virgo

QUADRATURE

CARDINAL	FIXED
Critical	*Ideal*
• Problems of challenge to self	• Quickening to pertinent meanings and values
• Direct call to specific action	• Concerned more with ideas than facts involved in any immediate issue
• Rejection of mediating factors	• Subjective mediation

Aries Cancer Libra Capricorn   Taurus Leo Scorpio Aquarius

COMMON

Practical

- Calls for adjustment to
others or relationships
with them in meeting a
need to mediate all experience in social terms (utilize
the culture and develop
resources of a civilization)

Gemini Virgo Sagittarius Pisces

TRIPLICITY

FIRE

Original

- Creative self-adequacy at
root
- Indomitable spontaneity
- Rising to an immediate
occasion (Cardinal)
- Ideal stimulating (Fixed)
- Socially eager (Common)

Aries Leo Sagittarius

EARTH

Efficient

- Gift for holding things in
the given reality
- Characteristically human
genius for continuing on
under handicaps (Cardinal)
- Human genius for self-realization in the midst of outside pressure (Fixed)
- Human genius for personal
exaltation of fundamen-
tally social potentials
(Common)

Taurus Virgo Capricorn

AIR	WATER
Ingenious	*Universal*

- Resourcefulness in improving a present situation (Cardinal)
- Adjusting to the conception of a present situation (Fixed)
- Sharing the fruits of a present situation (Common)

- Illimitable perspective in simple directness (Cardinal)
- Unlimited spread of associative ideas in memory (Fixed)
- Broadest possible awareness of personal relations or social responsibility (Common)

Gemini Libra Aquarius

Cancer Scorpio Pisces

FIRST AND SECOND HALVES OF SIGNS

1 - 15 DEGREES

Specializing

(Objective and to the point)

- Close
- Sharper implication
- Vicarious
- Specific

16 - 30 DEGREES

Generalizing

(Subjective and cumulative, or indirect)

- Remote
- Fuzzier implication
- Imaginative
- General

FIVE DEGREE UNITS OF EACH HALF SIGN

FIRST FIVE DEGREES	SECOND FIVE DEGREES
(1-5 AND 16-20)	(6-10 and 21-25)
Physical	*Social*

LAST FIVE DEGREES

(11-15 and 26-30)

Spiritual

The Hidden Genius of the Formula

Perhaps the most fascinating of all the aspects of working with the astrological formula is the *Fivefold Dimension of Self-Expression.*[8] For the astrologer working with the Sabian symbols at sunrise on a daily basis, there is the extra-dimensional genius of watching each five degree set in a sign unfold within the meanings of five of the astrological aspects, or the conjunction, opposition, trine, square and quintile. Starting with the first degree of each sign, the degrees are grouped in sets of five each, or 1-5, 6-10, 11-15, 16-20, 21-25 and 26-30. The first degree of each set (1, 6, 11, 16, 21, and 26) corresponds to the conjunction. The second degree of each set (2, 7, 12, 17, 22 and 27) corresponds to the opposition. The third degree of each set (3, 8, 13, 18, 23 and 28) corresponds to the trine. The fourth degree of each set (4, 9, 14, 19, 24 and 29) corresponds to the square. The fifth degree of each set (5, 10, 15, 20, 25 and 30) correspond to the quintile.

Accordingly, the first degree of a sign is the beginning of a new five day cycle. The second degree often brings opposition and awareness of what's happening or what has to be dealt with. The third degree brings momentum to what began on the first day of the cycle, and things can often seem overwhelming or demanding. The fourth degree can bring struggle and limitations that require effort and ingenuity to overcome.

The fifth degree is the culmination, and it reflects the genius of the potential indicated in the first degree of the cycle. Marc Jones' fivefold dimension of self-expression, the last part of his astrological formula, is as follows:

FIVEFOLD DIMENSION OF SELF-EXPRESSION

ONE

Experimental

(Naive and first outreaching in any or all experience.)

CONJUNCTION: *Emphasis*

TWO

Sensitive

(Reality is faced or stood against.)

OPPOSITION: *Awareness*

THREE

Receptive

(Responsiveness to potentials of being, together with a willingness to permit the flow of self into every realization of life's real complementation of a personal identity.)

TRINE: *Momentum*

FOUR

Responsible

(Reliability of man's conscious awareness of his state, ability to measure it's potentialities and attack its problems.)

SQUARE: *Construction*

FIVE

Inspired

(After each five-degree cycle, the individual, at
first concerned over his outreach into the separation of self-reality, is now turned back to the
cosmic certainty in which he finds himself in
union and partnership with the overall fact of
existence.)

QUINTILE: *Talent*

(the *genius* of the cycle)

Divinatory Techniques

Framing the Question: Everyone, even the nonastrologer, can use the
Sabian symbols to gain insight into a problem or situation. Framing the
question properly is the foundation of success in using any divinatory
technique. Open-ended or broadly-framed questions are always preferred
to a question that requires a simple yes or no answer. For instance, a
question that asks, "What will be the result if I accept this job offer?" will
give a fuller and more useful answer than "Should I accept this job offer?"
Writing your question down can help you frame your question more
effectively. It also preserves it, in case you can't remember exactly what
you asked.

    If you decide to use a method that assigns a number to each of the
360 Sabian symbols, instead of determining the symbol by sign and
degree, the table below can help you find the symbol that matches the
number.

Aries	1-30	Cancer	91-120
Taurus	31-60	Leo	121-150
Gemini	61-90	Virgo	151-180
Libra	181-210	Capricorn	271-300
Scorpio	211-240	Aquarius	301-330
Sagittarius	241-270	Pisces	331-360

Examples: 181 Libra is Libra 1; 209 is Libra 29; 33 is Taurus 3; 130 is Leo 10.

Some of the more common techniques used to derive a Sabian symbol are given below:

Calculator Method: Frame your question. Then concentrate on it while randomly punching five, single-digit numbers into a calculator. Divide the total sum of these numbers by 360. Round up anything over .5 to the next number. Round off anything under .5 and use the number to the left of the decimal point. For example, 180.84 would be read as 181, or Libra 1, while 180.36 would be read as 180, or Virgo 30.

Mental Focus: Frame your question and write it down or hold it in consciousness. Mentally relax and wait until one number from 1-360 (or an astrological sign and degree) forms in your mind. Record that number or sign and degree and read the Sabian symbol description for that answer.

Drawing Slips: Number small slips of paper from 1-360. Place these 360 slips in a container such as a bag, box or bowl and without looking, draw one of them. Find the correct Sabian symbol for that number from the table above and read the description for that symbol. Another method is to use two containers. Take 42 small slips of paper. Write one of each of the astrological signs on 12 of the slips and place them in one container. Number the remaining slips from 1-30 and place them in the other container. After framing your question, focus on it while drawing one slip from each container. Read the Sabian symbol for the sign and degree you have drawn.

Using a Clock: Using a technique similar to horary astrology, note the time a question arises in your mind. Use the time your question arose to determine the Sabian symbol. The hours (1-12) represent the astrological signs. The minutes (30 in each half of the clock) represent the degrees. Moving clockwise, the minutes from 12 to 6 represent the degrees from 1-30. The minutes from 6 to 12 also represent the degrees from 1-30. You never use anything over 30.

You do not need to consider whether it is AM or PM. For example, both 6:36 AM and 6:36 PM equate to Virgo 6.

By way of further explanation, *it makes no difference whether you subtract the minutes (degrees) from the next hour (sign), as in 24 minutes before 7:00 (Libra), or simply start counting from 1-30 again at the 6 on the bottom of the clock and count the minutes past the 6.* For example, the time 6:36, or Virgo 6 (i.e., six minutes past the 6 at the bottom of the clock), is the same as saying it's 24 minutes (or degrees) before 7:00 (Libra). If you subtract 24 degrees from Libra you still end up with Virgo 6. The result is the same.

To assist the nonastrologer, the signs are numbered below:

1 Aries	2 Taurus	3 Gemini
4 Cancer	5 Leo	6 Virgo
7 Libra	8 Scorpio	9 Sagittarius
10 Capricorn	11 Aquarius	12 Pisces

Using Dice: For those who like to use dice in divination, various game stores sell 30-sided and 12-sided dice that can be used to derive a Sabian symbol. Use the 12-sided die to derive the astrological sign and the 30-sided die to derive the degree.

Using Playing Cards: If you like the feel of cards, you can make yourself a Sabian symbol card deck. You will need 42 cards to work with. A set of blank cards can be ordered from one well-known card company. In this case, you can either write the astrological sign or draw the glyph for each sign on one of each of 12 cards. Then write the numbers from 1-30 on the remaining 30 cards. If you have a computer, you can also use clip art for the signs and numbers. Simply cut out the printed images and glue them to each card. It is recommended, if you use this method, that you also laminate or cover each card with self-adhering plastic film so your images won't curl and disturb your shuffling. Images can also be printed directly on self-adhering, clear labels and placed on the cards. If you would rather use a regular deck of playing cards, you can also do that and save yourself some time and labor. Dane Rudhyar first suggested this method; however, I prefer to use the Paul Foster Case assignment of suits for the cards and seasons and have used Case's assignment below for this technique.

First, remove the ace through the ten of spades from a regular deck of playing cars. They won't be used. Next, separate out all 12 face cards and place them in one stack. Then separate out the ace through the ten of hearts, diamonds and clubs and place them in a second stack. You now have two stacks (or packs)—12 face cards in pack #1 and 30 cards (1-10 of the hearts, diamonds and clubs) in pack #2. The astrological signs are assigned to the face cards, and the degrees are assigned to the numbered cards, in the following manner:

K Clubs (Spring)	Aries
Q Clubs (Spring)	Taurus
J Clubs (Spring)	Gemini
K Hearts (Summer)	Cancer
Q Hearts (Summer)	Leo
J Hearts (Summer)	Virgo
K Spades (Fall)	Libra
Q Spades (Fall)	Scorpio
J Spades (Fall)	Sagittarius
K Diamonds (Winter)	Capricorn
Q Diamonds (Winter)	Aquarius
J Diamonds (Winter)	Pisces

Clubs:	1-10
Hearts:	11-20
Diamonds:	21-30

Journals and Scrapbooks: When working with the Sabian symbols, it can be helpful, as well as fun, to keep a journal or scrapbook for photos, newspaper clippings or other pictures that help explain the way a symbol manifested or that captured the essence of a symbol.

Using Your Imagination: The key to effective divination is to use a method that feels natural and comfortable. And you can always use your imagination to invent your own Sabian symbol generator. Those who are talented in computer programming may prefer to write their own code to randomly generate a sign and degree. You can also carve the signs and degrees on gemstones, paint them on chopsticks or close your eyes, randomly open the book and put your finger on a symbol. Be creative and experiment.

3

The Sabian Symbols in Practical and Everyday Use

Cycles

Everything in life, from a sneeze to a career, has a cycle. And there are countless cycles within cycles. Like the *I Ching*, the Sabian symbols can help you determine where you are in a cycle. Symbols are actual facts of reality that allow you to bring diversity into pattern through mind. In a practical sense, the recognition of a symbol may be all that you need to solve a difficult problem or understand a confusing situation. For this reason, the astrologer may find it useful to use the Sabian symbols when working with progressed planets as well as natal planets.

Signatures

Symbols can also act as signatures, or intuitive indications that can help you understand situations and events. One of the events that I have learned to pay particular attention to, in working with the Sabian symbol at sunrise, is when the symbol for the sun holds over—or is the same for two days in a row. One such event happened in 1996 when 21 Taurus, "A finger pointing in an open book" was the symbol for the sun on both the 10th and 11th of May in Washington, D.C., the capital of our country and location for working with events on a national level. This symbol suggests a need to follow rules and verify information. It also alludes to a need to rectify some situation. On May 11th, the sun moved into 22 Taurus shortly after sunrise. I have come to anticipate that the symbol holding over for the sun at sunrise for two consecutive days acts as a background to some event that will be reflected by the Sabian symbol for the degree the sun next moves into, sometime during the second day. The Sabian symbol for 22 Taurus is "White dove over troubled waters." One of the things that this symbol can indicate is that there is a problem of some kind, or that trouble is brewing. It can also indicate complacency or obliviousness to imminent danger. On May 11th, ValuJet flight 592 took off from Miami, Florida and, minutes later, crashed in the Everglades about 17 miles northeast of Miami. One hundred and ten people died in the crash. Those who saw film footage of a similar plane said it looked strikingly like a dove.

A year later ValuJet reported it had evidence that a maintenance contractor who was anxious to pass an inspection by a potential client deliberately mislabeled oxygen canisters to get them off the shop floor in Miami. The canisters that should have been in specially-designed boxes with safety brackets and hazardous material labels were reported to have been moved to unmarked cardboard boxes and intentionally described on a manifest as "empty canisters." Those same canisters wound up as cargo on Flight 592. Federal investigators believed they somehow exploded and caused the deadly crash. The "finger pointing in an open book" was the background. The "white dove over troubled waters was the event. Rules weren't followed and a dangerous situation was completely ignored. The white dove fell.

Literal Interpretations

The Sabian symbol for the day can sometimes be quite literal. On April 23, 1996 the Sabian symbol for the sun at sunrise was 4 Taurus, "The rainbow's pot of gold." That same day there were two major news stories. One of the New York subway robbers who was shot by "subway vigilante" Bernard Goetz was awarded $43 million dollars by the jury in his personal injury case against Goetz. The other major news story concerned the exorbitant prices paid by bidders at a Sotheby's auction for clothing and other personal articles owned by Jacqueline Kennedy Onassis.

Astrological Charts

The Sabian symbol for the sun in an individual's chart can also be quite revealing. Remember that the sun represents *purpose*. Eva "Evita" Peron's sun was at 15° Taurus 46'. The Sabian symbol for her sun is 16 Taurus, "An old man attempting vainly to reveal the Mysteries." This symbol indicates a need to share the deepest part of self, and it frequently points to feelings of inadequacy and personal failure. Evita rose from impoverished obscurity as Eva Duarte, the illegitimate daughter of a married rancher and his cook/mistress in a small village in Argentina, to become an actress, mistress of a series of powerful men and, finally, the wife of Argentine dictator Juan Peron and acclaimed "saint" of the poor. Throughout her short life her insecurity was evidenced by her lavish expenditures for fine jewels and clothing and her insatiable need for recognition and adulation. Her purpose thus may be described in terms of her striving to be understood and recognized for her inner worth. Unfortunately, she chose the path of many individuals who overcompensate for their feelings of inferiority by surrounding themselves with material objects that represent outer achievement.

The ascendant in a chart represents the nascent personality and how society in general perceives the individual. It also provides insight into the individual's psychological struggle to establish his own unique identity. The Sabian symbol for Evita's ascendant is 28 Aries, "A large disappointed audience." This symbol dramatically reflects her fear of losing her popularity with the people of Argentina if she did not give them what they wanted and expected—a fear that was likely exacerbated in 1947 when, as Argentina's emissary, she bungled her way through Spain and several other European countries making one diplomatic *faux pas* after another.

The moon in a chart represents *feeling*, unconditioned responsiveness and emotions. It is inner and subjective. The Sabian symbol for Evita's moon is 21 Leo, "Chickens intoxicated." Marc Jones described this degree in his *Sabian Symbols* book as "a symbol of the inevitable distress of the human soul whenever it seeks stimulation from elements essentially alien to its own nature, dramatized in the reversed symbolism by the futility of a dependence on physical agency for spiritual results."

Perhaps Evita's greatest talent was her ability to motivate and inspire the public, particularly *los descamisados*, or the poor and shirtless ones. The theme in this book for 21 Leo is "Making Use of What You Have." This symbol focuses on transforming stumbling blocks into stepping stones. "What cannot be eliminated from the self must be used and glorified." Evita is a classic example of making use of what you have. After marrying Juan Peron, she capitalized on her poor and illegitimate origins at every opportunity, reminding the public over and over that "I am one of you." She took from the rich and gave to the poor and even held public lotteries where she sometimes gave away houses. When she died from cancer, at the young age of 33, the public went into national mourning and Evita was elevated to secular sainthood by her adoring and devastated public.

Subtlety

Sometimes the underlying significance of the Sabian symbols can be more subtle. One evening several years ago I was working on 20 Capricorn, "A hidden choir singing." An exposé on nursing home abuse was unfolding in the background on television. The interviewees had their faces blocked with those strange, aggregated little squares that are used to protect people who don't want their identities known. As I squinted and looked through my eyelashes to get a better look at these anonymous whistle-blowers, I suddenly understood this symbol in more practical terms. The hidden choir singing could also refer to those people who dare to "sing out" the truth about situations that need to be corrected but prefer to do it anonymously.

Divination

The Sabian symbols can also be used for divination, or to obtain a preview of coming events. As frequently happens, the members of one particular group had been struggling with issues revolving around its purpose and how the group should be functioning. The group was dividing itself into little camps and there had been more than a few personality clashes. The air was charged with apprehension as the group prepared to gather the coming weekend in the country for an informal affair. The question on everyone's mind was whether the individuals in the group would be able to overcome their personal differences and enjoy the occasion or go at it hammer and tongs. A Sabian symbol was randomly selected by one of the methods described in the chapter on techniques and the question posed: "What will be our experience when the group gathers this weekend?" The Sabian symbol derived was 17 Leo, "A nonvested church choir." The keyword for this symbol is "Communion." The theme concept for this symbol is "Cooperation," and the symbol itself speaks to the value of informal or unregimented group experience in learning cooperation and respect for personality. It also alludes to fellowship and a sense of community, group functioning in the absence of official rules and regulations, an exercise in self-discipline, and respect for the rights, contributions and idiosyncrasies of others. The opportunity in this symbol is found in learning to respect and appreciate difference—of opinion, personality and choice.

Whether it was self-fulfilling prophecy or a screen of prophecy, the promise of the Sabian symbol came to fruition. For the first time in years the group was able to confront their issues calmly and in practical, everyday terms. Despite a few strained moments, the group not only managed to avoid open confrontation but managed to make progress in resolving their differences and seeing things from the others' points of view. A communion of sorts had been achieved. The healing of the group had begun.

4

Negative or Reversed Symbols

No discussion on the practical use of the Sabian symbols would be complete without considering the "negative" or "reversed" symbols. Despite the best efforts of Marc Jones to keep out images that were moralized, or presented as essentially good or evil in their own nature, he labeled twenty-seven of the images as negative, in the sense that they portray tragedy and ill luck, such as 'An automobile wrecked by a train" and "A large disappointed audience." The way he approached his commentaries on these images was to present them as lessons in learning, and so he gave suggestions to the reader on how to handle these types of situations in a more productive manner. These negative, or reversed, symbols and their keywords are listed below:

Aries 13	An unsuccessful bomb explosion	*Impetuousness*
Aries 28	A large disappointed audience	*Disjunction*
Taurus 5	A widow at an open grave	*Reorientation*
Taurus 7	A woman of Samaria	*Awakening*
Taurus 16	An old man attempting vainly to reveal the mysteries	*Pertinacity*
Taurus 20	Wind clouds and haste	*Exaltation*
Gemini 8	An industrial strike	*Protest*
Gemini 10	An airplane falling	*Crisis*
Gemini 21	A labor demonstration	*Representation*
Gemini 28	A man declared bankrupt	*Deliverance*
Cancer 2	A man suspended over a vast level place	*Contemplation*
Cancer 5	An automobile wrecked by a train	*Dispersion*
Leo 1	A case of apoplexy	*Irresistibility*
Leo 2	An epidemic of mumps	*Infection*
Leo 8	A Bolshevik propagandist	*Leaven*
Leo 21	Chickens intoxicated	*Accentuation*
Leo 24	An untidy, unkempt man	*Imperturbability*
Libra 16	A boat landing washed away	*Respite*

Libra 18	Two men placed under arrest	*Consequence*
Libra 19	A gang of robbers in hiding	*Divergence*
Scorpio 2	A broken bottle and spilled perfume	*Permeation*
Scorpio 21	A soldier derelict in duty	*Deviation*
Sagittarius 13	A widow's past brought to light	*Rectification*
Capricorn 2	Three stained-glass windows, one damaged by bombardment	*Commemoration*
Aquarius 3	A deserter from the navy	*Defiance*
Aquarius 21	A woman disappointed and disillusioned	*Clearance*
Pisces 2	A squirrel hiding from hunters	*Caution*

Aries

♈

ARIES 1 A woman rises out of water, a seal rises and embraces her. KEYWORD: *Realization*

[handwritten] A woman rises out of water. A seal rises and embraces her

THEME: *The Way to Begin is to Begin.* This symbol speaks to birth, emergence and taking the first, faltering and naive steps on any journey. It also speaks to the stirring from within that signals the realization of potential and the possibilities of growth. The image, a woman rises out of water, a seal rises and embraces her, depicts the feminine, emotional and receptive or passive side of man embraced by the masculine, purposeful and initiating or active side of himself. This image also symbolizes the human spirit embraced by desire. The emphasis here is on the achievement of self-integration or that mystical union of all the elements of self. On a practical level, this image represents the first degree of the zodiac and thus spring, the beginning of a new cycle and freedom of choice. It also marks the starting point of the journey of self-discovery. Positive: At its highest, this symbol represents independence, initiative and openness to new experience. Negative: Willfulness or lack of discrimination.

TODAY: The accent is on change and new beginnings. You may be feeling bored, restless or lonely, or that something is missing in your life. Adventure beckons like the sweet scent of lilacs on a gentle spring wind. The novel and different have a special allure.

Opportunity: Your greatest advantage lies in being sensitive to what it is that you really need. Take a broader look at the options available to you, window shop and pay close attention to timing.

Risk: Guard against rashness and hasty decisions or making irrevocable commitments. Avoid jumping from the frying pan into the fire or being headstrong and stubborn in relationships with others.

STEPPING STONES: Birth, new beginnings, growth, self-integration, new cycles of experience, freedom of choice, receptivity.

ARIES 2   A comedian entertaining a group. KEYWORD: *Release*

A comedian entertaining a group

THEME: *Personification*. This symbol speaks to self-understanding through seeing the self's reflection in the mirror of life. The emphasis here is on the opportunity for self-discovery and personal growth through role-play. The image of a comedian entertaining a group dramatizes the necessity for a willingness to risk, here illustrated by a creative form of self-expression designed to elicit feedback and response to the self's outpouring. Implicit in this symbol is the importance of versatility and well-roundedness or the ability to function competently in a variety of situations. On a practical level, this symbol portrays humor and the ability to appreciate the ironies and incongruities of life. Positive: At its highest, this symbol represents sparkling wit and a keen sense of humor. Negative: Exhibitionism and silliness or an unwillingness to reveal the self.

TODAY: The accent is on self-discovery. You may see yourself in a new light or appreciate things you never realized about yourself. Communication skills should be at their peak.

Opportunity: Your greatest advantage lies in using a variety of approaches or techniques and keeping your sense of humor. Experiment with new ways of expressing yourself and pay careful attention to the feedback you get. Be innovative.

Risk: Guard against behavior that outrages community values. What may seem clever or funny at first thought may turn out to be highly offensive to others. On the other hand, this is not a time to be self-effacing or to hide your light under a bushel.

STEPPING STONES: Self-understanding, self-discovery, role play, creative self-expression, entertainment, humor, irony, versatility.

ARIES 3   A cameo profile of a man in the outline of his country. KEYWORD: *Exploitation*

THEME: *The Icon.* This symbol speaks to a broad but impersonal involvement in life with little of the inner self emphasized or revealed. The image of a cameo profile of a man in the outline of his country was written as "a cameo shows the profile of a man that suggests the outline of his country" in the astrological mimeograph version of this image. The implication is that the *profile* of the man *resembles* an outline of the country of his origin and that the man is perceived by others not as a unique individual but in terms of his collective identity or his heritage and the cultural traditions that he represents. On a practical level, this symbol illustrates the way in which such historical figures as Chief Sitting Bull, Queen Elizabeth and Lucky Luciano represent the American Indian, the British and the Mafia. While this symbol reflects a singular expression of group ideals it also implies a dedication to the achievement of social rather than personal goals. Positive: At its highest, this symbol represents personal distinctiveness as the result of epitomizing the highest ideals, traditions and talents of some particular group. Negative: Infamy as the result of portraying and perpetuating the worst stereotypes of a culture.

TODAY: The accent is on group identity, culture, customs and traditions. Social rather than personal goals take high focus at this time.

Opportunity: Your greatest advantage lies in working toward the achievement of group objectives. This could take the form of speaking up for or representing others in some matter, sharing your ideas or contributing your skills and talents to some community project.

Risk: Guard against personal behavior that could discredit or bring shame on a group that you are part of. Avoid accepting or taking personal credit for a group accomplishment or stereotyping any individual based on his group affiliations.

STEPPING STONES: Impersonality, resemblance, distinctiveness, identity, social ideals, leadership.

ARIES 4　　Two lovers strolling through a secluded walk. KEY-WORD: *Enjoyment*

Two lovers strolling through a secluded walk

THEME: *Privacy.* This symbol speaks to innocence, and to the experience of belonging with no sense of personal responsibility or obligation. It also speaks to the coming together of individuals out of mutual desire, simply to enjoy time together. The image of two lovers strolling through a secluded walk suggests peace, tranquility and seclusion. The two lovers are in their own world, or a reality of their own creation. The implication here is that reality is whatever we decide to make it, or that no experience is real until we give it meaning. On a practical level, this symbol indicates a preference for intimate, one-to-one relationships, rather than socializing with groups, and a desire for privacy and quiet surroundings. It also indicates a desire to avoid high pressure situations. Positive: At its highest, this symbol represents ingenuousness and an absence of premeditation. Negative: Inadequate social skills or possessiveness in relationships.

TODAY: The accent is on privacy, serenity and simplicity. You may find yourself wanting to put aside broader social obligations and responsibilities and withdraw from things.

Opportunity: Your greatest advantage lies in doing what comes naturally or following your instincts. Now is a good time to read, relax, work on a hobby or spend quality time with someone special. Take time for yourself and enjoy it without feeling guilty.

Risk: Guard against jealousy and possessiveness or trying to force your ideas and reality on someone else who doesn't see things the same way that you do. Be careful not to monopolize the person or time of others and resist the temptation to turn play into work.

STEPPING STONES: Innocence, freedom, peace, tranquility, privacy, intimacy, love.

ARIES 5   A triangle with wings. KEYWORD: *Zeal*

a triangle with wings

THEME: *Enthusiasm.* This symbol speaks to the ability of an individual to come through his experiences spiritually and psychologically intact as long as he remains true to self or acts purely from the center of his being. The image of a triangle with wings alludes to the three elements of an individual that make him unique, or his skills, loyalties and values. The basic desire of individuals is seen here as the achievement of spiritual enlightenment and self-transformation. The emphasis is on enthusiasm and a zest for living. On a practical level, this symbol indicates a "can do" attitude and a refusal to accept limitations. Positive: At its highest, this symbol represents high vision and a positive outlook on life, or a tendency to see life in terms of possibilities rather than actualities. Negative: Dissociation or a desire to escape from the practical realities of life through fantasy.

TODAY: The accent is on personal uniqueness and appreciating difference. An unusual opportunity or exciting challenge may present itself today and things may come in threes. High spirits and optimism are in the air. Ambition is the byword.

Opportunity: Your greatest advantage lies in keeping a positive attitude, being true to self, accepting only the best and focusing on the highest possible outcome in everything you do. Taking a fresh look at something as if it were the first time you were seeing it may bring unexpected rewards.

Risk: Guard against judging things prematurely or focusing on limitation. Refuse to give in to disappointment and avoid compromising your values, even when no one else seems to be sharing them. Above all, don't run away when the going gets rough.

STEPPING STONES: Enthusiasm, ambition, uniqueness, enlightenment, transformation, vision, possibilities, imagination.

ARIES 6   **A square brightly lighted on one side. KEYWORD:** *Set*

a square brightly lighted on one side

THEME: *Half of the Story.* This symbol speaks to the value of experience, and to the illusion of a materialistic reality. The image of a square brightly lighted on one side alludes to the dawning of awareness, or the early stages of insight, and it points to the limitations and dangers of looking at only one side of a situation. There is an implication in this symbol of a primitive type of thinking wherein the individual believes that he is what he possesses or that his worth is the sum total of the number and kinds of his possessions. He is unable to see that the real value is in his experience with the material, or only as he is able to use it to achieve his goals. Positive: At its highest, this symbol represents inner-directedness and a knack for making creative use of material resources to achieve personal objectives. Negative: Tendency to give up rather than struggle, or to underestimate the power of self to overcome physical limitations.

TODAY: The accent is on revelation. Something hidden may come to light or be exposed, or you may discover that you have been wrong about something. The emphasis is on the material and physical. Issues regarding ownership or possession of real or personal property may take center stage today.

Opportunity: Your greatest advantage lies in looking at both sides of an issue, listening to the whole story, then weighing the evidence carefully. If forced to choose between the aesthetic and the practical today, go with the practical or what is sensible, pragmatic or utilitarian.

Risk: Guard against illusion or being fooled by appearances. Jumping to conclusions or making decisions before you have all the facts can lead to regret. A thing may not be what it seems to be.

STEPPING STONES: Concrete or one-sided thinking, dawning of awareness, seeing half of a picture, materialism, physical experience.

ARIES 7   A man successfully expressing himself in two realms at once. KEYWORD: *Proficiency*

THEME: *A Doubling of Efforts.* This symbol speaks to versatility, and to an ability to function competently in more than one area. The image of a man successfully expressing himself in two realms at once also speaks to talent and to the self-confidence and sense of freedom that an individual feels when he knows he is in control of his life. The emphasis in this symbol is on duality. It is also the second symbol of the series of five in the astrological formula and thus it represents opposition, awareness and cooperation. On a practical level, two represents dexterity, diplomacy, and the ability to see both sides of an issue. Two can also represent duplicity, a double life, double-dipping or being two-faced. Positive: At its highest, this symbol represents a remarkable ability to competently handle a variety of projects at the same time. Negative: Indecisiveness, instability and easy distraction.

TODAY: The accent is on communication and your ability to deal effectively with different types of individuals and situations. You may find yourself trying to balance competing interests or facing the dilemma of being pulled in two directions at once.

Opportunity: Your greatest advantage lies in being flexible, articulate and diplomatic. Versatility and the ability to handle more than one thing at once will pay extra dividends.

Risk: Guard against being deceived by double-talk. Don't allow yourself to get distracted from your goal. Say no if you don't understand everything. Avoid getting caught in someone else's conflict.

STEPPING STONES: Duality, versatility, opposition, awareness, dexterity, diplomacy, balance, duplicity, doubling.

ARIES 8   A large hat with streamers flying, facing east. KEY-
WORD: *Excitation*

A large hat with the

streamers flying

Facing East

THEME: *The Winds of Change*. This symbol speaks to anticipation,
expectation, and an innocent eagerness to experience the fullness of life.
The image of a large hat with streamers flying, facing east can easily
conjure up a mental picture of a woman. But there is no mention of a
woman on the index card pertaining to this degree, or even whether the
hat is being worn. Elsie Wheeler could have seen this hat hanging on a
fence post or perched on the head of a sailor in the 1925 post-Victorian
era when this image came through. The very lack of mention of the hat
being worn suggests potentiality. For what occasion will it be worn? The
wind blowing from the east symbolizes change, and the implication in
this image is that change is being welcomed for the new opportunities it
brings. The fact that the hat faces into the wind indicates a readiness to
cooperate and meet new challenge. Positive: At its highest, this symbol
represents friendliness and an innocent love of adventure and new
experience. Negative: Overconcern with appearance or disingenuousness.

TODAY: The accent is on excitement and the anticipation of change and
adventure. Now is a time of waiting and watching. Expect the unexpected.

Opportunity: Your greatest advantage lies in staying alert to the early
signs and indications of change. Be patient and prepared. An answer or
offer may come from the east or someone associated with the east.

Risk: Guard against focusing so intently on appearances or other trivial matters that you miss an important cue.

STEPPING STONES: Anticipation, expectation, readiness, change, opportunity, friendliness, new experience.

ARIES 9   A crystal gazer. KEYWORD: *Acuteness*

a crystal gazer

THEME: *Divination.* This symbol speaks to global perspective, and to the capacity to quickly grasp the significance of all the facets of a situation at once and understand the meaning in coincidental events. The image of a crystal gazer emphasizes the world of potential as intuited or perceived through clairvoyance and vision. Implicit in this symbol is the concept of dual imagery or a mirroring effect wherein man and his universe reflect each other and thereby create a means for predicting the future. On a practical level, this degree can symbolize a situation where all ordinary means for solving a problem have been exhausted and divinatory techniques are turned to. Positive: At its highest, this symbol represents psychic sensitivity, prophetic insight and the ability to organize and plan in such a manner that facilitation and convenience precede actual need. Negative: Snooping and prying or foolish impracticality.

TODAY: The accent is on sensitivity and the need to find information or immediate answers to problems. Logic and reason may not work well at this time. Solutions are discovered intuitively or through psychic means. You are especially alert today and may surprise yourself and someone else by tuning in to something that was being kept secret.

Opportunity: Your greatest advantage lies in looking ahead to what is going to be needed in the not-too-distant future.

Risk: Guard against being intrusive or violating others' rights to privacy. Mind your own business unless you are specifically asked to get involved.

STEPPING STONES: Intuition, clairvoyance, vision, reflection, sensitivity, global perspective, potential.

ARIES 10   **A man teaching new forms for old symbols. KEY-WORD:** *Interpretation*

a man Teaching new forms for old symbols

THEME: *Update.* This symbol speaks to the rectification of thinking, or new understanding gained through practical, hands-on experience in the everyday world. The image of a man teaching new forms for old symbols is perhaps better understood in the context of the astrological mimeograph version of this degree. The unmodified word "symbols" was expanded there to read "symbols that have lost their meaning." The implication is that the passage of time, cultural evolution and modern ways of doing things can change the meaning of words and images. On a practical level, a good example is the difficulty of interpreting runes or ancient Mayan and Egyptian hieroglyphics in light of present day experience. The concepts they represent still exist but there is little or no frame of reference for these older symbols in a modern age. Thus new symbols are continually being created as the concepts they represent are dramatized in the common experience of individuals in every new age. Positive: At its highest, this symbol represents a genius for understanding and creating analogies and translating experience into symbolic imagery. Negative: Dislogic and an inability to understand the meaning of experience or the link between cause and effect.

TODAY: The accent is on psychology and communication. You may need to find new ways to get your message across due to a generation gap in experience or language difficulties.

Opportunity: Your greatest advantage lies in being creative, innovative and alert. Something you see or hear today could be the key that solves a mystery, facilitates your understanding or helps you communicate more effectively with others. Listen closely.

Risk: Guard against the inclination to turn a deaf ear or blind eye to what doesn't make sense to you at first hearing or sight. Resist the temptation to hold on to old ways of doing things that no longer work, just because they're familiar and comfortable. Don't sell yourself short or underestimate your ability to learn new skills.

STEPPING STONES: Rectification, new understanding, updating, substitution, progress, analogy, explanation, translation, education.

ARIES 11   **The president of the country. KEYWORD:** *Idealization*

The President of the Country

THEME: *Ambition.* This symbol speaks to ambition, and to a desire to achieve notoriety as the established representative of some group ideal. It also points to a desire to attain a lifestyle that would be difficult to achieve in the role of an ordinary citizen. The image of the president of the country suggests that the position sought is one of high responsibility and that the individual seeking such a position is willing to make sacrifices in exchange for the opportunity to rule or lead. On a practical level, this symbol describes the individual who puts all his eggs in one basket and puts aside every interest and involvement to achieve one major goal. Positive: At its highest, this symbol represents leadership and conscientious stewardship of group ideals. Negative: Autocratic or dictatorial approach to achieving final ends.

TODAY: The accent is on aspiration, plans and objectives. You may be feeling quite capable and on top of it all today. Volunteering for some job or project is definitely within the realm of possibility.

Opportunity: Your greatest advantage lies in your ability to do what is necessary for the good of the group and sacrifice short-term pleasure for long-term gain.

Risk: Guard against being bossy, telling others how to do their jobs, or taking on more responsibility than you can properly handle.

STEPPING STONES: Ambition, high ideals and goals, leadership, responsibility, stewardship, conscientiousness.

ARIES 12   A flock of wild geese. KEYWORD: *Insouciance*

a flock of white geese

THEME: *High Flight*. This symbol speaks to the desire of an individual to lift himself above the superficial limitations of everyday living. The image of a flock of wild geese suggests a yearning for light-hearted freedom such as might be experienced by the geese in flight but eventually, like migrating geese, every individual who achieves such a state must eventually come back down to earth and take up where he left off. Although this symbol can indicate a naive attempt to mentally or physically escape unpleasant or difficult situations, there is a "safety in numbers" quality in this image. The implication here is that the individual prefers the security of the group and would be reluctant to strike out on his own on any journey to freedom. Positive: At its highest, this symbol represents naive detachment, optimism and idealism. Negative: Superficial thinking or overdependence on the opinions of others.

TODAY: The accent is on travel, social events and freedom. You may be dreaming about faraway places or feeling a need to get away from it all and do something light and fun. Where you are doesn't seem to be where you want to be. Responsibility weighs heavily on your shoulders and you're simply not in the mood for deep thinking or serious decision-making.

Opportunity: Your greatest advantage lies in keeping a positive attitude and helping others do the same.

Risk: Guard against the impulse to abandon your responsibilities and ignore things you would rather not have to face. Going along with the crowd to avoid confrontation or letting others do your thinking for you can create even bigger problems.

STEPPING STONES: Light-heartedness, lack of concern, escape, detachment, naïveté, optimism, idealism, aspiration, freedom.

ARIES 13   An unsuccessful bomb explosion. KEYWORD: *Impetuousness*

An unsuccessful bomb explosion

THEME: *Haste Makes Waste.* This symbol speaks to failed initiative, and to the supremacy of good over evil. It also speaks to the ability of the world to protect itself against the destructive acts of individuals. The image of an unsuccessful bomb explosion is one of the destructive images that came through Elsie Wheeler and that Marc Jones tried to keep out. Each of these images were described as "reversed symbolism" in his 1953 book. The focus in this symbol is on poor planning and the need to find better ways to accomplish objectives. The negative implications of this image are downplayed. The implication here is that evil is only punished when an individual is successful in accomplishing an evil deed and that there is little penalty in life for simply attempting to carry out an evil plan that fails. As long as he is unsuccessful, there is still hope for such a misguided individual. On a practical level, this symbol speaks to the old adage, "Haste makes waste." Positive: At its highest, this symbol represents perfectionism, or a tendency to regard any result or outcome that doesn't fully square to plan as a failure, and a refusal to stop trying until success is at hand. Negative: Impulsive and careless planning.

TODAY: The accent is on carelessness and unpredictability. The tendency is to rush through things and overlook important details. Overconfidence or neglect is likely to be at the bottom of things not turning out as expected. It may also be that someone else's mistake is a lucky one for you.

Opportunity: Your greatest advantage lies in being patient and thorough. Take a deep breath and relax. Go over those plans one more time and don't stop trying.

Risk: Guard against impulsiveness, or acting before you think things through. Avoid setting unrealistic deadlines or trying to beat the clock. "Haste makes waste" is the caution of the day.

STEPPING STONES: Impulsiveness, impatience, carelessness, haste, recklessness, rashness, experimentalism, poor planning.

ARIES 14   A serpent coiling near a man and a woman.
            KEYWORD: *Revelation*

A serpent coiling near a man and a woman

THEME: *Higher Wisdom.* This symbol speaks to raising the physical, emotional and mental natures of man to their highest level of functioning. The image of a serpent coiling near a man and woman symbolizes the rising of the kundalini or serpent power and the achievement of higher wisdom through a mystical union of mind and emotions or head and heart. The coiled snake also represents the spiral of spiritual evolution that lifts the expression of physical satisfaction and pleasure to higher levels where they manifest as devotion and dedication to universal ideals. This image further alludes to the biblical allegory of Adam and Eve and the serpent in the garden, and so it symbolizes not only a desire for knowledge but physical temptation. Positive: At its highest, this symbol represents sublimation, or the channeling of the libido and socially unacceptable impulses into higher and spiritual or creative modes of expression such as art, poetry and the sciences. Negative: Sexual promiscuity and lust or impulsiveness and an inability to delay physical gratification and pleasure.

TODAY: The accent is on temptation and compulsion. Passions run high. This could take the form of a desire to overindulge in food, drink, sex or other physical activities. You could find yourself thinking about retaliating for some perceived hurt or wrong. The battle is between the heart and head or what you want to do versus what is in your own best interest. Today is a day for learning through experience.

Opportunity: Your greatest advantage lies in channeling your energy creatively and productively, perhaps through yoga, athletics, artistic projects or even intellectual pursuits. Put your reason and creativity together and aim for the highest.

Risk: Guard against impulsiveness and excess. Resist the urge to throw caution to the wind and give in "just this once."

STEPPING STONES: Desire, union, temptation, higher wisdom, marriage of head and heart.

ARIES 15   An Indian weaving a blanket. **KEYWORD**: *Diligence*

An Indian weaving a blanket

THEME: *Active Participation*. This symbol speaks to pride and personal fulfillment as achieved through creative self-expression. The image of an Indian weaving a blanket focuses on the preservation of cultural values and traditions through art. At the same time, it depicts the pleasure and satisfaction an individual can experience through meeting the needs of others. This symbol is similar to the meaning of the Eight of Pentacles in the Rider-Waite Tarot deck in that it expresses the pride of a skilled craftsman who is able to artistically express himself and his values through his work in some tangible manner and, at the same time, produce goods that meet a basic need in human society. In this symbol, the weaver is creating something that will provide protection from the elements as well as express his skills as an artist. The figure of the weaver also reflects patience and concentration, and as such it symbolizes the stability and peace of mind that an individual can achieve through being an active and contributing member of the society that sustains him. In modern terms, this is called being part of the process. Positive: At its highest, this symbol represents self-fulfillment and enjoyment through opportunities to use personal skills and talents for the benefit of others. Negative: Insecurity and a willingness to live a dull and predictable life rather than face the uncertainties of commitment.

TODAY: The accent is on ethnicity, pride in workmanship and creative self-expression. This is a good time for visiting museums, taking an art class, delving into the history and traditions of different cultures or working on your own personal project.

Opportunity: Your greatest advantage lies in putting your talents to practical use for the benefit of others. Go for the conventional or traditional rather than the innovative or fancy. Fill a need and warm a heart.

Risk: Guard against oversensitivity or letting your work become a convenient excuse for avoiding social relationships and involvements.

STEPPING STONES: Pride, conscientiousness, creativity, skill, artistry, craftsmanship, productivity, patience, concentration, work, tradition.

ARIES 16   Brownies dancing in the setting sun. KEYWORD: *Invigoration*

Brownies dancing in the setting sun

THEME: *The Dance of Life.* This symbol speaks to getting back to the raw, unrefined and natural source of things for clarification, understanding and self-renewal. The image of Brownies dancing in the setting sun depicts nature spirits reveling just before day turns to night when, symbolically, the source of their life goes home or returns to its source. In a very real sense, this image depicts a celebration of life or the end of a cycle and an honoring of whatever this cycle signified. But it also depicts an eagerness to move into the next cycle, and so it alludes to transitions or that point where the old gives way to the new and the end and beginning are one. Here, the implication is of a naive optimism and a willingness to face the unknown. This symbol also implies rejuvenation in the form of getting back to nature and the physical source of life. It illustrates not only the friendly relationship between man and his universe but the indestructible link or bond between any source and its progeny. On a practical level, this symbol can apply to an Irish wake, a bachelor party, a graduation dance, a retirement dinner and all other rituals and celebrations of life's most significant transitions. Positive: At its highest, this symbol represents a rich and rewarding life as a result of appreciating and accepting new opportunities for growth. Negative: Inability to recognize when change or improvement is needed or naive fatalism.

TODAY: The accent is on the celebration of endings and beginnings and the natural cycles of life. You could find yourself laughing and crying at the same time. A wistful sense of nostalgia at having to close the door on the past mingles with the excitement of opening wide the gateway to a new cycle of activity. Here is a bittersweet blending of regret and eagerness. Time stands still in this moment of celebration where today meets tomorrow and the past and the future are one.

Opportunity: Your greatest advantage lies in recognizing when a cycle has ended and in being able to release, let go and move on. Getting back to nature can help clear the mind. In matters of health, natural remedies are favored.

Risk: Guard against crystallizing yourself by refusing to accept change. Try not to cling to the past or hang on to what has long since served its time.

STEPPING STONES: Animation, vitality, strength, energy, activity, life force, health, nature, happiness, celebration, renewal, rejuvenation, the end and beginning in one, portal of the solar mysteries.

ARIES 17   Two prim spinsters. **KEYWORD:** *Divorcement*

Two prim spinsters

THEME: *Seclusion.* This symbol speaks to detachment and withdrawal from society, or retreat into a private reality of the self's own making. The image of two prim spinsters depicts two unmarried women who appear to be linked to each other in some way. Their primness emphasizes excessive attention to propriety, and thus there is a certain suggestion of judgmentalism or a fixation on the right and wrong way of doing things. The implication here is that the two spinsters, seemingly removed from the rest of the world, symbolize subjective thinking and a conscious disdain or rejection of the ideas and opinions of others as well as a willingness to give up the rewards of normal social relationships in exchange for the privilege of being left alone to do as they please. On a practical level, this symbol describes the individual who neither wants nor seeks advice and prefers his own company to that of others. Positive: At its highest, this symbol represents independent thinking and faithfulness to the self and its ideals. Negative: Isolationism and a superior-to-others attitude.

TODAY: You may find yourself in a more serious or critical mood or thinking in terms of rights and wrongs or goods and bads. In fact, you may prefer to be left alone with your thoughts right now. The initial response today could easily be, "I don't like it." And you might be thinking, "If I can't have it my way I would rather not have it at all."

Opportunity: Your greatest advantage lies in keeping an open mind and listening to all sides of an issue before making a decision.

Risk: Guard against alienating others through excessive criticism and negativity.

STEPPING STONES: Detachment, withdrawal, rejection, retreat, seclusion, separation, propriety, judgmentalism, subjectivity, self-sufficiency.

ARIES 18   An empty hammock. KEYWORD: *Rumination*

An empty hammock

THEME: *Pause.* This symbol speaks to self-confidence, and to a growing awareness that it's time to make a change—inwardly, outwardly or both—and at a time when there is absolutely no perceived reason or pressure to make one. The image of an empty hammock beautifully illustrates a state of suspension between deciding whether to dash off and do something on wild impulse or retreat to the inner recesses of mind and memory to meditate, reflect or ponder. The hammock is empty and waiting. The decision is yet to be made. On a practical level, this symbol alludes to that static moment of hesitation or pause just before something happens or someone starts a ball rolling in one direction or another. Positive: At its highest, this symbol represents tranquility, poise and harmony. Negative: Cowardice or laziness and indecision.

TODAY: The accent is on contemplation, reorientation and transition. You may feel that a change is needed but you're more inclined to take a "wait and see approach." The mood is one of anticipation and suspense.

Opportunity: Your greatest advantage lies in being patient. Timing is the key. Pay attention to unusual convergences and signatures that will tell you when it's time to take action or what kind of action you should take.

Risk: Guard against failing to act when you should or delaying a decision until it's too late.

STEPPING STONES: Reflection, ponderment, meditation, suspension, waiting, pause, hesitation, poise, harmony, balance.

ARIES 19   **The magic carpet. KEYWORD:** *Panorama*

The magic carpet

THEME: *But I Can Dream, Can't I?* This symbol speaks to the magic of fantasy, and to that marvelous capacity of man to fulfill his dreams in his imagination and enjoy playing various roles without the assumption of any responsibility. The image of a magic carpet symbolizes freedom, optimism and aspiration. It also suggests broad perspective and the ability to see experience in the context of the whole in which it occurs. The "rising above" aspect of this symbol points to detachment and an ability to vicariously enjoy experience without becoming personally involved. On a practical level, this symbol can indicate attempts to alleviate stress or simply wish fulfillment, as when a prisoner dreams of being with a loved one, a child imagines he is the president of the country or an office worker fantasizes about lying on a warm, sunny beach. Positive: At its highest, this symbol represents vision, creativity and a gift for seeing the world in terms of possibilities and endless opportunities. Negative: Escapism and emotional detachment.

TODAY: The accent is on imagination and enjoyment. Your creative energies are flowing and you may find yourself daydreaming and fantasizing more than usual or wanting to get away from it all. Your detached and carefree attitude helps you see things from a higher point of view. Opportunities and possibilities that were unrecognizable when you were too close to the picture or too personally involved can now be seen.

Opportunity: Your greatest advantage lies in your ability to visualize and hold a clear image in your mind of what you want to accomplish. Use your imagination, aim for the sky and expect success. Anything that can be dreamed of can be achieved. Wishes do come true.

Risk: Guard against focusing on limitations, problems and obstacles. Telling yourself that there's no way to reach your goal or no way out of a situation is a sure guarantee of failure. Running away isn't the answer.

STEPPING STONES: Vision, broad perspective, possibilities, fantasy, wish-fulfillment, magic, freedom, enjoyment, optimism, aspiration.

ARIES 20   A young girl feeding birds in winter. KEYWORD: *Hospitality*

THEME: *Social Conscience*. This symbol speaks to generosity and nurturance, and to the process of maturation and the development of a social conscience. The image of a young girl feeding birds in winter illustrates the natural desire of man to help those less fortunate than himself, and it implies a certain sympathy and awareness of the needs of others. It also alludes to the self-assurance and satisfaction that an individual gains from helping others grow. The young girl symbolizes youth and innocence and the birds in winter symbolize the hope and aspiration that seek to survive the harsh or barren and seemingly unfruitful periods of life. On a practical level, this symbol suggests charity, or assistance with no strings attached. Positive: At its highest, this symbol represents a unique gift for knowing exactly what others most need or want, or what is required in any particular case to ensure continued survival and success. Negative: Low self-esteem manifested as attempts to buy love and appreciation or be all things to all people.

TODAY: The accent is on assistance. The needs of others take high priority at this time. You may feel unusually concerned and sympathetic or inclined to be especially generous.

Opportunity: Your greatest advantage lies in being able to tell the difference between helping and interfering, or between what is asked for and what is needed.

Risk: Guard against being a soft touch or letting yourself get talked into something you may later regret because you hate to say no or you're afraid someone will get angry with you if you refuse.

STEPPING STONES: Helpfulness, generosity, giving, kindness, altruism, care, concern, social conscience, sympathy, innocence.

ARIES 21   A pugilist entering the ring. KEYWORD: *Exertion*

a pugilist entering the ring

THEME: *The Prize Fighter.* This symbol speaks to a belief in the self's invincibility on all levels, a natural immunity to criticism, and a willingness to risk. The image of a pugilist entering the ring uses the figure of a boxer or fist-fighter to conceptualize a readiness to attack or defend a position in public. It also alludes to a need to be actively involved in life or be where the action is. On a practical level, this symbol can indicate a very forceful and dominant personality that particularly enjoys controversy and challenge. Positive: At its highest, this symbol represents self-assertion, courage and a willingness to fight for rights and principles. Negative: Foolhardiness and daredevil antics or achievement of goals through crude bully tactics or aggressive takeovers.

TODAY: The accent is on opposition, controversy and conflict. Strong feelings may be expressed. Pride and fear of losing a position of some kind can result in arguments and differences of opinion over who is the best or who is right and wrong.

Opportunity: Your greatest advantage lies in looking at things from the other fellow's point of view and listening carefully to what he has to say so you can understand where he's coming from.

Risk: Guard against being oversensitive and defensive or critical of your fellows. This is not a good time to order others around or issue ultimatums.

STEPPING STONES: Self-confidence, strength, self-assertion, courage, force, competition, activity, combat, conflict, defense.

ARIES 22   The gate to the garden of desire. KEYWORD: Prospect

The gate to the garden of desire

THEME: *Exercising Options.* This symbol speaks to a complete openness to life, and to a childlike belief that the world was created for personal enjoyment. The image of the gate to the garden of desire suggests that whatever is desired can be easily obtained with little effort; however, there is nothing in this image to indicate any pressure or incentive to take action. Instead, there is an almost lyrical quality in this image that suggests the individual may be completely satisfied knowing that whatever he wants or needs is within his reach and waiting to be used at his leisure but making no effort to obtain it. Positive: At its highest, this symbol represents a heightened alertness to opportunity and a natural instinct for knowing the right time to make a move or exercise an option. Negative: Loss of opportunity through procrastination, deliberate inaction or inhibition.

TODAY: The accent is on openings and opportunities. Something you have been waiting for is now within reach, but it's up to you to make the first move.

Opportunity: Your greatest advantage lies in looking before you leap and making your move at the right time.

Risk: Guard against letting an opportunity slip through your fingers because you're afraid to speak up or reach out and accept what is being offered to you. Don't take too long to make up your mind. The offer may be withdrawn.

STEPPING STONES: Opportunity, possibilities, opening, alertness, enjoyment, temptation, desire, option.

ARIES 23   A woman in pastel colors carrying a heavy and valuable but veiled load. KEYWORD: *Reticence*

A woman in pastel colors carrying a heavy and valuable but veiled load

THEME: *Behind the Scenes*. This symbol speaks to privacy, and to the unreliability of superficial appearances. The image of a woman in pastel colors carrying a heavy and valuable but veiled load presents a contrast between the light and gentle appearance of the woman and the heavy but disguised burden she carries. The implication here is that the load she carries is an important obligation and, despite the weight of it, she is committed and not willing or ready give it up or share it. On a practical level, this symbol cautions against judging by appearances. It also implies that the truth of a matter may be hidden, or that some important secret is being kept. Positive: At its highest, this symbol represents integrity, discreteness and a willingness to accept responsibility without complaint. Negative: Hidden agendas or deception.

TODAY: The accent is on mystery and things that are hidden or not what they appear to be.

Opportunity: Your greatest advantage lies in keeping quiet and not revealing too much at this time—but demand full disclosure in your dealings with others.

Risk: Guard against underestimating the value or importance of what hasn't been said. Buying a pig in a poke or saying yes before you get all the facts could prove costly.

STEPPING STONES: Shyness, privacy, reluctance, secrets, concealment, camouflage, discreteness, confidentiality, hidden strength, responsibility, burden.

ARIES 24   **An open window and a net curtain blowing into a cornucopia. KEYWORD:** *Munificence*

An open window and a net curtain blowing into a cornucopia

THEME: *Reciprocity*. This symbol speaks to the extraordinary gifts of life that come to the individual who generously gives of the fullness of himself without thought of return. The image of an open window symbolizes openness to new experience. The net curtain blowing into a cornucopia dramatizes the world's enthusiastic response to this openness in the form of prosperity and opportunity. In his 1953 commentary, Marc Jones described this symbol in terms of the "continued outer manifestation of what at times may seem to be an unmerited good fortune," and he explained that this apparent phenomena is more of a joyful tipping of the hats between an individual and the cosmos. The focus here is on the richness of life available to those individuals who welcome all experience for the value to be gained from it. Positive: At its highest, this symbol represents a lack of inhibition, friendliness and good fortune created through positive expectations. Negative: Self-serving generosity.

TODAY: The accent is on lavishness, abundance and unexpected gifts of all kinds.

Opportunity: Your greatest advantage lies in being generous. Cast your bread upon the waters. Think positively. Expect the best and you'll get it.

Risk: Guard against being cavalier or flaunting your possessions in front of those who are less fortunate.

STEPPING STONES: Abundance, prosperity, bounty, charity, generosity, gifts, good fortune, benevolence, philanthropy.

ARIES 25   **A double promise. KEYWORD:** *Sensibility*

A double promise promise

THEME: *On the Other Hand.* This symbol speaks to duplication, "twoness" and everything that the two represents. It also speaks to resourcefulness in finding options or alternatives. The image of a double promise alludes to choice, and here the choice is between two options that hold equal promise. The emphasis on duality highlights the fact that everything in life has both a literal and symbolical value, and that every option open to an individual can be viewed in terms of its inner or subjective value (what it means to the individual) and its outer or objective value (what it means to others). Positive: At its highest, this symbol represents flexibility, the capacity to see both sides of an issue, and a talent for getting all things and people to cooperate and work together in harmony. Negative: Duplicity and trickery.

TODAY: The accent is on choice and options. There is also an emphasis in this symbol on security and being doubly careful to protect things.

Opportunity: Your greatest advantage lies in looking at both sides of an issue. Carefully weigh the pros and cons and examine alternatives.

Risk: Guard against making a decision too quickly. Don't accept things at face value. They may not be what they appear to be.

STEPPING STONES: Duality, choice, alternatives, equality, cooperation, assurance, literal and symbolical meanings, inner and outer, visible and invisible.

ARIES 26   **A man possessed of more gifts than he can hold.**
KEYWORD: *Equipment*

THEME: *The Dynamo.* This symbol speaks to exceptional talent and self-confidence. The image of a man possessed of more gifts than he can hold illustrates the concept of the renaissance man, or the man for all seasons. The challenge in this symbol is in learning when and where to set limits on the demands of others and how to avoid spreading the self too thin, or trying to handle too many things at once. There is an inclination indicated here to try to be all things to all people and to grow restless or bored when things slow down to a lull. There may also be a tendency to overestimate how much can be handled at one time and to overburden the self with too many responsibilities or projects. Positive:

At its highest, this symbol represents extraordinary competency and talent, independence, and an insatiable desire to explore and develop all of the self's potential. Negative: Obsessive-compulsive behavior and flights of fancy or an inability to sit quietly alone in a room and relax.

TODAY: The accent is on excess and abundance. The indication here is that whatever the day brings, there will be plenty of it—perhaps too much. Activity is the byword.

Opportunity: Your greatest advantage lies in capitalizing on your high level of competency. Your talents and skills should be at their peak today. Stay focused on your own projects and goals.

Risk: Guard against letting others unload their problems or responsibilities on you. Avoid overdoing or taking on more than you can handle. Learn to say no—gracefully but firmly.

STEPPING STONES: Abundance, excess, prosperity, richness, fruitfulness, affluence, competence, talent, versatility, success, fortune, blessings.

ARIES 27   Lost opportunity regained in the imagination. KEY-
              WORD: *Reformulation*

Lost opportunity regained in the imagination

THEME: *Learning from Experience.* This symbol speaks to new insights gained through the process of reflecting on past experiences from the vantage point of maturity and the passage of time. It also speaks to new opportunities created by putting the pieces of the past together in new and productive ways. The image of lost opportunity regained in the imagination refers to gaining understanding, learning from experience, remembering things long forgotten and the chance to reestablish broken connections, or take up something that was rejected or passed over on the first encounter, within a new framework of hope and optimism. Positive: At its highest, this symbol represents keen perception and the courage to make changes or start over again when it is obvious that the present approach can't bring about the desired result. Negative: Remorse or crying over spilled milk and blaming the past for present failures.

TODAY: The accent is on rectification. Rethinking things brings new insights and understanding. Moving forward toward success should be easier now.

Opportunity: Your greatest advantage lies in your willingness to start over or make changes if you discover that you were wrong or that what you have been doing isn't working.

Risk: Guard against burying yourself in guilt or agonizing over mistakes. Make the necessary amends or corrections and move on.

STEPPING STONES: Repossession, recapture, reclamation, recovering, understanding, remembrance, reestablishment, rescue.

ARIES 28   A large disappointed audience. KEYWORD: *Disjunction*

a large disappointed audience

THEME: *Nothing Lasts Forever.* This symbol speaks to the disillusionment that can occur when too great a dependence is placed on things external to self. The image of a large disappointed audience alludes to an expectation that wasn't met, as when something that is being enjoyed ends prematurely or when something that is anticipated or expected to occur fails to materialize. Thus this symbol also speaks to the unpredictabilities of life and to changes in taste or preference. This is one of the images that Marc Jones described as "reversed symbolism," or as carrying a negative connotation, and he commented there on the danger of an individual becoming disillusioned as a result of "making the momentary mood of the masses any proper guide for the values he should pursue." In modern terms, this degree emphasizes being true to self. Positive: At its highest, this symbol represents the courage to do what is best for the self and resist emotional appeals and pressures from others. Negative: Self-annihilation through pessimistic thinking and false perceptions of rejection.

TODAY: The accent is on a shift in attitudes and values. What worked yesterday may not hold up well today.

Opportunity: Your greatest advantage lies in being self-reliant and pleasing yourself. Think independently and objectively.

Risk: Guard against letting criticism, disapproval or the opinions of others get you down or stop you from doing what you know is right for you. Avoid self-pity and negative thinking.

STEPPING STONES: Disattunement, disillusionment, chagrin, dissatisfaction, dismay, frustration, letdown, discouragement, unpredictability, disappointment, lack of harmony.

ARIES 29   A celestial choir singing. KEYWORD: *Veneration*

a celestial choir singing

THEME: *In Tune with the Infinite*. This symbol speaks to the capacity of individuals to become channels of the highest values and ideals that sustain society and the world. The image of a celestial choir singing symbolizes inspiration and spiritual upliftment. The implication here is of an effort to encourage positive change and the development of a social conscience. Positive: At its highest, this symbol represents the ability to inspire others to higher ways of living by lifting the simple and ordinary acts of everyday life to greater significance. Negative: Pretense to spiritual superiority or singing one's own praises.

TODAY: The accent is on inspiration, group harmony and encouragement. Little acts of kindness work wonders.

Opportunity: Your greatest advantage lies in being thoughtful of others and focusing on the good things in your life. Express appreciation and be thankful.

Risk: Guard against talking down to others or appearing to be condescending and patronizing.

STEPPING STONES: Encouragement, inspiration, upliftment, spirituality, exaltation, celebration, devotion.

ARIES 30   A duck pond and its brood. KEYWORD: *Reliability*

duck

a duck pond and its brood

THEME: *Contentment*. This symbol speaks to everything flowing smoothly when an individual is in tune with himself and the universe. The image of a duck pond and its brood speaks to natural order or pattern. A duckling's behavior is based on imprinting instinct. After birth, each little duck bonds himself to the first thing he sees that moves, usually his mother. Thus, ducks ordinarily swim in the pond as family units. The ducks are doing what comes naturally and their world is in order. The suggestion here is that individuals also find their world in order when they act in accord with their own special genius. It is possible that the turn-of-the-century, American slang expressions "everything is just ducky"(meaning fine and satisfactory) and "having one's ducks lined up" (or in order) provided the basis for the early commentary on this image. Positive: At its highest, this symbol represents an easy-going, unaffected disposition and a certain calmness and surety in handling things. Negative: Lack of polish and refinement or a lack of sensitivity to danger and personal deficiencies.

TODAY: The accent is on contentment and satisfaction with the status quo. Business as usual is the byword of the day.

Opportunity: Your greatest advantage lies in organizing and putting things in order. Follow established routines and be consistent.

Risk: Guard against complacency. Don't take things for granted or ignore something that is out of pattern.

STEPPING STONES: Alignment, satisfaction, complacency, calm, naturalness, accord, stability, conformity, uniformity, fitness, belonging, contentment.

Taurus

♉

TAURUS 1   A clear mountain stream. KEYWORD: *Resourcefulness*

A clear mountain stream

THEME: *Self as the Source of Strength*. This symbol speaks to the impossibility of restraining the human spirit and to the purity of the spiritual fountainhead from which all life flows. The image of a clear mountain stream emphasizes spontaneity, creativity and freedom. Just as a stream accepts the limitations of rocks and obstacles only as they help it reach its destination, so the individual is free from all requirement to accept unnecessary limitation or live his life according to any predetermined pattern, except as he chooses for the purpose of helping him achieve his objectives. Positive: At its highest, this symbol represents a clear and deep understanding of the self's destiny, and the determination to achieve it. Negative: Self-dissipation through a tendency to scatter the resources of self or go out in all directions at once.

TODAY: The accent is on light-hearted spontaneity and freedom. You may be experiencing an inner urge to break pattern and try something new. Rules and regulations may feel especially burdensome. Adventure beckons.

Opportunity: Your greatest advantage lies in capitalizing on your creative energy. Write down the new ideas and thoughts that come to you today. Knock again on that door that has been closed.

Risk: Guard against going out in all directions or trying to do too many things at once. Curb that urge to throw caution to the wind and overspend your time, energy and money.

STEPPING STONES: Source, purity, clarity, spontaneity, freedom, lack of constraint, liveliness, creativity, inspiration.

TAURUS 2   An electrical storm. KEYWORD: *Transformation*

An electrical storm

THEME: *Tension Release*. This symbol speaks to impact, and to man's ability to influence the course of events by effectively meeting crises with the full of himself. The image of an electrical storm inspires awe and fear of potential destruction. In the same way, men also fear themselves and their own potential for violence or destruction when they experience their anger rising or their emotions getting out of control. The release of stress by nature alludes to the fact that individuals also need to release their tensions that build up over time, especially in climactic moments of high intensity. The emphasis in this symbol is on catharsis, transformation, and the process of clearing away of all that has outlived its usefulness or is no longer needed. Positive: At its highest, this symbol represents a special talent for dramatizing the most important issues at hand, and calling attention to those likely to arise in the future. Negative: Extreme shyness and sensitivity to criticism or fear of letting emotions get out of hand.

TODAY: The accent is on climax. Things may culminate or come to a head today in a most dramatic way. Tension that has been building in some area is likely to be released today.

Opportunity: Your greatest advantage lies in keeping your head when all about you may be losing theirs. Pay particular attention to the symbolic significance of any crisis that occurs today and see how it applies to your own life.

Risk: Guard against losing your temper or saying something you might later regret. Emotions are at full tide. Try not to let criticism or what others say get you down.

STEPPING STONES: Crisis, impact, climax, discharge, outburst, explosion, drama, clearance, release of tension, catharsis.

TAURUS 3   **Steps up to a lawn blooming with clover. KEY-WORD:** *Hopefulness*

Steps up to a lawn blooming with clover

THEME: *The Higher Path.* This symbol speaks to man's growing realization of divinity in the beauty that surrounds him, and to the fact that nothing can stop an individual from pursuing his goals or dreams when he believes they can be realized The image of steps up to a lawn blooming with clover alludes to a desirable goal within easy reach. Clover symbolizes prosperity, enjoyment and freedom from care. Its three-leaf structure also represents the Holy Trinity. The stairs or steps leading upward symbolize ambition, optimism, inspiration and questing. The way and means to reach the goal is present in this image, but the suggestion here is that the individual must take the initiative, set his foot on the path and put forth the effort required to reach it. Positive: At its highest, this symbol represents vision, optimism and the determination to keep going until a goal is reached. Negative: Unrealistic expectations or unrealized hopes and dreams as the result of laziness or a foolish dependence on luck.

TODAY: The accent is on beauty and enjoyment, and the tendency is to view things through rose-colored glasses. The mood is upbeat and optimistic. Goals seem to be within reach.

Opportunity: Your greatest advantage lies in taking the initiative and putting forth the effort to accomplish what it is that you want to achieve. Be willing to struggle.

Risk: Guard against taking things for granted or laying back and expecting things to fall into place by themselves. Opportunity could pass you by.

STEPPING STONES: Opportunity, quest, vision, hope, optimism, beauty, enjoyment, promise.

TAURUS 4   The rainbow's pot of gold. KEYWORD: *Faith*

The rainbow's pot of gold

THEME: *The Promise of Treasure.* This symbol speaks to wealth and prosperity as the lower sign of a higher mastery of values. The wording in this image of the rainbow's pot of gold is a subtle rearrangement of the familiar "pot of gold at the end of the rainbow" and it places the emphasis on the rainbow, or the promise of spiritual treasure, rather than on the pot of gold or material wealth. The image of the rainbow's pot of gold implies that the pot of gold is more of a carrot on a stick, or an incentive, and that when an individual focuses on keeping the spiritual covenant between himself and God, or "the universal matrix of life itself," the rewards are guaranteed. Positive: At its highest, this symbol represents prosperity and happiness as the natural result of spiritual faithfulness and personal effort. Negative: Disappointment and unhappiness as the result of frivolous living and a lack of commitment to any worthwhile purpose.

TODAY: The accent is on fulfillment. Something you have worked hard for, or have been hoping to receive, may be realized or come to you today.

Opportunity: Your greatest advantage lies in refusing to give up hope. Have faith that what you have put your effort into will work out in your best interest.

Risk: Guard against deception through get-rich schemes or false promises of getting something for nothing. If it looks too good to be true, it probably is.

STEPPING STONES: Incentive, prosperity, happiness, treasure, value, wealth, abundance, reward, success, fulfillment, victory, accomplishment, promise, covenant.

TAURUS 5   A widow at an open grave. KEYWORD: *Reorientation*

a widow at an open grave

THEME: *Letting Go and Moving On.* This symbol speaks to the great sense of deprivation and grief that an individual can experience when he makes anything physical the entire focus of his reality and affection and then loses it. The image of a widow at an open grave is one of the images Marc Jones described as "reversed symbolism," and he commented that there is an implication here of a need to release the self from all "outworn elements of experience," or let go of that which is dead and gone and get on with living. The emphasis here is on the need to adjust. The individual is asked to focus on what he still has, rather than on what has been lost, and to count his blessings. Positive: At its highest, this symbol represents the ability to maintain equilibrium and flexibility in the face of change, material loss, disappointment or premature endings. Negative: Pessimism, discouragement, and feelings of helplessness or a lack of self-confidence.

TODAY: The accent is on refocusing, transition and change. It's time to let go of what once was and take notice of new opportunities that lie at hand. Life is what you make of it.

Opportunity: Your greatest advantage lies in looking ahead to the future. Take stock of your skills and talents and all the resources around you. You may have overlooked something you can use.

Risk: Guard against letting disappointment get you down. Fretting over what has been lost can prevent you from recognizing that new opportunity.

STEPPING STONES: Reorientation, adjustment, reorganization, reassignment, transition, change, loss, disappointment, release, letting go.

TAURUS 6   **A bridge being built across a gorge. KEYWORD:** *Channelship*

a bridge being built across a gorge

THEME: *Transcending Limitation.* This symbol speaks to ingenuity, and to the fact that any limitation or obstacle can be overcome when an individual puts his mind to work on finding a solution. The image of a bridge being built across a gorge dramatizes man's ability to overcome impediments. It also emphasizes the fact that man's freedom can be limited or taken away only when he refuses to do something about an unpleasant or unhealthy situation. There is no handicap or disadvantage that can't be eliminated, surmounted or transformed into an asset with a little clever planning and determination. Positive: At its highest, this symbol represents a very practical "can-do" attitude and the ability to get a job done quickly and efficiently. Negative: A tendency to seek quick and easy rather than competent answers to the problems of life.

TODAY: The accent is on overcoming difficulties and obstacles. Solutions to problems may be found through partnerships and alliances. New paths may soon open up for you.

Opportunity: Your greatest advantage lies in believing in yourself and your ability to accomplish what it is that you want to achieve. Prioritize. Put first things first and keep your eye on the goal.

Risk: Guard against trimming to excess or taking short cuts that could turn out to be pitfalls. Avoid the temptation to skimp on quality to save money or eliminate something that may be critical to success just to save time. Acting too quickly may be regretted.

STEPPING STONES: Linkage, connection, merger, unification, effort, ambition, passage, transition, conduction, overcoming difficulties.

TAURUS 7   A woman of Samaria. **KEYWORD:** *Awakening*

A woman of Samaria

THEME: *Upreach.* This symbol speaks to the basic goodness of man, and to his never-ending quest to find the highest experiences in everyday living. The image of a woman of Samaria alludes to the biblical story of Jesus revealing his Messiahship to a woman at a well who is both a stranger and an outcast. It illustrates the concept of upreach or the principle that the individual who seeks the fulfillment of a higher way of life cannot permit himself to be pulled down and conditioned by the opinions of others or succumb to social pressures to conform to the lowest common denominator of his fellows. This is another of the images that Marc Jones described as negative or "reversed symbolism," but it suggests that it isn't necessary to go to the mountain to find spiritual enlightenment. Rather it is found in simple fellowship with others in the most ordinary and common circumstances of life. Positive: At its highest, this symbol represents hospitality, service and a warm and giving nature. Negative: Lack of self-respect or moral decadence and a willingness to sell the self too cheaply.

TODAY: The accent is on outreach and service. Help may come from an unexpected source. The mood today is altruistic. Personal differences are forgotten as people join together in a common effort to help others.

Opportunity: Your greatest advantage lies in putting aside fear or personal prejudices and reaching out to someone who could use your help. Genuinely offering your assistance, or just being willing to listen to someone in distress, may bring unsuspected rewards.

Risk: Guard against letting yourself be used rather than useful. Avoid the temptation to overextend yourself by taking on more than you can handle.

STEPPING STONES: Charity, hospitality, service, compassion, altruism, sympathy, understanding, fellowship.

TAURUS 8   A sleigh without snow. KEYWORD: *Sustainment*

a sleigh without snow

THEME: *The Magic of Believing*. This symbol speaks to having faith that anything is possible and refusing to fall victim to the idea that everything is contingent on the happening of some prior event, or that there is only one way to get a job done. The image of a sleigh without snow suggests insurmountable obstacles and difficulties to the person who accepts limitation, yet this symbol alludes to magic and the power of imagination. The challenge in this degree is in recognizing that nature is generous with her resources and that there are illimitable solutions and alternatives for achieving any goal. On a practical level, this degree refers to serendipity or the fortuitous convergence of events in time and space in a relevant and significant but inexplicable manner. Positive: At its highest, this symbol represents creativity and a magical ability to make wishes come true or a knack for being at the right time and place when things come together in harmony. Negative: Pollyannaism or a fatalistic acceptance of disappointments as one's lot in life.

TODAY: The accent is on miracles and magic. Help may come from an unexpected source. The solution is there if you will only see it.

Opportunity: Your greatest advantage lies in being open and receptive. Use your imagination and be creative. Experiment with every idea. One of them will work.

Risk: Guard against accepting defeat too easily by telling yourself and others that things just weren't meant to be. Avoid rejecting possible solutions because they don't seem logical.

STEPPING STONES: Faith, magic, miracles, transcendence of difficulty, imagination, resourcefulness, support.

TAURUS 9   A Christmas tree decorated. KEYWORD: *Symbolization*

a christmas tree decorated

THEME: *The Magic of Sharing*. This symbol speaks to spiritual self-renewal, and to revitalization through fellowship with friends and family. The image of a Christmas tree decorated is a sentimental and nostalgic symbol that tends to stimulate a process of reverie and remembrance of an individual's earliest childhood experiences with his family. The evergreen tree symbolizes the immortality of the Christ spirit while the lights symbolize hope. The decorations are a sign of preparation, anticipation and excitement. The ritual of gift-giving, implicit in this image, alludes to the fact that possessions gain their greatest value as they are shared with others and made the basis of fellowship. Positive: At its highest, this symbol represents generosity, optimism and self-fulfillment found through sharing the resources of self with others. Negative: Giving with strings or conditions attached and feelings of entitlement.

TODAY: The accent is on joy and fellowship. Fulfillment is found in sharing time and memories with friends and family.

Opportunity: Your greatest advantage lies in making this day special for others. Brighten someone's life by giving them an anonymous gift or doing a thoughtful deed. Call an old friend or spend time with a shut-in.

Risk: Guard against feeling resentful if someone doesn't reciprocate in kind. Avoid reminding others of the things you have done for them or hinting that they owe you.

STEPPING STONES: Sharing, giving, abundance, enjoyment, celebration, hope, renewal, joy, beauty, fullness, spiritual gifts.

TAURUS 10   A Red Cross nurse. KEYWORD: *Enlistment*

a red cross nurse

THEME: *The Magic of Service.* This symbol speaks to spiritual service or the concern and care for others that characterizes the highest form of self-giving. The image of a Red Cross nurse is an international symbol of humanitarianism, mercy and compassion and it emphasizes simple kindness as a path to self-realization. Positive: At its highest, this symbol represents altruism, benevolence and unselfish service to others. Negative: False charity or self-serving do-goodism.

TODAY: The accent is on healing and service. Humanitarian concerns and efforts to bring things into balance and alignment take priority. Volunteer organizations are emphasized.

Opportunity: Your greatest advantage lies in being part of the cure. Make amends or help others find common ground on which to work together.

Risk: Guard against the temptation to accept some position of authority because the title or honor might improve your self-esteem or flatter your ego. Avoid neglecting yourself or your family because of a misplaced sense of obligation to others.

STEPPING STONES: Humanitarianism, service, compassion, concern, care, help, aid, assistance, healing, amelioration, restoration, rehabilitation, remedy.

TAURUS 11   A woman sprinkling flowers. KEYWORD: *Care*

A woman sprinkling flowers

THEME: *The Green Thumb*. This symbol speaks to creativity as an outbreathing of self that increases the value and enjoyment of life, and to a desire to pour the self into everything that offers the potential for growth. The image of a woman sprinkling flowers dramatizes the concept of nurturance or affectionate care and attention. On a practical level, this image illustrates the care required to bring any creative project to fruition. An individual gets out of life what he is willing to put into it. Positive: At its highest, this symbol thoughtfulness, conscientiousness and a natural gift for bringing out the best in others. Negative: Superficial involvements and an inability to grasp the deeper meaning of things.

TODAY: The accent is on nurturance. Things seem to demand your attention today. Children and others who rely on you tend to be especially demanding. You may be worrying more than usual about the health and growth of your special projects.

Opportunity: Your greatest advantage lies in reviewing or looking over those things that you are responsible for. Make sure all is in order. Give attention where it is needed.

Risk: Guard against wasting your time and energy on trivial matters. Try not to worry yourself to death over things that may never come to pass.

STEPPING STONES: Caretaking, attention, thoughtfulness, considerateness, generosity, nurturance, conscientiousness, responsibility, concern, worry.

TAURUS 12   Window-shoppers. KEYWORD: *Visualization*

Window shoppers

THEME: *Looking at Options.* This symbol speaks to the role of imagination and mental rehearsal in helping an individual evaluate whether or not he is likely to succeed or be happy with any particular choice that is open to him. The image of window shoppers alludes to fact-finding, idea gathering and looking at options, but the implication here is that no goal can ever be reached unless the individual makes a decision and acts on it. Positive: At its highest, this symbol represents ingenuity and a natural gift for spotting potential. Negative: Indecisiveness and an inability to follow through and keep commitments.

TODAY: The accent is on looking at options. Gathering information for decisions may occupy your time today. Have fun and enjoy stretching your imagination. Appreciate the many opportunities for self-expression that are available for you to choose from.

Opportunity: Your greatest advantage lies in taking the time to look at all the possibilities you can see in a thing. Turn it around in your mind as if you were looking at it through the lens of a camera. Visualize it in different settings. Think of its usefulness at different times or for different purposes. Be creative.

Risk: Guard against self-defeat and ruining all chances of success and happiness by telling yourself that what you really want is beyond your reach, or that you are not deserving enough to have it.

STEPPING STONES: Mental rehearsal, preparation, choice, looking at options, imagination, visualization, research, examination, inquiry, investigation.

TAURUS 13   A man handling baggage. **KEYWORD:** *Industry*

A man handling baggage

THEME: *Putting Forth the Effort.* This symbol speaks to self-fulfillment through work, and to each individual's search for a special niche in life. The image of a man handling baggage dramatizes the fact that every individual ultimately must depend on his own inner resources, put forth an effort and make adjustments if he expects to take his place in society. This image also refers to a need to feel useful. The suggestion here is that no job or function is superior to another when it comes down to filling a need. Positive: At its highest, this symbol represents self-confidence, responsibility, dignity and competency. Negative: Low self-esteem and a preference for menial labor as a way of avoiding greater responsibility or challenge.

TODAY: The accent is on responsibility. Trying to get everything done could be a challenge. Your workload may be unusually heavy. Whatever happens, you should experience a genuine feeling of accomplishment before the day is over.

Opportunity: Your greatest advantage lies in making the effort. It can be done.

Risk: Guard against taking on other people's responsibilities or letting yourself be talked into accepting any new responsibilities that will affect your ability to get the work you already have done. Remember the straw that broke the camel's back.

STEPPING STONES: Work, effort, assistance, responsibility, competency, industriousness, performance, accomplishment.

TAURUS 14   Shellfish groping and children playing. KEYWORD:
Emergence

*Shellfish groping
and children playing*

THEME: *Respect for Personality*. This symbol speaks to the opportunities for self-discovery at every level and stage of life. The image of shellfish groping and children playing shows two different life forms engaged in exploring their own worlds or "doing their own thing," and it dramatizes the concept of being true to self or the principle that each individual must develop his own potential without concern as to what others think or say. The emphasis here is on a relaxed and playful approach to self-realization and personal growth, and on respect for personality or the appreciation of individual difference and the beauty of diversity. Positive: At its highest, this symbol represents curiosity, independence and the achievement of individual potential through following the self's inner urgings and respecting others' rights to do the same. Negative: Confusion and lack of accomplishment as the result of trying to do too many things at once.

TODAY: The accent is on exploration and discovery. Outreach and trial-and-error methods set the tone for the day. The movement is upward and outward.

Opportunity: Your greatest advantage lies in being willing to experiment and try things out. Make a game of it.

Risk: Guard against letting your curiosity and eagerness to sample every new thing within reach interfere with your ability to accomplish the task at hand. Avoid following the Pied Piper.

STEPPING STONES: Experimentation, exploration, growth, self-sufficiency, discovery, individual difference, curiosity, interest.

TAURUS 15 A man muffled up, with a rakish silk hat.
KEYWORD: *Sophistication*

a man muffled up with a rakish silk hat

THEME: *Nonchalance*. This symbol speaks to the ability to maintain aplomb or poise, even in the most trying situations. The image of a man muffled up with a rakish silk hat portrays a dramatic effort to radiate dignity and personal distinction. The implication here is of a strong sense of self and a refusal to settle for being just another face in the crowd. This degree also suggests a sophisticated ability to use whatever resources lie at hand to achieve a goal or overcome obstacles. Positive: At its highest, this symbol represents self-composure and resourcefulness in meeting the challenges of everyday life. Negative: Arrogance or a cavalier refusal to take life seriously.

TODAY: The accent is on role-play and impressions or the appearance of things. The recommendation is to put your best foot forward. Individuals and groups are not likely to let others dictate what is or is not appropriate.

Opportunity: Your greatest advantage lies in acting "as if." Create yourself anew by visualizing yourself as you would like to be and dramatize that self to the world. Maintain your dignity no matter what difficulties you face.

Risk: Guard against becoming overconfident or cocky. Avoid making promises that you can't keep or creating expectations that you can't live up to.

STEPPING STONES: Sophistication, finesse, poise, impression, aplomb, polish, savoir-faire, refinement, resourcefulness, self-sufficiency.

TAURUS 16   An old man attempting vainly to reveal the Mysteries.
                KEYWORD: *Pertinacity*

An old man attempting vainly to reveal the Mysteries

THEME: *Finding the Right Way to Get the Message Across.* This symbol speaks to a need to share whatever has been the most important and life-sustaining factor in an individual's life, or what made him who he is. The image of an old man attempting vainly to reveal the Mysteries describes one individual's attempt to transmit knowledge, or his understanding of the meaning of life, and it dramatizes the difficulty of teaching or putting into words that which can only be learned from experience. It also illustrates the frustration felt when any effort fails or is found to be inadequate. This is another reversed or negative symbol, but the suggestion here is that any effort or attempt is a sign of hope or expectation of success. Implicit in this degree is a sense of urgency that this information be passed on while there is still time. Positive: At its highest, this symbol represents spiritual enlightenment and wisdom and a desire to share it with others. Negative: Lost opportunity through an inability or unwillingness to communicate at a level others can understand.

TODAY: The accent is on communication and getting your message across. Trying to share your most intimate thoughts and ideas with others could prove to be a frustrating experience.

Opportunity: Your greatest advantage lies in communicating with people at their level of understanding and experience, or in their own language. Ask for feedback and be patient.

Risk: Guard against talking above people's heads or being too abstract. Avoid complicated explanations or you will lose your audience.

STEPPING STONES: Communication, teaching, determination, purpose, resoluteness, persistence, stubbornness, effort.

TAURUS 17   **A battle between the swords and the torches. KEY-WORD:** *Resolution*

a battle between the swords and torches

THEME: *Competing Factors.* This symbol speaks to the eternal conflict between the ideal and the practical. The image of a battle between the swords and the torches depicts a battle between spiritual forces on the one hand and physical or mental forces on the other. The swords symbolize force or compulsion and the torches symbolize enlightenment. The emphasis here is on finding ways to reconcile conflicting goals or competing interests that won't require compromising personal integrity. On a practical level, this image can represent a true-life dilemma in which an individual is tempted to sacrifice some cherished ideal in order to satisfy a compelling physical urge or desire. Positive: At its highest, this symbol represents highly refined negotiation or mediation skills, exceptional skill in reconciling differences and a natural gift for helping individuals or groups at odds with each other understand and appreciate their differences. Negative: Inability to act decisively or find peace of mind as the result of inner conflict and confusion.

TODAY: The accent is on opposition. There is a tendency to go to extremes in trying to accomplish goals today. The challenge is found in finding the proper means to achieve your ends.

Opportunity: Your greatest advantage lies in understanding the motivation behind conflict and reconciling your differences with others.

Risk: Guard against trying to force things. Refusing to cooperate or find middle ground could be costly.

STEPPING STONES: Struggle, competition, conflict, contention, dispute, strife, rivalry, contest, opposition, challenge.

TAURUS 18   A woman holding a bag out of a window. KEY-WORD: *Facilitation*

A woman holding a bag out a window

THEME: *Making Things Better*. This symbol speaks to service as the highest path to self-fulfillment. The image of a woman holding a bag out of a window refers to the now almost abandoned practice of removing stale and musty odors from clothing and other items by placing them outside in the fresh air. The earliest commentary on this image used the words "linen bag." The implication here is that by performing even the most routine tasks conscientiously, life is made easier and more enjoyable for others. On a practical level, the table set with flowers or the freshly scrubbed floor may not seem important in the total scheme of things but the message received by those who enjoy the fruits of the labor is that someone cared enough to take the time to make life a little brighter, a little lovelier and a little friendlier. Positive: At its highest, this symbol represents a unique gift for enhancing everyday experience and making people feel special. Negative: Nitpicking and complaining or a pervasive negative outlook and frequently expressed belief that nothing is right with the world.

TODAY: The accent is on service and the personal touch. This could involve helping others clean up or clear away the old.

Opportunity: Your greatest advantage lies in making yourself useful. Tend to the little things and take pleasure in the results.

Risk: Guard against fault-finding and nitpicking. Avoid making yourself unwelcome by pointing out what is wrong rather than expressing appreciation for what is right.

STEPPING STONES: Service, assistance, helpfulness, facilitation, thoughtfulness, concern, enhancement.

TAURUS 19   A newly formed continent. KEYWORD: *Originality*

A newly formed continent

Tangible

THEME: *Fresh Opportunity*. This symbol speaks to the fact that experience ultimately conforms to desire and expectation. The image of a newly formed continent was described by Marc Jones as symbolizing "the raw substance of existence," and he emphasized the fact that reality is constantly being reworked "through the course of successive, overall cycles." The implication here is that experience expands awareness and with each new realization or understanding of reality in any given situation man is called upon to make adjustments or reestablish himself and look for new opportunities. Positive: At its highest, this symbol represents creative and sweeping vision with the potential to transform the world. Negative: Restlessness and inner turmoil or difficulty in learning from experience.

TODAY: The accent is on evolution and changes in the environment. You may suddenly notice some new thing or situation that has been quietly developing or taking form for quite some time.

Opportunity: Your greatest advantage lies in adjusting to changing circumstances. Identify the potential and your place in the new scheme of things. Start planning now.

Risk: Guard against making things more difficult for yourself by resisting change. Try not to expect the worst or fight what may turn out to be a change for the better.

STEPPING STONES: Creativity, manifestation, establishment, innovation, novelty, originality, transformation, reconstruction, alteration, opportunity, revelation.

TAURUS 20   Wind clouds and haste. KEYWORD: *Exaltation*

Wind clouds and haste

THEME: *Holding to Center.* This symbol speaks to the inclination of the average person to skim over the surface of life and avoid deeper involvements. It also speaks to the instability and insecurity that result from a successful avoidance of commitment and responsibility. The image of wind clouds and haste symbolizes change, ephemerality and impatience. This is yet another image designated by Marc Jones as a negative or reversed symbol, and it emphasizes the importance of staying poised and holding steady in the midst of temporary turmoil and confusion. Positive: At its highest, this symbol represents the ability to stay centered in the face of sudden change and crisis and a gift for recognizing and seizing the opportunities that are stirred up by excitement. Negative: Inability to accomplish anything of long-term value as the result of a tendency to get lost in superficial details.

TODAY: The accent is on confusion. Things are in flux and it may be difficult to get a grasp on which direction to take or what to focus your attention on.

Opportunity: Your greatest advantage lies in waiting it out, keeping your eye open for unexpected opportunities, and staying calm.

Risk: Guard against trying to do things too fast or trying to handle too many things at once. Failing to take the time to investigate thoroughly could prove fatal.

STEPPING STONES: Change, instability, agitation, diffusion, disturbance, transiency, turmoil, confusion, scatter, excitement.

TAURUS 21   A finger pointing in an open book. **KEYWORD:** *Confirmation*

a finger pointing in an open book

THEME: *Reconsideration.* This symbol speaks to rectification, seeing things in new ways and correcting misconceptions or gaining insight into experiences that have been misinterpreted or are not fully understood and appreciated. The image of a finger pointing in an open book alludes to authority, guidance, instruction and the process of verifying information. It also emphasizes the importance of long-range planning and foresight. The implication here is that individuals tend to ignore whatever has no immediate relevance. On a practical level, this image can refer to a literal need to go by the book or that some important rule has been broken or procedure not followed. The suggestion here is that a lack of sensitivity to higher laws can result in serious consequences. Positive: At its highest, this symbol represents self-discipline, good judgment and a remarkable ability to see to the heart of any matter. Negative: Rule-driven or rigid behavior and fear of making mistakes.

TODAY: The accent is on validation and rectification. A feeling that things are not quite right may lead you to investigate and take corrective action.

Opportunity: Your greatest advantage lies in paying attention to the meaning and purpose of things. When in doubt, check things out or consult a higher authority.

Risk: Guard against taking things for granted or depending on others to take care of things. Avoid overlooking small details or fine print that could be important.

STEPPING STONES: Guidance, authority, rules, going by the book, confirmation, verification, affirmation, sanction, corroboration, proof, substantiation, verification, validation, rectification.

TAURUS 22   White dove over troubled waters. KEYWORD: *Guidance*

White dove over troubled waters

THEME: *A Higher Call*. This symbol speaks to the fact that every individual comes into the world with a spiritual mission or purpose that guides him, whether or not it is recognized. The image of a white dove over troubled water symbolizes divine protection, the triumph of spirit over matter, peace of mind and the ability to transcend emotional turmoil and psychological stress. Implicit in this symbol is the freedom and strength that can be gained from listening to the inner voice for guidance and direction. The suggestion here is that the individual who knows his purpose and sets out to fulfill it will succeed. On a practical level, this symbol can represent peace or an end to war, dissension, enmity or conflict. Positive: At its highest, this symbol represents a strong sense of personal destiny and the ability to rise above superficial difficulties and keep focused on a goal until it's achieved. Negative: Confusion and lack of direction or absent-mindedness and daydreaming.

TODAY: The accent is on rising above difficulties and emotional stress.

Opportunity: Your greatest advantage lies in minding your own business, working on your own goals, and refusing to get involved in the problems of others.

Risk: Guard against not paying attention or letting your mind wander. You may miss an important message.

STEPPING STONES: Guidance, direction, message, advice, help, protection, mission, transcendence, peace.

TAURUS 23   A jewelry shop. KEYWORD: *Preservation*

a jewelry Shop

THEME: *All that Glitters*. This symbol speaks to practical or material values, and to man's desire to own and possess those things that affirm or validate his personal concept of who he is. The image of a jewelry shop full of precious gems and minerals emphasizes luxury, wealth and beauty. Jewelry is used to commemorate special events such as engagements, coronations, graduations and weddings. Thus, it alludes to achievement, accomplishment and special status. It also symbolizes aspiration, romance and reward. Positive: At its highest, this symbol represents wealth, as a lower sign of a higher mastery of values, and a unique talent for creating beauty through imaginative enhancements of the ordinary. Negative: Greed and materialism or bad taste and gaudy overadornment.

TODAY: The accent is on possessions. You may be tempted to overspend or be extravagant with your resources. A change in status is indicated.

Opportunity: Your greatest advantage lies in focusing on quality. Work for and expect the best that can be achieved.

Risk: Guard against excess or losing something of value by taking more than you need or going overboard in some direction. Don't bite off more than you can chew.

STEPPING STONES: Luxury, wealth, beauty, values, reward, elegance, lavishness, extravagance, splendor.

TAURUS 24   A mounted Indian with scalp locks. KEYWORD: *Command*

a mounted Indian with scalp locks

THEME: *The Conqueror.* This symbol speaks to ingenuity, accomplishment, and pride in the ability to gain a superior position of authority over others. The image of a mounted Indian with scalp locks is an aggressive symbol, and it suggests a primitive need to conquer and rule. The horse, which is alluded to but not specifically mentioned, represents power, the senses, and the lower or animal instincts of man. The scalp locks symbolize thought, mind, imagination and intelligence. The Indian is depicted in a position of control over himself and others. Interestingly, this image was not designated by Marc Jones as one of the images that came through as "reversed symbolism." From this it can be implied that this is not an ominous symbol but rather an indication of earned authority and achievement. In modern times, this symbol could represent a corporate headhunter. Positive: At its highest, this symbol represents self-discipline and mastership. Negative: Tyranny, or a ruthless "off-with-their-heads" approach to life, and an obsession with controlling the thoughts and minds of others.

TODAY: The accent is on conquest and self-mastery. There is a chance that things could get aggressive today and heads might roll.

Opportunity: Your greatest advantage lies in staying calm and exercising self-discipline.

Risk: Guard against losing your temper or being too controlling. Avoid power struggles.

STEPPING STONES: Authority, control, power, dominion, leadership, superiority, command, mastery, skill, achievement, aggression, headhunting.

TAURUS 25 A large well-kept public park. KEYWORD: *Recreation*

THEME: *Group Work.* This symbol speaks to a division of labor, and to the benefits to be gained by working with others in a common group endeavor. The image of a large well-kept public park describes a community gathering place, and it dramatizes the fact that there are some things in life that an individual can't accomplish by himself or that require cooperative effort to establish and maintain. It also emphasizes the fact that self-worth can be realized only in the ordinary, everyday world as the individual discovers when and how he needs others and they in turn need him. Positive: At its highest, this symbol represents community leadership and an unselfish dedication to the welfare of all people. Negative: Lack of self-confidence and a tendency to be easily swayed or influenced by the thoughts and opinions of others.

TODAY: The accent is on enjoyment. Take time to savor the fruits of your labor. Community or social gatherings bring special pleasure.

Opportunity: Your greatest advantage lies in working on group, rather than personal projects at this time. Focus on aesthetics and add a touch of beauty to the world around you.

Risk: Guard against giving in to pressure from others against your better judgment. Don't waste your time arguing over trivial matters.

STEPPING STONES: Common ground, cooperative effort, shared resources, group project, division of labor, beautification.

TAURUS 26   A Spaniard serenading his señorita. KEYWORD: *Constancy*

a Spaniard serenading his señorita

THEME: *Romance*. This symbol speaks to resourcefulness and to man's ability to make himself at home and find whatever he needs, wherever he is. The image of a Spaniard serenading his señorita romantically illustrates the pursuit of an ideal, and the suggestion here is that reality is self-created or that anything becomes real and possessed only as the individual contributes to its creation and becomes a part of it. On a practical level this degree suggests that the harder a thing is worked for, the more it is valued and appreciated. Positive: At its highest, this symbol represents idealism, a deep passion for life, and a refusal to give up until a goal is reached. Negative: Laziness and a preference for getting ones way through manipulation, sweet talk and flattery.

TODAY: The accent is on creative resourcefulness. You may find it hard to say no.

Opportunity: Your greatest advantage lies in finding new and clever ways to use what you have to accomplish your goals. Emotional appeals are the most effective.

Risk: Guard against letting yourself get talked into agreeing to something that you may later regret. Try not to let your heart rule your head. Put off making important decisions until you have time to think them over.

STEPPING STONES: Romance, desire, passion, courtship, pursuit, resourcefulness, design, orchestration.

TAURUS 27   A squaw selling beads. KEYWORD: *Detachment*

a squaw selling beads

THEME: *Intrinsic Value.* This symbol speaks to a basic lack of concern with trivialities and superficial appearances and to a focus on an inner reality of skills and talents, meaning and significance, values and ideals. The image of a squaw selling beads alludes to wisdom gained through experience, and to the preservation and sharing of cultural knowledge and traditions. It also denotes arts, crafts and commerce. Payment for the beads dramatizes the principle of value given for value received. Positive: At its highest, this symbol represents creative talent, originality, poise and dignity. Negative: Social isolation and low self-esteem.

TODAY: The accent is on skill. You may be feeling an urge to express yourself in some dramatic way. Production takes high focus.

Opportunity: Your greatest advantage lies in being creative. Take the time to work on that special project that you enjoy so much.

Risk: Guard against selling yourself short or undervaluing what you have to contribute. Withdrawing is not the solution.

STEPPING STONES: Creativity, skill, experience, cultural traditions, depth of character, industry, commerce, arts and crafts.

TAURUS 28 A woman pursued by mature romance. KEYWORD: *Persuasion*

a woman pursued by mature romance

THEME: *No Time Like the Present.* This symbol speaks to appreciation, and to the fact that there is no point beyond which the fullness of life cannot be experienced. It also speaks to faith and a refusal to accept defeat or loss as the end of a matter. The image of a woman pursued by mature romance expresses the deeper joy to be found in experience when it comes after its appointed time has passed. There is no time like the present for seizing opportunity. If the potential exists it can be realized. Positive: At its highest, this symbol speaks to unquenchable hope, patience and a refusal to recognize limitations. Negative: Disillusionment and a refusal to take chances, or a willingness to accept a lesser that is available today rather than wait for the better that may come tomorrow.

TODAY: The accent is on serendipity. Something you may have given up hoping for may suddenly appear on your doorstep.

Opportunity: Your greatest advantage lies in recognizing opportunity when it knocks. Everything comes at its own appointed time.

Risk: Guard against giving up too soon or accepting second best because you're afraid you won't get what you really want.

STEPPING STONES: Inducement, appeal, plea, solicitation, petition, allure, attraction, enchantment, hope, opportunity, prospect, chance, appreciation, ripeness.

TAURUS 29   Two cobblers working at a table. KEYWORD: *Capability*

Two cobblers working at a table

THEME: *Different Points of View*. This symbol speaks to brainstorming, and to the old adage that "two heads are better than one." The image of two cobblers working at a table alludes to those situations where people talk things over as they work with their hands. The table is a place where people come together to discuss matters, share their views and weigh the pros and cons of things. Feet represent understanding. The act of repairing shoes thus symbolizes an attempt to strengthen the frame of reference in which learning can take place. The emphasis here is on reason, dialogue and cooperative problem-solving. Positive: At its highest, this symbol represents good judgment, objective thinking and a willingness to look at all sides of an issue. Negative: Psychological blocks in perception and understanding or a lack of ambition and initiative.

TODAY: The accent is on decision-making. Meetings and discussions could occupy your time today.

Opportunity: Your greatest advantage lies in listening to both sides before making up your mind. Talking things over with someone you trust or whose opinion you value may help.

Risk: Guard against idle gossip and believing everything you hear. Don't waste your time arguing over petty things.

STEPPING STONES: Cooperation, discussion, brainstorming, communion, different points of view, sharing, assistance, problem-solving, skill, labor, effort.

TAURUS 30   A peacock parading on an ancient lawn. **KEYWORD:** *Aloofness*

A peacock parading on an ancient lawn

THEME: *Pride*. This symbol speaks to pride in accomplishment, and to the importance of honoring or recognizing even the smallest achievements of an individual. The image of a peacock parading on an ancient lawn is symbolic representation of the collective ideals of others as manifested in one individual. The colorful display of the peacock is an attention-getting device that serves to encourage or motivate those individuals who haven't as yet recognized the existence of greater values toward the achievement of at least the outer, or superficial, symbols of success. In modern times, this symbol might stand for the "carrot on the stick," or the clever marketing ploy. Positive: At its highest, this symbol represents poise, presence and a natural gift for dramatizing and exalting the highest and best of society or astute historical insight and the ability to profit from the failures and successes of others. Negative: Pretentiousness, narcissism and vanity, or social isolation, detachment and haughtiness.

TODAY: The accent is on motivation. You may be encouraged and inspired by the achievements of others to do something to improve your own position.

Opportunity: Your greatest advantage lies in studying how others have succeeded. Develop a plan for accomplishing your objectives.

Risk: Guard against offending others by appearing vain or trying to act superior. Avoid the temptation to boast or gloat over your victories. It won't be appreciated.

STEPPING STONES: Pride, vanity, dignity, standing on tradition, drama, exaltation, exhibition, display, collective ideals, enticement.

Gemini

♊

GEMINI 1   A glass-bottomed boat in still water. KEYWORD: *Curiosity*

a glass-bottomed boat in still water

THEME: *Window of Opportunity*. This symbol speaks to sensitivity or a heightened awareness of the need to take timely action or seize the moment when it arises, if the opportunity is not to be lost. The image of a glass-bottomed boat in still water suggests an open eye, and it symbolizes perception and the ability to see things clearly. Still water symbolizes emotional poise, detachment and the unconscious. The emphasis in this symbol is on objectivity or the absence of mind-set, prejudice and preconceptions. It also emphasizes discrimination and the necessity that an individual be able to distinguish his own opportunities from another's. On a practical level, this symbol can indicate the entrepreneur or the opportunist. Positive: At its highest, this symbol represents clairvoyance, psychological insight and a remarkable talent for quickly recognizing opportunities. Negative: Voyeurism and intrusiveness or aloofness and emotional detachment.

TODAY: The accent is on perception. Something you have been trying to understand may suddenly become clear to you today.

Opportunity: Your greatest advantage lies in using this time of clear seeing to look into new opportunities. Strike while the iron is hot.

Risk: Guard against overstepping your bounds and sticking your nose in where it doesn't belong.

STEPPING STONES: Awareness, perception, vision, insight, clairvoyance, voyeurism, curiosity, emotional poise, detachment, aloofness.

GEMINI 2   Santa Claus filling stockings furtively. KEYWORD: *Prodigality*

Santa Claus filling stockings furtively

THEME: *The Magic of Giving*. This symbol speaks to the universal giver of gifts or the ultimate and illimitable Source of all. The image of Santa Claus filling stockings furtively focuses on the element of surprise, and it dramatizes the seemingly magical manner in which gifts sometimes appear. This Christmas scene alludes to compensation and the rewards given to those who have earned them. The emphasis in this symbol is on reciprocity and the necessity of appreciation. It also suggests the importance of maintaining the traditions and rituals that celebrate spiritual values, such as Christmas gift-giving. Positive: At its highest, this symbol represents generosity, largesse, and a clever knack for finding the gifts that bring the most joy to individuals. Negative: Hoarding and greed.

TODAY: The accent is on reward and compensation. Someone may express his gratitude by surprising you with a gift.

Opportunity: Your greatest advantage lies in showing appreciation. Concentrate on giving.

Risk: Guard against selfishness or demanding more than you've earned or have a right to ask for.

STEPPING STONES: Gifts, reward, generosity, secret giving, surprise, covertness, surreptitiousness.

GEMINI 3   The garden of the Tuileries. KEYWORD: *Luxury*

The garden of the Tuilleries (Paris)

THEME: *The Fruits of Privilege*. This symbol speaks to artistry, and to aesthetic self-expression. It also speaks to the self-confidence and authority that come from social power and wealth. The image of the gardens of the Tuileries focuses on the magnificent gardens constructed in the time of Louis XIV at the former royal palace in Paris and it emphasizes grace, luxury and beauty. It also alludes to the historical preservation of those things that express the values of any group of people. On a practical level, this image suggests the incidental benefits that flow through to society through a creative use of time and money. Positive: At its highest, this symbol represents philanthropy and the support and encouragement of all forms of creative self-expression. Negative: Hedonism, boasting and pretense to social superiority.

TODAY: The accent is on aesthetics and artistry. A visit to a museum or other cultural institution can lift your spirits and stimulate your imagination.

Opportunity: Your greatest advantage lies in enhancing the beauty of your surroundings. Try hanging a new painting, buying some flowers or even rearranging your furniture.

Risk: Guard against name dropping or trying to impress others with your social standing. Trying to curry favor will be seen for what it is.

STEPPING STONES: Luxury, leisure, aesthetics, culture, beauty, artistry, wealth, social position, creative self-expression.

GEMINI 4   Holly and mistletoe. KEYWORD: *Ritualization*

Holly and mistletoe

THEME: *The Magic of Anticipation.* This symbol speaks to the role that preparation plays in stimulating a change of mood or attitude and in calling forth a heightened anticipation of the joy to be found in the special celebrations of every culture. The image of holly and mistletoe stresses the traditions of Christmas and the inspirational effect of decorating or stage setting. The holly, with its green leaves and red berries, reflects a passion for new life and fresh beginnings. The sprigs of mistletoe symbolize romance and the immortal values that society preserves in its rituals. The emphasis here is on the special opportunities for spiritual self-renewal and time to share with friends and family. Positive: At its highest, this symbol represents a special talent for adding plussage to the lives of others by transforming even the most ordinary events into delightful occasions. Negative: Loss of touch with meaning and significance through an overconcern with details.

TODAY: The accent is on celebration. You may feel especially inspired as you look forward to some traditional gathering of friends or family.

Opportunity: Your greatest advantage lies in being prepared. Is there something you forgot about or neglected to do in a moment of excitement?

Risk: Guard against ruining what should be a special occasion by obsessing over trivial details and appearances. Avoid scheduling more than you can possibly handle.

STEPPING STONES: Christmas, tradition, ritual, anticipation, preparation, new beginnings, celebration, romance, self-renewal.

GEMINI 5   A radical magazine. KEYWORD: *Tangency*

A radical magazine

THEME: *Personal Statements.* This symbol speaks to the dramatic changes that can occur in life with the arrival of unexpected things or events that are needed for a deepening of understanding, or for learning a valuable lesson through some new experience. This symbol also points to the tendency of individuals to exalt whatever they have found significant and meaningful in their lives, perhaps through some memorable event that left an emotional imprint. The image of a radical magazine refers to a periodical that expresses extreme viewpoints or contains statements that depart considerably from the average or traditional point of view, and it dramatizes the desire of individuals to assert themselves and make their marks on life in ways that will announce to others who they are and what they value. On a practical level, this symbol is exemplified in the use of nicknames, the endowment of scholarships, bumper stickers on cars, personal logos, editorials and personal essays. Positive: At its highest, this symbol represents a personal distinctiveness that leaves the individual's trademark on everything he touches. Negative: Perverse pleasure in offending others or destroying those things and ideas that they hold dear.

TODAY: The accent is on freedom of speech. Strong statements and extreme viewpoints are likely to be heard today.

Opportunity: Your greatest advantage lies in daring to be yourself. Do it your way.

Risk: Guard against attacking the foundations and belief systems of others. Don't be insensitive to the rights of others to form their own opinions and have their own value systems.

STEPPING STONES: Extremism, speaking out, protest, assertion, iconoclasm, non-conformity, activism, dissidence, fanaticism, liberalism, free-thinking, heresy, radicalism, quarrelsomeness.

GEMINI 6   Drilling for oil. KEYWORD: *Speculation*

Drilling for oil

THEME: *Taking a Risk.* This symbol speaks to exploration, and to the extraordinary lengths that individuals will go to in order to find and acquire everything that can possibly be used to enhance their physical experience. The image of drilling for oil dramatizes man's ingenuity, persistence, and willingness to risk all or undergo any hardship in order to thoroughly plumb the depths of whatever he perceives to offer unusual potential or opportunity. The emphasis here is on speculation or the gambling of time, effort and money in the hope of obtaining greater reward. On a practical level, this symbol can represent the gambler, detective, scientist or even the simple gold digger. Positive: At its highest, this symbol represents an uncanny ability to find the right tools and methods needed to accomplish any objective, and the capacity for sustaining a sharp and concentrated focus on any goal until it's achieved. Negative: Reckless gambling or wasting personal resources through a lack of foresight and planning.

TODAY: The accent is on speculation and exploring new opportunities.

Opportunity: Your greatest advantage lies in being willing to take a chance. Nothing ventured, nothing gained.

Risk: Guard against being reckless with your resources. Don't risk more than you can afford to lose.

STEPPING STONES: Gambling, risk taking, penetration, investigation, exploration, discovery, venture.

GEMINI 7   An old-fashioned well. KEYWORD: *Recompense*

an old fashioned well

THEME: *Regeneration.* This symbol speaks to self-renewal, and to organic integrity or the fact that each individual retains his own unique identity, no matter how many times and ways he enters into relationships with others or assimilates their reality into his own. The image of an old-fashioned well symbolizes the source of all life and it emphasizes regeneration, nourishment and revitalization. Implicit in this symbol is the suggestion that man must give of himself in order to renew or refresh himself, and that individuals who try to keep a status quo or resist change eventually stagnate or run dry. Positive: At its highest, this symbol represents inner strength, resourcefulness and the wisdom to know when to go with the flow. Negative: Inadequacy, indifference and impassiveness.

TODAY: The accent is on revitalization and sustainment.

Opportunity: Your greatest advantage lies in taking the time to fill your own well, or take care of your own needs. Do something for yourself today.

Risk: Guard against losing touch with what it is that sustains you. Avoid giving too much.

STEPPING STONES: Source of life, purity, self-renewal, depth, regeneration, nourishment, revitalization, compensation, sustainment.

GEMINI 8   An industrial strike. **KEYWORD:** *Protest*

an industrial strike

THEME: *A Call for Change.* This symbol speaks to the necessity that individuals act in their own best interest and do whatever is necessary to extricate themselves from situations that provide no opportunity for personal growth. The image of an industrial strike is another of the reversed symbols, and it emphasizes disruption, uncertainty and instability as change agents that bring about reorganization, restructuring and the establishment of a new order. On a practical level, this degree challenges the seeker to do something about it if he isn't satisfied or with his life. The reference to "the dignity of a personality" in the 1953 commentary alludes to the difference between being useful and being used, and to having the courage to do what is necessary to maintain personal dignity while, at the same time, respecting the dignity of others. Positive: At its highest, this symbol represents strength of character, assertiveness, courage and a refusal to sacrifice principles for short-term comfort. Negative: Giving up too easily or selling the self short in order to avoid struggle or confrontation.

TODAY: The accent is on dissatisfaction and dissidence. You may be feeling that you are being taken advantage of in some way and decide to put your foot down.

Opportunity: Your greatest advantage lies in standing on principle and saying what is on your mind. If you feel trapped in some situation, do something about it.

Risk: Guard against giving in against your better judgment. Avoid closing your eyes to reality or adopting a long-suffering attitude to escape confrontation.

STEPPING STONES: Protest, self-assertion, disruption, challenge, demonstration, disapproval, dissent, grievance, objection, outcry, resistance, repudiation, complaint.

GEMINI 9   A quiver filled with arrows. KEYWORD: *Preparation*

A quiver filled with arrows

THEME: *Survival*. This symbol speaks to a sensitivity to personal opportunity, initiative, and an individual's ability to know what it is that he wants or needs and go after it. The image of a quiver filled with arrows refers to the tools and skills needed for hunting and it alludes to the self-discipline, training and ambition required to accomplish objectives. Implicit in this degree is an emphasis on the right of every person to have what he needs in order to survive and make his contribution to the society in which he lives. Positive: At its highest, this symbol represents readiness and high competency in meeting the challenges of life. Negative: Criticism and fault-finding or unusual quirks and eccentricities.

TODAY: The accent is on hitting your target or achieving your goal.

Opportunity: Your greatest advantage lies in being properly prepared before you set out to accomplish your objective. Check everything out and make sure it works before you begin.

Risk: Guard against offending someone or hurting their feelings by being too critical. Watch your tongue. Others could be especially sensitive today.

STEPPING STONES: Objectives, goals, hunting, pursuit, quest, preparation, readiness, skills, ambition.

GEMINI 10   An airplane falling. KEYWORD: *Crisis*

An aeroplane - falling

THEME: *Free Fall.* This symbol speaks to diving into experience without hesitation or any thought of failure, and with the attitude that whatever difficulties or problems are encountered can be successfully resolved when and if they arise. The image of an airplane falling is another of the reversed symbols, but here it illustrates the concept "unclutch and let go." What can't be comprehended from one point of view can be understood from another. On a practical level, this symbol suggests relaxing, going with the flow, and being willing to risk or take a chance. It also alludes to the fact that overcontrol and fear can limit opportunity. Positive: At its highest, this symbol represents learning through doing and an intuitive knack for handling crises competently. Negative: Helplessness, lack of self-direction, and a defeatist attitude or a refusal to get involved in anything that requires effort or risk.

TODAY: The accent is on impulsiveness or diving into experience without thinking. You may have to take corrective action or deal with some unexpected crisis.

Opportunity: Your greatest advantage lies in keeping your head and concentrating on the task at hand. Go with the flow and stay calm.

Risk: Guard against panic. Avoid the temptation to bale out or quit in defeat before the situation has a chance to right itself.

STEPPING STONES: Crisis, decline, downfall, collapse, decrease, descent, plunge, breakdown, collapse, defeat, failure, drop.

GEMINI 11   A new path of realism in experience. KEYWORD: *Identification*

A new path of realism in experience

THEME: *Practical Involvement.* This symbol speaks to the expansion of awareness and understanding through involvement in everyday activities. It also speaks to the advantages that can be gained by being flexible and open to experimenting with different ways of doing things—or even starting over if present methods aren't working. The image of a new path of realism in experience was described in the 1931 mimeograph version of the Sabian symbols as "a new real-estate subdivision is revealed with wide paved streets." In light of the fact that Marc Jones mentioned that Elsie Wheeler was chosen to channel the degree images because she was not burdened with an abstract mind, and this description is an abstract interpretation or description rather than a concrete image, it is possible that the image described in the earliest version is closer to what Elsie actually saw. The emphasis in this degree is on objectivity, or keeping an open mind, looking at all sides of any issue, and determining the value of things on the basis of what works or what is useful. It also alludes to the necessity that an individual frequently and honestly evaluate his personal skills and resources in light of those that are needed to obtain his goals and objectives. Positive: At its highest, this symbol represents a remarkable ability to adapt to new situations and the foresight to identify and acquire the necessary information and resources required, ahead of the need to use them. Negative: Denial of reality and a refusal to acknowledge or deal with anything regarded as unpleasant or stressful.

TODAY: The accent is on objectivity. You may decide it's time to take matters into your own hands and change the direction of some situation.

Opportunity: Your greatest advantage lies in taking a practical approach. Analyze the situation and gather information. Use the right tools to get the job done.

Risk: Guard against psychological denial or refusing to face reality. Looking the other way could make matters worse.

STEPPING STONES: Opportunity, new beginnings, practicality, objectivity, functionalism, experimental, fundamental, pragmatic.

GEMINI 12   A Topsy saucily asserting herself. KEYWORD: *Growth*

THEME: *Self-Assertion.* This symbol speaks to the need of every individual to strike a healthy balance between giving in to the demands of those who support or sustain him and asserting his own rights as an individual. The image of a Topsy saucily asserting herself is a vintage description from the early part of the 20th century. Topsy was a fictional character, a black slave child, in the novel *Uncle Tom's Cabin* by Harriet Beecher Stowe. Her unconscious humor provided comic relief to the story and her name thus became a symbol of that which originates spontaneously. The emphasis in this symbol is on the necessity that an individual develop the courage to speak up when others attempt to undermine his rights or violate his dignity. It is only by taking risks and standing up for himself and what he believes in that man can grow to his fullest potential. Positive: At its highest, this symbol represents self-assertion and an intuitive gift for knowing the right time and place to take advantage of an opportunity. Negative: Perverse pleasure in being contrary or belligerent and quarrelsome.

TODAY: The accent is on spontaneity. Someone may surprise you by suddenly telling you what they really think.

Opportunity: Your greatest advantage lies in speaking out at the right time. Stand up for yourself.

Risk: Guard against being flippant or impudent. Be careful not to rub someone the wrong way by appearing to challenge his authority.

STEPPING STONES: Self-assertion, courage, spontaneity, risk-taking, contrariness, capriciousness, candidness, impetuousness.

GEMINI 13   A great musician at his piano. KEYWORD: *Achievement*

a great musician at his piano

THEME: *Creative Fulfillment*. This symbol speaks to artistic self-expression as it inspires individuals toward the refinement of their own personal excellence. The image of a great musician at his piano suggests the fulfillment that can be experienced by any individual who is willing to put the time and effort into improving his skills and talents. It also alludes to the joy to be found in a welcoming response, or genuine appreciation. Positive: At its highest, this symbol represents creative brilliance, self-assurance, and the drive and self-discipline necessary to develop a natural talent to the level of genius. Negative: Loss of all opportunity for achievement through an inability to distinguish the difference between polite applause and genuine admiration.

TODAY: The accent is on excellence and accomplishment. Appreciation of the achievements of others provides incentive for your own self-refinement.

Opportunity: Your greatest advantage lies in spending the time and energy to develop your skills and talents. Practice makes perfect.

Risk: Guard against mistaking social politeness for genuine appreciation. Try not to set your goals too low.

STEPPING STONES: Artistry, self-expression, creativity, accomplishment, self-refinement, skill, talent, achievement.

GEMINI 14   A conversation by telepathy. KEYWORD: *Intimation*

a conversation by telepathy

THEME: *Invisible Ties*. This symbol speaks to the very real but invisible level of communication that sustains the link between an individual and his fellows and provides the means for overcoming superficial limitations that can impede understanding. The image of a conversation by telepathy symbolizes sensitivity, psychic attunement and invisible fellowship. It also emphasizes the fact that reality consists of more than that which can be seen and touched. Positive: At its highest, this symbol represents an exceptional capacity for comprehending and sharing the higher meaning and significance of experience. Negative: Cheating, or the use of dishonest and unscrupulous means to accomplish personal objectives.

TODAY: The accent is on attunement. You may be extremely sensitive to undercurrents and what other people are really thinking at this time.

Opportunity: Your greatest advantage lies in listening with the ears of your heart. Pay attention to mood and focus on *how* things are said rather than *what* is said.

Risk: Guard against deception. Don't be fooled by innuendo or misled by an intentional twisting of facts.

STEPPING STONES: Transcendence, clairaudience, sensitivity, psychic attunement, invisible fellowship, communication, messages, knowing.

GEMINI 15   Two Dutch children talking. KEYWORD: *Clarification*

Two Dutch Children Talking

THEME: *Common Interests.* This symbol speaks to a vicarious sharing of experience, planning and the creative exploration of perceived possibilities and opportunities. The image of two Dutch children talking alludes to the common tendency of individuals to seek out others who share similar backgrounds, values, and interests, and their attempt to establish friendships and alliances that will build self-confidence and facilitate success. On a practical level, this image can symbolize communications that may not be understood by others (speaking Dutch). It can also represent behind-the-scenes discussions of a small group or clique that are secret, confidential or not open to the public. Positive: At its highest, this symbol represents a special capacity for self-establishment in a broad variety of situations as the result of highly-developed human relations skills and social sensitivity. Negative: Clannishness and separatism or an inability to clearly communicate thoughts and ideas.

TODAY: The accent is on communication and talking things over. You may feel a need to seek advice from someone who has experience in handling a situation you are trying to understand.

Opportunity: Your greatest advantage lies in being discreet and not repeating everything you hear. If you have to get something off your chest, seek out someone you trust not to betray your confidence to hear you out.

Risk: Guard against failing to communicate some important piece of information clearly and fully. Be careful not to reveal more than you should to a gossip.

STEPPING STONES: Communication, discussion, clarification, sharing experience, planning, exploration of ideas, commonality, friendship.

GEMINI 16   A woman suffragist haranguing. KEYWORD: *Indignation*

a woman suffragist haranguing

THEME: *Liberty and Justice for All.* This symbol speaks to the eternal struggle of the disenfranchised to be fully-accepted members of society, with all the accompanying rights and privileges. The image of a woman suffragist haranguing symbolizes all efforts to end discrimination and separatism in whatever form they appear. The emphasis here is on the necessity that men learn to cooperate, or mutually give and take when differences arise, and respect the rights of others to form their own opinions and make their own decisions. This symbol also stresses the importance of objectively balancing personal rights against the rights of others. Positive: At its highest, this symbol represents a strong sense of justice and an unswerving commitment to the preservation of human dignity. Negative: Prejudice and self-elevating discrimination.

TODAY: The accent is on discontent. Things may not seem to be fair or equitable and you may be feeling left out.

Opportunity: Your greatest advantage lies in making sure you have all your facts straight before presenting your case or voicing your complaint. Try to understand the other person's point of view.

Risk: Guard against being overbearing or pushy. Appeal to reason and be willing to negotiate. If you demand all or nothing, it's likely you'll get nothing.

STEPPING STONES: Complaint, protest, indignation, displeasure, anger, annoyance, resentment, dissatisfaction, disapproval, exasperation, bitterness.

GEMINI 17   The head of health dissolved into the head of mentality. KEYWORD: *Development*

The head of health dissolved into the head of mentality

THEME: *Maturation*. This symbol speaks to the process of maturation, or growth from youthful self-involvement to the development of a social conscience. The image of the head of health dissolved into the head of mentality suggests spiritual growth, self-awareness and the ability to see the world through the eyes of others. This degree also implies that physical and mental well-being are the result of a well-rounded and very practical grounding in the everyday world of fact. Positive: At its highest, this symbol represents self-integration, broad vision and wisdom. Negative: Peter Pan syndrome or an obsession with youthfulness and a simple refusal to grow up.

TODAY: The accent is on maturity and expansion of consciousness. It's time to put selfish concerns aside and focus on the welfare of the whole.

Opportunity: Your greatest advantage lies in looking to the future and to what you can expect to experience if you continue in your present direction or course of action.

Risk: Guard against relying on others to take care of your needs or handle your responsibilities. Don't get caught unprepared.

STEPPING STONES: Maturation, adulthood, development, growth, evolution, completeness, wholeness, well-roundedness, self-integration, well-being, wisdom.

GEMINI 18   Two Chinese men talking Chinese. KEYWORD: *Difference*

THEME: *Specialization.* This symbol speaks to distinctiveness, or the type of uniqueness that separates an individual from the rest of his fellows in terms of intelligence, education or interests. It also speaks to the strength and comfort that can be found in affiliating with other like-minded individuals. The image of two Chinese men talking Chinese suggests an exclusivity of the type that is often misunderstood or viewed with suspicion; however, the emphasis here is on specialization and a refinement of skills that serves to protect an individual from scattering himself too thinly. On a practical level, this degree refers to the scholar, the scientist and other specialists. Positive: At its highest, this symbol represents a highly developed expertise in some unusual area. Negative: Lack of success in life due to an unfortunate tendency to repeatedly get involved in activities and relationships that are totally unsuited to the self's potential.

TODAY: The accent is on specialization and exclusiveness. You may find it necessary to find an expert to help you with a project.

Opportunity: Your greatest advantage lies in appreciating and refining your own uniqueness. Find others who share your interests. Be true to self.

Risk: Guard against trying to be something you're not. Don't try to force yourself into a groove that you don't fit.

STEPPING STONES: Uniqueness, difference, specialization, exclusiveness, distinctiveness, communication, conversation.

GEMINI 19   A large archaic volume. KEYWORD: *Background*

a large archaic volume

THEME: *History Lessons.* This symbol speaks to learning, and to knowledge gained through the repetition of experience. The image of a large archaic volume emphasizes the principle that experience can't be destroyed, and that each time an experience is repeated it gets easier. This symbol also alludes to ancient wisdom, the akashic records and the insight that can be obtained from examining the history or background of any situation. The 1953 commentary on this image states that "man achieves best as he cultures a real sense of obligation to his own roots," and it suggests that an individual should be guided by what he learns from his own experiences before he relies on the advice of others. Positive: At its highest, this symbol represents a special talent for reestablishing the self in any situation of prior advantage with a minimum of effort, and exceptional skill in solving difficult problems. Negative: Crystallization or ruining all opportunity for growth by living in the past and trying to preserve a stale status quo.

TODAY: The accent is on learning from experience and looking at things from a historical perspective.

Opportunity: Your greatest advantage lies in paying attention to the background of a situation. An answer you are looking for may be found in a book or library.

Risk: Guard against ruining all chance for growth and progress by insisting that things stay as they are and always have been. Older isn't necessarily better.

STEPPING STONES: Knowledge, education, heritage, history, background, frame of reference, experience, guidance.

GEMINI 20   A cafeteria. KEYWORD: *Supply*

a cafeteria

THEME: *A Full Supply for Here and Now.* This symbol speaks to the division of labor in any society whereby each individual benefits all the others by contributing his own special skills and talents to the pool of resources. The image of a cafeteria emphasizes abundance, variety and the importance of using discrimination in satisfying personal needs and wants. Positive: At its highest, this symbol represents versatility and personal enrichment through full participation in the give-and-take situations of life. Negative: Vacillation, indecision, and an inability to keep long-term commitments.

TODAY: The accent is on self-help. Everything you need is at hand. All you have to do is choose.

Opportunity: Your greatest advantage lies in taking care of your responsibilities and being willing to ask for help if you need it.

Risk: Guard against letting yourself get confused by the number of choices available to you. Know what you want and don't dwell on trying to get things you don't need.

STEPPING STONES: Nourishment, abundance, supply, profusion, variety, choice, diversity, self help, division of labor.

GEMINI 21   A labor demonstration. KEYWORD: *Representation*

a labor demonstration

THEME: *Protest.* This symbol speaks to breaking free of the restrictions and limitations that undermine the basic rights and freedom of men. The image of a labor demonstration is another of the reversed or negative symbols and it dramatizes the universal spirit as the source of all protests against social injustice. The implication here is that civil or human rights cannot be established and maintained without conscious effort, and that constraints, controls and regulations are justified only as they benefit society as a whole. Positive: At its highest, this symbol represents the courage to speak out against inequity and injustice, and a willingness to make personal sacrifices for the welfare of the group. Negative: Hostility and contentiousness or simple trouble making.

TODAY: The accent is on justice and human dignity. Some incident today may be the straw that breaks the camel's back.

Opportunity: Your greatest advantage lies in standing up for your rights and those of others. Be willing to put up with a little discomfort and inconvenience to bring about positive change.

Risk: Guard against being manipulated into fighting someone else's battle for them. Avoid taking an all or nothing position. Leave room for negotiation.

STEPPING STONES: Protest, strike, riot, rally, campaign, grievance, objection, outcry, dissent, breaking free, courage, injustice, inequity.

GEMINI 22   A barn dance. KEYWORD: *Gregariousness*

a barn dance

THEME: *A Good Time.* This symbol speaks to finding happiness through full participation in everyday community activities. The image of a barn dance describes a free-spirited and carefree social event where all personal differences and problems are put aside or temporarily forgotten. The suggestion of a square dance alludes to the give-and-take interchange of individuals on equal footing and it emphasizes friendliness, cooperation and a lack of inhibition. Positive: At its highest, this symbol represents extroversion, enthusiasm, a love of socializing and a preference for working in groups. Negative: Constant need for excitement and attention from others or an inability to function independently and spend quiet time alone.

TODAY: The accent is on interchange. Social activities take center stage.

Opportunity: Your greatest advantage lies in participating. Relax, enjoy, communicate and get involved.

Risk: Guard against making busyness an excuse for not dealing with your personal problems. Don't depend on others to make your life interesting.

STEPPING STONES: Celebration, fun, enthusiasm, congeniality, sociability, gregariousness, happiness, interchange, friendliness, cooperation.

GEMINI 23   Three fledglings in a nest high in a tree. **KEYWORD:** *Elevation*

Three fledglings in a nest high in a tree
NEST

THEME: *Give It a Try.* This symbol speaks to a dawning awareness of potentiality or what can be achieved, along with a desire to succeed and the willingness to try. The image of three fledglings in a nest high in a tree symbolizes activity, creativity and aspiration in their initial stages of growth. The little birds are realizing that it is possible to fly—but how? The emphasis here is on innovation. If one method doesn't work then try another. Each individual is constantly himself, and the intimation or revelation of his own special genius can be found in his earliest and unconditioned hopes and dreams. Positive: At its highest, this symbol represents free-spirited optimism and boundless creativity. Negative: Lack of common sense and an inability to recognize or accept responsibility.

TODAY: The accent is on aspiration. High hopes and expectations may have you on your toes and holding your breath.

Opportunity: Your greatest advantage lies in giving it a try. Put fear behind you and expect the best. Be innovative.

Risk: Guard against rash or hasty decisions. Don't be in such a hurry to get going. Look before you leap.

STEPPING STONES: Potential, promise, prospect, hope, possibility, anticipation, aptitude, aspiration, immaturity.

GEMINI 24   Children skating on ice. KEYWORD: *Fun*

Children skating on ice

THEME: *Adventures in Experience*. This symbol speaks to excitement, the heightened anticipation of enjoyment, and the ever-present danger of neglecting or failing to properly maintain foundations. It also speaks to the need to be ready and prepared to handle all unexpected demands that may arise. The image of children skating on ice dramatizes the spirit of adventure as well as an innocent but somewhat naive obliviousness to the realities of "skating on thin ice," or the hazards present in any risky situation. The emphasis in this symbol is on having clearly established goals and recognizing that every success is merely a stepping stone to greater achievement. On a practical level, this means never surrendering to a "things-are-fine-as-is" level of complacency or succumbing to delusions of adequacy. Positive: At its highest, this symbol represents joy in self-discovery through endless adventure. Negative: Thrill seeking and an inability to sense real danger.

TODAY: The accent is on caution. There could be hidden danger in some adventure.

Opportunity: Your greatest advantage lies in making sure you are standing on solid ground or a firm foundation before you perform any intricate maneuver. Be prepared for the unexpected.

Risk: Guard against complacency or assuming that because things were fine the last time you looked that they still are. Don't press your luck. It isn't always the other fellow who gets hurt.

STEPPING STONES: Danger, hazard, thrill-seeking, risk, fun, adventure, escapade, excitement, obliviousness.

GEMINI 25   A man trimming palms. KEYWORD: *Enhancement*

a man trimming palms

THEME: *Dedication*. This symbol speaks to effort, and to the pride in workmanship that helps an individual make his personal mark in the world. The image of a man trimming palm trees depicts the shaping and enhancement of natural resources to man's purposes. The process of trimming dead palm fronds from the trees also symbolizes the elimination of those things that have no immediate value or purpose, or that burden and impede future growth. Implicit in this symbol is the necessity that an individual become intimately familiar with the raw materials of his work and know how to use them to achieve his goals. Positive: At its highest, this symbol represents a special talent for obtaining the cooperation and resources needed to accomplish objectives. Negative: Naive satisfaction in making things look good rather than doing a job properly.

TODAY: The accent is on cutting back and sprucing up.

Opportunity: Your greatest advantage lies in getting rid of excess or things you don't really need in your life. Streamline and refine. Remember that sometimes less is more.

Risk: Guard against wasting valuable time on trivial details or trying to make a silk purse out of a sow's ear.

STEPPING STONES: Beautification, care, betterment, cultivation, enhancement, perfection, refinement, cutting back, reduction, labor, effort.

GEMINI 26   Winter frost in the woods. KEYWORD: *Splendor*

Winter frost in the woods

THEME: *Temporary Setback*. This symbol speaks to the significance of interruption, temporary loss or delay, and the upsetting of plans or the smooth flow of things. It also speaks to the principle of priorities, or first things first, and the need and power of the universe to sustain itself over the demands of men that everything conform to their personal convenience. The image of winter frost in the woods alludes to a suspension of normal activities, or a sudden freeze in the motion forward, and it emphasizes a need to change perspective. It also signals a moment of wonder and a time for appreciating the magic and splendor to be found in the fulfillment of cosmic purpose. Positive: At its highest, this symbol represents transition and realignment, or the process of transformation where the old gives way to the new. Negative: Elimination or the sweeping away of all that has no further use or value.

TODAY: The accent is on interruption. Things may be canceled or delayed today through no fault of your own.

Opportunity: Your greatest advantage lies in finding the meaning and opportunity in postponement, or having to wait for what you want. Appreciate the unexpected.

Risk: Guard against crystallization. Don't miss the magic moments that inevitably occur in the unexpected disruptions of plans and schedules.

STEPPING STONES: Transformation, wonderment, beauty, pause, temporary setback, interruption, delay, suspension, freeze.

GEMINI 27   **A gypsy coming out of the forest. KEYWORD:** *Expenditure*

THEME: *In Search of Success*. This symbol speaks to an individual's first realization that he is a person in his own right, and to his naive self-confidence and eagerness for success and recognition. The image of a gypsy coming out of the forest symbolizes the emergence of selfhood and a certain childlike but optimistic readiness for new experience and adventure. The emphasis here is on expansion of consciousness and the development of competency through outreach and learning how to cooperate with others. Positive: At its highest, this symbol speaks to joy in the ability to express the self freely and delight in personal accomplishment. Negative: Nonconformity and iconoclasm, or social mistrust and an inability to cooperate or feel comfortable in normal social relationships.

TODAY: The accent is on curiosity and enthusiasm. Naive optimism may be the catalyst that launches you on a new adventure.

Opportunity: Your greatest advantage lies in having faith in your ability to succeed. Trust that whatever you need will be there when you need it.

Risk: Guard against trying to be too self-sufficient. Rejecting assistance or an offer of help can deprive another of a chance to be of service.

STEPPING STONES: Expansion of experience, adventure, curiosity, inquisitiveness, interest, emergence, quest, aspiration, ambition, naïveté, nonconformity.

GEMINI 28   A man declared bankrupt. KEYWORD: *Deliverance*

a man declared bankrupt

THEME: *Starting Over.* This symbol speaks to the end of a cycle, and to the need to start over or begin anew whenever all present opportunities for growth or sustainment have been exhausted. The image of a man declared bankrupt is another reversed symbol and it symbolizes a release from unbearable responsibilities and pressures that can no longer be endured or tolerated. It also alludes to impermanence and the basic principle that nothing lasts forever. Here is a call to recognize that good and bad times come and go. Reward and penalty are merely moral judgment words that describe cause and effect in terms of consequence. And, in reality, consequence is simply "a convenient convergence of relationships" in time and space. Positive: At its highest, this symbol represents resourcefulness or the ability to find solutions to even the most difficult problems. Negative: Avoidance of responsibility and self-betrayal.

TODAY: The accent is on turning points. When one door closes another opens.

Opportunity: Your greatest advantage lies in realizing when it's time to quit and start over. Learn from your mistakes and move forward.

Risk: Guard against abusing privilege or imposing on others by making them pay your way or assume your responsibilities.

STEPPING STONES: Rescue, release, fresh start, end of a cycle, loss, starting over, new opportunity.

GEMINI 29   The first mockingbird in spring. KEYWORD: *Quickening*

The first mockingbird in spring

THEME: *Awakening*. This symbol speaks to self-strengthening, and to refinement through the aesthetic experience. The image of the first mocking bird in spring symbolizes the awakening of an individual to his own potential, and it emphasizes the necessity that an individual be able to articulate or clarify to himself what it is that he hopes to achieve in life. This degree also alludes to rehearsal, imitation and the value of vicarious experience. The implication here is that aspiration is the springboard to success. On a practical level, this image suggests a wake-up call or the need to pay attention to something that has been overlooked or neglected. Positive: At its highest, this symbol represents a natural talent for inspiring and motivating others and an intuitive gift for recognizing opportunity before it fully develops. Negative: A tendency to irritate others by being too pushy or bossy.

TODAY: The accent is on hearing the call to action. A new opportunity or important news may be announced today.

Opportunity: Your greatest advantage lies in paying attention. The early bird catches the worm.

Risk: Guard against speaking up too soon or irritating those around you by voicing your opinions too loudly or strongly.

STEPPING STONES: Awakening, announcement, wake-up call, greeting, articulation, imitation, stimulation, inspiration, revitalization, quickening, beckoning.

GEMINI 30 Bathing beauties. KEYWORD: *Charm*

THEME: *The Appearance of Things.* This symbol speaks to personal excellence that is innate or genetic in nature. It also speaks to the necessity that man learn to stand on his own two feet and become self-reliant. An individual falls short, or betrays himself, when he refuses to make his own decisions and accept responsibility for his own acts and behavior. The image of bathing beauties alludes to vanity, superficial appearances and the ephemeral nature of all physical things. Implicit in this degree is the principle that men gain self-confidence and are willing to be themselves only as they accept and appreciate those elements of themselves that cannot be changed or destroyed. On a practical level, this image can indicate overconcern with appearances or what others think and say. Positive: At its highest, this symbol represents charm and an ability to transform the normal and ordinary into the exceptional and beautiful. Negative: Immaturity or narcissism and conceit.

TODAY: The accent is on superficial appearance.

Opportunity: Your greatest advantage lies in making what you have work for you. Use your charm and put your best foot forward.

Risk: Guard against accepting things at face value. They may not be what they appear to be. Try not to let praise go to your head.

STEPPING STONES: Appearances, endowments, charm, charisma, allure, self-confidence, beauty, attractiveness, vanity, conceit.

Cancer

♋

CANCER 1   A furled and an unfurled flag displayed from a vessel.
KEYWORD: *Adaptability*

a furled and unfurled flag displayed from a vessel

THEME: *Decision.* This symbol speaks to a dramatic change of heart and to realignment, or a turning point in life. The image of a furled and an unfurled flag displayed from a vessel alludes to a change in authority or a transfer of allegiance. The indication here is that the vessel, which can also symbolize the individual, is about to sail under a new flag or align itself with a new or different cause. The suggestion in this image is that nothing is irrevocable and that if an individual discovers that he has been untrue to himself in his commitments, or finds that he can make no further progress towards achieving his ultimate goal or purpose, then he is justified in changing his loyalties. On a practical level, this degree can indicate a change in political parties, group affiliation, lifestyle or even citizenship. Positive: At its highest, this symbol represents flexibility and a willingness to risk temporary upsets or endure the hardships associated with any extreme change in order to maintain self-integrity. Negative: Indecisiveness or spinelessness and irresponsibility.

TODAY: The accent is on a major change of commitment and realignment. The realization that you have outgrown some experience or that your objectives are better served elsewhere may cause you to close the door on something in your life and take different path.

Opportunity: Your greatest advantage lies in recognizing when change is in your best interest and having the courage to make it.

Risk: Guard against being afraid to let go of the familiar, or feeling that others will be upset with you if you leave. You don't have to go down with the ship or sacrifice yourself just to please others.

STEPPING STONES: Change of allegiance or loyalty, transition, adaptability, flexibility, compromise, vacillation, indecision.

CANCER 2   A man suspended over a vast level place. KEYWORD: *Contemplation*

a man suspended are a vast level place

THEME: *Circumspection.* This symbol speaks to looking over situations and examining all options, opportunities and possible consequences before making commitments or getting involved. The image of a man suspended over a vast level place is one of the reversed or negative symbols, but here it suggests poise, circumspection, and a look-before-leaping approach to decision-making, or making wise choices. Positive: At its highest this symbol represents calm and reasoned judgment, broad vision and the ability to perceive the interconnectedness of all things. Negative: Impracticality or flightiness and fear of commitment.

TODAY: The accent is on perspective. You may be trying to get a broader overview of some situation before making a commitment or making a decision.

Opportunity: Your greatest advantage lies in taking all the time you need to gather your facts and weigh your options.

Risk: Guard against trying to avoid commitment by thinking an idea to death or ignoring the need to make a decision. Don't set deadlines you're not prepared to meet.

STEPPING STONES: Contemplation, study, thought, consideration, deliberation, reflection, examination, decision, circumspection, vision, observation, overview, perspective.

CANCER 3   **A man all bundled up in fur leading a shaggy deer.**
KEYWORD: *Indomitability*

a man all bundled up in fur leading a shaggy deer

THEME: *Trailblazing.* This symbol speaks to a pioneer spirit and rugged individualism. The image of a man all bundled up in fur leading a shaggy deer expresses hardiness, strength of character and courage. It also portrays the independent thinker or one who insists on doing things his way, even if it means going it alone. Positive: At its highest this symbol represents inner conviction, strongly held principles and a deep sense of purpose. Negative: Self-defeating behavior or a tendency to create the same self-limiting problems as a way of avoiding the new, the unfamiliar and the unknown.

TODAY: The accent is on rugged individualism and determination. The urge to break free from some frustrating situation may result in someone you know setting out alone in an entirely new direction.

Opportunity: Your greatest advantage lies in following your instincts and doing what you believe is in your own best interest, even if it doesn't accord with what the rest of the world would be inclined to do.

Risk: Guard against making things difficult for yourself by getting into situations where your options and freedom are limited.

STEPPING STONES: Determination, strength, conviction, purpose, hardiness, pioneering spirit, individualism, independence, challenge.

CANCER 4   A cat arguing with a mouse. KEYWORD: *Justification*

a cat arguing with a mouse

THEME: *Savvy*. This symbol speaks to mind-set and to planning or having a specific objective or purpose in view before taking concrete action. It also emphasizes the fact that preparing for an event is often more exciting and enjoyable than the event itself. The image of a cat arguing with a mouse depicts a setup, or baiting and manipulation. Here a cat is toying with a mouse in an attempt to evoke the response that will justify killing it. The image thus dramatizes the natural tendency of men to seek outer sanction or approval before acting on their inner desires, or their need to rationalize and find logical support for their values and behaviors. On a practical level, this symbol says "I did this because . . . ." Positive: At its highest this symbol represents psychological insight and a charismatic gift of persuasion. Negative: Dissatisfaction, manipulation and argumentativeness.

TODAY: The accent is on setting up or manipulating situations in order to produce a desired outcome. Clever attempts to win approval for some action are likely to be made today.

Opportunity: Your greatest advantage lies in having a plan of action for achieving your goals. Make sure you have the support of others.

Risk: Guard against being baited into an argument or fight today. Don't play into someone else's hands by losing your temper.

STEPPING STONES: Harassment, provocation, teasing, torment, baiting, badgering, goading, mind-set, excuse, justification.

CANCER 5   An automobile wrecked by a train. KEYWORD: *Dispersion*

An auto wrecked by a train

THEME: *Knowing When to Stop.* This symbol speaks to a compelling sense of urgency or obligation to complete or finish something that has been started or set in motion. In a broad sense, this symbol speaks to a desire to obtain closure. The image of an automobile wrecked by a train is another of the reversed symbols, and it dramatically illustrates the dangers of trying to rush things or bring any situation to a premature end. The earliest description of this image was "A man in an automobile, maddened by the lust for speed, races with a fast train and loses; he is killed." The emphasis in this symbol is on self-control, self-preservation and the need to understand that at all times the ultimate obligation of any individual is to himself rather than the outcome of any objective. The seeker is ill-advised to continue any course of action to the point of self-annihilation. Positive: At its highest this symbol represents a remarkable talent for finding solutions to difficult problems by reevaluating prior experience in terms of current needs. Negative: A tendency toward obsession that can lead to recklessness or foolish decision-making.

TODAY: The accent is on rushing to finish or get through things.

Opportunity: Your greatest advantage lies in knowing when to stop or take a break. Stay in control of the situation and don't be pressured by artificial or self-created deadlines.

Risk: Guard against endangering your health by living your life on the fast track or forgetting that your first obligation is to yourself.

STEPPING STONES: Haste, recklessness, carelessness, rashness, foolhardiness, negligence, short-sightedness, compulsion, obsession.

CANCER 6   Game birds feathering their nests. KEYWORD: *Meticulousness*

THEME: *Group Dynamics.* This symbol speaks to group spirit, and to the satisfaction that can be found in learning how to go with the flow and use the natural course of things to best advantage. The image of game birds feathering their nests depicts the building of a community and it dramatizes the opportunities for developing the skills and talents that are needed in any group project or cooperative division of labor. More importantly, this symbol alludes to pride, self-esteem, and the importance of being part of the process. Every individual needs to know that he has his own task or special role to play in a group and that he is respected and appreciated for having done a good job. Positive: At its highest this symbol represents a remarkable gift for identifying and assuming responsibility for the tasks in life that offer the greatest potential for personal growth. Negative: Insecurity and an unwillingness to assume responsibility or work independently.

TODAY: The accent is on improving home and community.

Opportunity: Your greatest advantage lies in making it a group effort or dividing up the responsibilities of some important project with each person doing what he does best. Cooperation is the key.

Risk: Guard against making yourself miserable by worrying about what you don't have rather than enjoying what you do have.

STEPPING STONES: Fastidious, conscientious, responsibility, concern, cooperation, group organization, division of labor, community.

CANCER 7   Two fairies on a moonlit night. KEYWORD: *Ascendancy*

Two faires on a moonlit night

THEME: *Unifying Magic*. This symbol speaks to transformation, lightness of heart, and the need of every individual to take a break and do something restful and relaxing when functioning under stress or strain. The image of two fairies on a moonlit night alludes to the healing power of nature and the hidden, unifying magic behind all things. The emphasis here is on imagination as a springboard to self-realization and on quiet reflection as the path to understanding and inner peace. On a practical level, this symbol may indicate the granting of a wish. Positive: At its highest this symbol represents an intuitive awareness of what needs to be done in order to maintain a proper balance or restore a situation to wholeness. Negative: Refusal to deal with reality and escape through fantasy and denial.

TODAY: The accent is on magic. Release from pressure and stress or a healing of some situation or condition brings welcome relief. Romance is in the air.

Opportunity: Your greatest advantage lies in using your creativity and imagination and following your intuition. Believe in miracles.

Risk: Guard against refusing to look at a situation as it really is, or telling yourself that it will go away if you just refuse to recognize it. Don't let someone pull the wool over your eyes by telling you what you want to hear.

STEPPING STONES: Imagination, magic, fantasy, illusion, reverie, romance, wishes, dreams, vision, escape, transcendence, inspiration.

CANCER 8   Rabbits   dressed   in   clothes   and   on parade.
KEYWORD: *Appropriation*

Rabbits dressed in clothes and on parade

THEME: *Let's Pretend.* This symbol speaks to aspiration and ambition, and to the necessity that an individual's everyday experience contribute in some manner to the formulation and clarification of his value system. The image of rabbits dressed in clothes and on parade emphasizes the importance of imagination, experimental role-play and mental rehearsal in the achievement of practical goals. Whatever can be articulated or dramatized in some way can become tangible reality. Here the rabbits are creating the reality they hope to establish for themselves. Positive: At its highest this symbol represents positive thinking, unwavering self-confidence, and an ever-continuing upliftment of self into broader and higher levels of accomplishment. Negative: Wishful thinking and a tendency to make up stories or fabricate the truth rather than admit to failure or exert the effort to make a dream come true.

TODAY: The accent is on ambition. The desire to fulfill a dream may lead you to do something concrete to achieve an important goal you previously abandoned.

Opportunity: Your greatest advantage lies in living your ideals. Experiment, role play and rehearse.

Risk: Guard against being fooled by appearances or believing everything you hear. Just because someone says a thing is so doesn't mean that it is. Avoid stretching the truth or exaggerating things. Don't make claims you can't substantiate.

STEPPING STONES: Pretense, aspiration, ambition, affectation, masquerade, charade, disguise, false claim, appropriation, plagiarism.

CANCER 9   A tiny nude miss reaching in the water for a fish.
        KEYWORD: *Inclination*

A Tiny nude miss reaching in the water for a fish

THEME: *Beginner's Luck.* This symbol speaks to the first innocent outreach of an individual into new experience, and to the importance of trying. The image of a tiny nude miss reaching in the water for a fish dramatizes naive curiosity and a complete absence of the fear and inhibitions that lead to failure. It also alludes to an alertness to opportunity. On a practical level, this symbol describes the principle of beginners luck as it is played out when an individual jumps into a situation on a whim and, with little or no knowledge of the rules or procedures, comes up a winner. Positive: At its highest this symbol represents irresistible charm and spontaneity. Negative: Rash behavior or lack of discretion.

TODAY: The accent is on experimentation and reaching out. Curiosity may get the best of your today and cause you to try something new.

Opportunity: Your greatest advantage lies in taking a chance. Think positively. The way to begin is to begin.

Risk: Guard against telling yourself all the reasons why something won't work or you can't succeed. Don't let fear stop you from enjoying yourself.

STEPPING STONES: Beginner's luck, new experience, expectation, effort, curiosity, alertness, spontaneity, enthusiasm, impulsiveness, inclination, disposition.

CANCER 10   A large diamond not completely cut. KEYWORD: *Latency*

a large diamond not completely carved

THEME: *Hidden Promise*. This symbol speaks to cultural and intellectual self-refinement, and to service in the form of a creative and personal contribution to society. The image of a large diamond not completely cut depicts work in progress on something of great value and it symbolizes evolution, transformation, self-actualization and the process of striving toward perfection. The emphasis here is on the development of potential. Positive: At its highest this symbol represents a special gift for discovering and bringing out the hidden beauty and purpose in things. Negative: Difficulty in recognizing possibilities or a tendency to place too much stock in things that have no potential for growth.

TODAY: The accent is on actualizing potential. You may suddenly recognize a possibility you never noticed before and decide to do experiment with it.

Opportunity: Your greatest advantage lies in finding the hidden promise in things. Concentrate on self-improvement. Refine your skills and talents. You may need them soon.

Risk: Guard against judging things by appearance. You may miss a great opportunity or end up with a pig in a poke.

STEPPING STONES: Work in progress, possibility, potential, development, hope, incompletion.

CANCER 11   A clown making grimaces. KEYWORD: *Inimitability*

[handwritten: A clown making grimaces]

THEME: *Keeping a Sense of Humor.* This symbol speaks to self-expression and to the continual refinement of individual personality through trial-and-error experimentation in the practical and everyday world. The image of a clown making grimaces (or frowning) symbolizes exaggerated or dramatic self-ridicule, and it emphasizes the importance of being able to acknowledge deficiencies, find the humor in situations and laugh at trivial mistakes and failures. On a practical level, this symbol can refer to clowning around or acting silly. Positive: At its highest this symbol represents a good sense of humor, personal distinctiveness and the ability to make a dramatic impact on others. Negative: Exaggeration or irritating grandstanding that erodes credibility.

TODAY: The accent is on hyperbole and drama. Everything may seem magnified today. Look behind the masks you see.

Opportunity: Your greatest advantage lies in keeping your sense of humor.

Risk: Guard against crying wolf or overstating your case or point once too often. You will lose your audience. Watch out for someone trying to cover up something with ridicule.

STEPPING STONES: Drama, exaggeration, ridicule, humor, comedy, parody, burlesque, hyperbole, overstatement, enhancement, embellishment, imitation.

CANCER 12   A Chinese woman nursing a baby with a message.
KEYWORD: *Materialization*

a chinese woman nursing a baby with a message

THEME: *Universal Brotherhood*. This symbol speaks to brotherhood and to broadening personal opportunities by reaching out and beyond the artificial boundaries of the immediate social milieu to embrace all the peoples of the world. The image of a Chinese woman nursing a baby with a message emphasizes nurturance, service and the sharing of personal resources. The baby has a "message" that was not further described in the first recorded description of this image, but the inference can be made that the message represents something to be learned or intuitively understood. In the 1931 mimeograph version of this image, the baby was described as having about it "the glorious nimbus of divine incarnation." It is thus possible that this message pertains to universal fellowship and love. Positive: At its highest this symbol represents service and a special gift for bringing culturally diverse people together in harmony. Negative: Smug pretense to spiritual superiority and a demand that others acknowledge it.

TODAY: The accent is on brotherhood and reaching out to others. Messages come in many forms.

Opportunity: Your greatest advantage lies in being open and willing to listen to what others have to say. You may be pleasantly surprised at what you hear.

Risk: Guard against insisting that your way is the only way. Don't close the door to opportunity by refusing to extend the hand of friendship.

STEPPING STONES: Brotherhood, fraternity, unity, fellowship, nurturance, service, harmony, peace, good will, emergence, unfoldment, message.

CANCER 13   One hand slightly flexed with a very prominent thumb. KEYWORD: *Determination*

One hand slightly flexed with a very prominent thumb

THEME: *Will Power.* This symbol speaks to man's belief in his personal supremacy over all other life forms and his unshakeable confidence in his ability to handle whatever arises in the practical and everyday world. The image of one hand slightly flexed with a very prominent thumb symbolizes will-power, determination and stubbornness. There is a certain caution indicated here. Although the hand is slightly flexed, indicating receptivity and flexibility, the prominent thumb alludes to forcefulness and control. Overall, the hand suggests an open invitation that if accepted could lead to subjugation or a potential loss of personal freedom; however, as the 1953 commentary suggests, "Any individual must rule his environment or surrender his own potentialities forever." Positive: At its highest this symbol represents exceptional self-discipline, self-control, responsibility and inner strength. Negative: Ruthlessness and tyrannical behavior or authoritativeness and a refusal to cooperate with others.

TODAY: The accent is on determination. People are not inclined to give in today. Getting people to cooperation may be difficult.

Opportunity: Your greatest advantage lies in exercising self-discipline. Believe in yourself and radiate self-confidence.

Risk: Guard against forcing others against their will. Even a good imposed on another is an evil.

STEPPING STONES: Determination, strong will, stubbornness, rigidity, inflexibility, tenacity, persistence, volition, resoluteness, insistence, confidence, conviction, obstinacy, ruthlessness.

CANCER 14   A very old man facing a vast dark space to the northeast. KEYWORD: *Sanction*

[handwritten] A very old man facing a vast dark space to the NE

THEME: *Hidden Reserves.* This symbol speaks to inner strength, and to the fact that man is always free to choose his beginnings. Future events can never limit present aspiration. The image of a very old man facing a vast dark space to the northeast has a somewhat lonely feel to it but the emphasis here is on fearlessness, courage and an inner assurance that arises out of experience, wisdom and faith. The vast dark space to the northeast symbolizes the spiritual reality that supports all of existence. The message in this symbol is that no individual is ever truly alone, even in the darkest moments of his soul. Positive: At its highest this symbol represents invisible sustainment and an ability to move forward into the unknown with dignity and courage. Negative: Fear of the future and an inability to understand the higher purpose in things.

TODAY: The accent is on invisible sustainment. Help may come from an unexpected source.

Opportunity: Your greatest advantage lies in your willingness to face the unknown and trust in the ultimate value of every experience.

Risk: Guard against losing sight of your purpose. Don't lose hope.

STEPPING STONES: Expectation, the unknown, courage, fearlessness, assurance, wisdom, faith, confidence, hope, trust, invisible sustainment.

CANCER 15   A group of people who have overeaten and enjoyed it.
KEYWORD: *Satiety*

a group of blackle who have overeaten and enjoyed it

THEME: *Satisfaction*. This symbol speaks to man's enjoyment of the fruits of his labor while at the same time cautioning against hoarding, gluttony and overindulgence. The image of a group of people who have overeaten and enjoyed it dramatizes the fullness of a shared experience with others, but it also points to the necessity of using discretion and the inevitable consequences of overcompensating for a lack in one area by going overboard in another. This image also suggests that the individual who develops an inner richness of being will never feel empty and deprived or try to make a present moment last forever out of a fear of a barren tomorrow. Positive: At its highest this symbol represents exceptional competence and a passion for life. Negative: Lack of self-control and a tendency to engage in excess.

TODAY: The accent is on overindulgence. You may be inclined to over-do or go overboard in some manner today.

Opportunity: Your greatest advantage lies in knowing when it's time to stop. Be moderate.

Risk: Guard against living too fast or too hard out of a fear that time and things are running out for you. Don't be greedy.

STEPPING STONES: Satiation, gratification, satisfaction, enjoyment, abundance, fullness, extravagance, luxury, over-indulgence, gluttony, excess, indiscretion, hedonism, intemperance.

CANCER 16   A man before a square with a manuscript scroll before him. KEYWORD: *Profundity*

[handwritten: A man before a square with a M.S scroll before him]

THEME: *Bringing Things Up to Standard.* This symbol speaks to intellectual experience as a challenge to self-competency, and to an attempt to improve things, or make *what is* square with *what could be.* The image of a man before a square with a manuscript scroll suggests editorial revision. The square is a measure, standard, pattern or model, and the inference here is that life is a continuing process of trying to bring all things into conformity with their ideal or highest potential. The implication is that individuals need to frequently examine their ideas, beliefs and opinions and make adjustments whenever they discover that their subjective perceptions are out of sync with objective reality. The emphasis is on structure, logic and objectivity. At its highest this symbol represents extraordinary organizational and analytical skills, reasoned judgment and self-discipline. Negative: Rigid thinking and lack of imagination, or an inability to think creatively and recognize the potential of things.

TODAY: The accent is on logic, system and structure. Comparisons, judgments and evaluations are emphasized. You may find yourself put to the test or having to answer the question, "Are you who you say you are?"

Opportunity: Your greatest advantage lies in making sure your behavior squares with your ideals.

Risk: Guard against expecting others to measure up to your standards or demanding a perfection that is unrealistic to the circumstance.

STEPPING STONES: Knowledge, erudition, intelligence, wisdom, conformity, squaring to standard, compliance, comparison, analysis, judgment, logic, structure.

CANCER 17 **The germ grows into knowledge and life.** KEY-
WORD: *Unfoldment*

*The germ grows into
knowledge and life*

THEME: *Self-actualization.* This symbol speaks to a dynamic will to live and achieve immortality through some lasting and significant contribution to the world. The image, the germ grows into knowledge and life, was compared by Marc Jones to the concept of the philosopher's stone that alchemists sought for the purpose of transforming base metals into gold or silver, or that occult philosophers seek as the knowledge by which all problems of objective life may be solved. It also symbolizes the uniqueness or distinctiveness that constitutes "self." The emphasis here is on a determination to not only survive but to reach the goal of a maximum fulfillment of personal potential or make the most of what the self can be. Positive: At its highest this symbol represents self-actualization, self-understanding and a total involvement of the self in every aspect of immediate concern. Negative: Baseless self-aggrandizement and a persistent demand for recognition.

TODAY: The accent is on growth and development. Things that have been at a standstill may suddenly take off and develop a life of their own today.

Opportunity: Your greatest advantage lies in capitalizing on the momentum present at this time and moving forward with your plans. Stay in the driver's seat and do it your way.

Risk: Guard against acting "holier than thou" or giving the impression that you think others are lacking in integrity. Avoid pontificating or proselytizing.

STEPPING STONES: Growth, development, maturation, transformation, metamorphosis, evolution, expansion, progress, emergence, advancement, formation, unfoldment, change.

CANCER 18   A hen scratching for her chicks. **KEYWORD:** *Provision*

a hen scratching for her chicks

THEME: *Nurturance.* This symbol speaks to personal protection and survival and to the principle that life supports life, or that assistance is available in any situation of need. The image of a hen scratching for her chicks emphasizes industriousness and persistence, and it dramatizes the necessity that the older and more experienced help the younger and less capable until they can stand on their own. It also alludes to responsibility and the importance of following up desire with action, or putting the shoulder to the wheel and keeping a forward motion. On a practical level, this image suggests mothering, nurturing and concern for those who have yet to establish themselves in life. Positive: At its highest this symbol represents stewardship and a remarkable gift for finding the advantage in even the bleakest of situations. Negative: Tendency to fret and worry or stir up confusion and turmoil over trivial issues.

TODAY: The accent is on assistance and helping those who can't yet stand on their own two feet.

Opportunity: Your greatest advantage lies in thinking ahead to what you're going to need very soon and getting it ready. Be resourceful and willing to do a little extra work.

Risk: Guard against making matters worse by digging up things that are better left buried. Don't waste valuable time on trivial or inconsequential matters.

STEPPING STONES: Provision, nurturance, care, assistance, sustainment, support, concern, stewardship, industriousness, preservation, foresight.

CANCER 19 A priest performing a marriage ceremony. KEY-WORD: *Conformity*

a priest performing a marriage ceremony

THEME: *Commitment.* This symbol speaks to spiritual stewardship as it is assumed by those individuals and institutions that have dedicated themselves to preserving the highest values of society. The image of a priest performing a marriage ceremony emphasizes moral integrity and a commitment to upholding community standards by living its ideals. On a practical level, this degree can refer to going along with the crowd or giving in to group pressure. Positive: At its highest this symbol represents a special gift for inspiring cooperation and finding ways to bring diverse elements and people together in a harmonious and functioning whole. Negative: Ritualistic behavior or obsession with the appearance rather than substance of things.

TODAY: The accent is on unification and integrity. Loyalty and commitment to common ideals may help people resolve their differences.

Opportunity: Your greatest advantage lies in helping people find what they have in common. Seek cooperation.

Risk: Guard against pretending things are okay when they're not or trying to make things look good on the surface for the sake of appearance. Don't be satisfied with the illusion of truth. Live it.

STEPPING STONES: Commitment, conformity, tradition, moral integrity, unification, harmony, integration, blessing, ritual.

CANCER 20   Gondoliers in a serenade. KEYWORD: *Sentiment*

Gondoliers in a serenade

THEME: *High Romance.* This symbol speaks to courtship, emotional idealism and an enjoyment of the social side of life. The image of gondoliers in a serenade symbolizes cooperation, harmony, the flowering of romance and creative self-expression. The implication of Venice and its water canals alludes to creativity, imagination and the undercurrent of sentimentality present in this degree. Positive: At its highest this symbol represents the perfection of those personal skills and talents that bring pleasure and happiness to others. Negative: Tendency to live in a world of fantasy.

TODAY: The accent is on romance. You may be feeling especially nostalgic and sentimental today.

Opportunity: Your greatest advantage lies in using your imagination and appealing to the heart. You'll catch more flies with honey than vinegar.

Risk: Guard against letting yourself be sweet-talked into something against your better judgment. Avoid making decisions based on sympathy.

STEPPING STONES: Romance, affection, desire, sentiment, love, courtship, passion, pleasure, self-expression.

CANCER 21   A prima donna singing. KEYWORD: *Excellence*

a prima donna singing

THEME: *Encouragement to Perfection.* This symbol speaks to the fulfillment of an opportunity to make a significant and lasting contribution through personal skills and talent. The image of a prima donna singing alludes to the importance of using a popular medium to reach the common man and awaken him to higher values and his own potential for success through a vicarious experience of excellence he can relate to at his own level or understand in familiar terms. The emphasis in this degree is on self-perfection as the dynamic for a continuation of personal existence. Positive: At its highest this symbol represents the blossoming of selfhood as the result of a fully self-directed development of personal potential. Negative: Delusions of adequacy or inappropriate self-display.

TODAY: The accent is on excellence. You may be inspired by someone whose skills and talents speak to you at your soul level.

Opportunity: Your greatest advantage lies in recognizing that the time is ripe to start that self-improvement program. Tailor it to your own needs and situation.

Risk: Guard against drawing negative attention to yourself by violating socially accepted standards of behavior. Try to avoid offending conservatives with bohemian or avant-garde opinions and behaviors. You won't be appreciated.

STEPPING STONES: Skill, talent, artistry, mastery, excellence, perfection, encouragement, inspiration, motivation, incentive.

CANCER 22   A woman awaiting a sailboat. KEYWORD: *Equanimity*

THEME: *The Right Time and Place.* This symbol speaks to waiting for the right opportunity or time to act. It also alludes to the ability to stay poised and focused in the present while anticipating that which is yet to come. The image of a woman awaiting a sailboat emphasizes the importance of positive thinking. It is not present fact but the creative power of idea that establishes enduring reality. On a practical level, this image stresses the need for patience and the ability to hold up under stress or maintain emotional composure. Positive: At its highest this symbol represents an intuitive understanding of the meaning to be discovered in synchronicity, or the convergence of chance events, and the vision required to accurately predict the outcome of any current situation. Negative: Superstitious behavior or lack of initiative and a blind dependence on luck.

TODAY: The accent is on anticipation. You may find yourself frustrated by delays. Being in the right place at the right time is important.

Opportunity: Your greatest advantage lies in being patient. The wait will be worth it. Make sure you know what you are looking for or you may not recognize it when it gets here.

Risk: Guard against expecting things to fall in your lap without putting forth the effort to get them. You could be disappointed in the end.

STEPPING STONES: Anticipation, patience, poise, composure, focus, perspective, vision, positive thinking, faith, confidence, trust, hope, conviction.

CANCER 23   Meeting of a literary society. KEYWORD: *Criticism*

Meeting of a literary society

THEME: *Learning to Talk About It.* This symbol speaks to imagination, creativity and resourcefulness in finding new ways to raise the level of consciousness and stimulate others to broaden their horizons and set more rewarding goals in their lives. The image of a meeting of a literary society focuses on the critical review and analysis of the world's intellectual arts, or writings, as a means for enhancing self-awareness and understanding others. The emphasis in this degree is on the objective discussion of experience, and it dramatizes the need to examine personal attitudes and behaviors and talk about things in order to properly understand them. Positive: At its highest this symbol represents personal growth and the achievement of objectives through learning how to struggle and cooperate with others within the context of a group. Negative: Tendency to avoid risks by talking about life rather than living it.

TODAY: The accent is on critical discussion. Awareness is enhanced and opinions and perspectives are revealed, as ideas are threshed out with others.

Opportunity: Your greatest advantage lies in using group discussion, another's experience, or a great piece of literature as a frame of reference against which to examine your own attitudes and behaviors. Compare them to the values you profess. Do your actions match what you say you believe?

Risk: Guard against being a Walter Mitty or living in a dream world. Avoid criticizing others for their failures and mistakes if you have never walked in their shoes.

STEPPING STONES: Analysis, discussion, assessment, evaluation, criticism, review, examination, appraisal, intellectual pursuits, culture.

CANCER 24 **A woman and two men on a bit of sunlit land facing south. KEYWORD:** *Inception*

THEME: *Being Prepared.* This symbol speaks to decision-making as it applies to allegiances and loyalties, and deciding which demands will be answered. The image of a woman and two men on a bit of sunlit land facing south emphasizes mediation and the need to balance competing interests. The woman symbolizes emotions and the two men symbolize the mental and physical or habit nature. Together they represent the Platonic three souls of man. The south symbolizes passion, the libido, and freedom or lack of constraint. The three figures all face in the same direction, suggesting unity of purpose and cohesiveness. Implicit in this symbol is the concept of self-integration or the idea that an individual must pull himself together and be prepared to seize opportunity when it knocks. Positive: At its highest this symbol represents organizational skills and an exceptional ability to gain the advantage and win the confidence of others by demonstrating the potential to handle whatever is presented. Negative: Dependency, or a tendency to feel helpless and incompetent without the support of others.

TODAY: The accent is on making plans for a journey or trip. You may find that instead of prioritizing things and making choices you are trying to have things both ways, or have your cake and eat it too.

Opportunity: Your greatest advantage lies in demonstrating your competency and skills and proving you are the right one for the job.

Risk: Guard against letting your emotions get out of hand. Use your reason. You really can make it on your own if you try.

STEPPING STONES: Cohesion, congruity, agreement, accord, consistency, inception, beginnings, commencement, decision, mediation.

CANCER 25   A dark shadow or mantle thrown suddenly over the right shoulder. KEYWORD: *Destiny*

A dark shadow or mantle thrown suddenly over the right shoulder

THEME: *Leadership.* This symbol speaks to the fact that no individual can successfully ignore or reject his obligation to whatever he is a part of. Reality cannot be denied. The image of a dark shadow or mantle thrown suddenly over the right shoulder was described in the 1931 mimeograph version of these symbols as an "invisible mantle of power," indicating an unanticipated or abrupt assumption of leadership. The emphasis here is not so much on leadership per se as on the spiritual stewardship that it implies. At the same time this symbol alludes to the satisfaction that an individual experiences when he fulfills his potential by assuming a responsibility through which he can demonstrate his competency in practical and everyday terms. Positive: At its highest this symbol represents spectacular leadership and outstanding service. Negative: Exaggeration and delusions of grandeur.

TODAY: The accent is on an unexpected assumption of leadership and authority. You may be worrying about how to handle a new responsibility today.

Opportunity: Your greatest advantage lies in doing what you believe is best for all concerned, even if it isn't popular.

Risk: Guard against abusing your power or authority. What goes around comes around.

STEPPING STONES: Responsibility, accountability, commitment, assignment, duty, obligation, leadership, power, stewardship, service.

CANCER 26   Contentment and happiness in luxury, people reading on davenports. KEYWORD: *Repose*

Contentment and happiness in luxury Peple reading on davenports

THEME: *Time Out*. This symbol speaks to interlude, relaxation, a rest well-earned, and the contentment that follows an individual mastery of experience. The image of contentment and happiness in luxury, people reading on davenports also cautions against complacency and self-indulgence. The emphasis here is on the need to realize that when life slows down, it's time to gather strength for the greater task ahead. On a practical level, this degree advises the seeker to enjoy the moment while it lasts. Positive: At its highest this symbol represents revitalization, self-renewal and relief from stress and strain. Negative: Laziness or lack of motivation and mindless dissipation of potential.

TODAY: The accent is on leisure. Enjoy it while you can.

Opportunity: Your greatest advantage lies in taking time to rest and relax. Enjoy your accomplishments and smell the flowers while the blossoms last.

Risk: Guard against complacency or taking things for granted. Getting caught unprepared could spell defeat.

STEPPING STONES: Leisure, comfort, ease, peace, relaxation, composure, serenity, tranquility, complacency, freedom, enjoyment, interlude.

CANCER 27   **A storm in a canyon. KEYWORD:** *Intensification*

A storm in a canyon

THEME: *Crisis.* This symbol speaks to intensification, and to a sharp awakening from complacency through some event that cannot be ignored. It also alludes to the divine aspect of terror and violence when they strike to the core of the soul and ignite the passion of the individual's highest ideals. Here the individual is brought to a full realization of what he truly values as he struggles to preserve and protect those things he holds dear. The image of a storm in a canyon symbolizes a dramatic cleansing or catharsis. As such it strengthens integrity and clarifies the ultimate purpose of all things. Whatever holds no value is here swept away. Positive: At its highest this symbol represents the ability to rise above crisis and bring every resource of self to hand in meeting the greater challenges of life. Negative: Thrill seeking and a tendency to create chaos or stir up trouble.

TODAY: The accent is on crisis and the release of tension. Things that have been building to a climax may come to a head in a dramatic way.

Opportunity: Your greatest advantage lies in protecting those things you value the most. Look for positive and productive ways to work off anger, relieve anxiety or calm your nerves.

Risk: Guard against losing your temper or getting caught in the middle of an emotional confrontation. Don't add fuel to a fire by picking this time to get everything off your chest or let off steam.

STEPPING STONES: Crisis, terror, fear, turmoil, awakening, intensification, heightening, amplification, magnification, exacerbation, cleansing, catharsis, elimination.

CANCER 28   **A modern Pocahontas. KEYWORD:** *Compatibility*

A modern Pocahontas

THEME: *Assimilation.* This symbol speaks to cooperation between the old and the new or the conventional and the experimental. The image of a modern Pocahontas symbolizes self-integration, flexibility, and an acceptance of the ideas, traditions and customs of others. It also alludes to broad-mindedness and the ability to function effectively in more than one world at once. Positive: At its highest this symbol represents an ability to bring attention to forgotten or neglected values and ideals and demonstrate their usefulness for enhancing present-day living. Negative: Refusal to release the past or a foolish clinging to outworn traditions and an inability to cope with change.

TODAY: The accent is on progress, advancement and bringing things up to date or looking at new ways of doing things.

Opportunity: Your greatest advantage lies in recognizing when doing things the way you have always done them is holding you back or ruining your chance for happiness. Be willing to make needed changes and move forward.

Risk: Guard against crystallization. Avoid clinging to stale or obsolete ideas that affect your ability to function effectively in a present situation. Don't live in the past because you're afraid to deal with change.

STEPPING STONES: Synthesis, cooperation, union, assimilation, broad-mindedness, consolidation, integration, alliance, accord, progress, growth.

CANCER 29 A Muse weighing twins. KEYWORD: *Value*

a muse weighing twins

THEME: *Reconciliation of Opposites.* This symbol speaks to man's ability to connect with his guiding genius, or his source of inspiration, and to his ongoing process of self-integration and spiritual growth. The image of a Muse weighing twins refers to decision-making and inner reconciliation. A Muse is any of the nine sister goddesses in Greek mythology who oversee music, poetry, the arts and sciences. To muse on something is to ponder or contemplate it. Here the twins, or intuition and reason, are weighed in an attempt to achieve a balance in thinking that will ultimately help the individual recognize the universe as the unified and spiritual whole that it is. The emphasis in this symbol is on maintaining personal integrity through a continual process of self-examination and evaluation. Positive: At its highest this symbol represents exceptional judgment and the ability to fairly weigh both sides of an issue before coming to conclusions. Negative: Perfectionism, or a tendency to get lost in trivial detail and lose sight of the ultimate objective.

TODAY: The accent is on contemplation and decision-making. You may find yourself trying to reconcile conflicting values or information.

Opportunity: Your greatest advantage lies in combining intuition and reason in order to solve a problem or make a choice. Act with integrity and do what is right and just, even if it isn't easy or it creates a minor hardship.

Risk: Guard against putting off making a decision about some situation until it's too late to do anything about it. Don't fall into the trap of believing that there is only one right and perfect way to get a job done.

STEPPING STONES: Balancing, weighing, pondering, comparison, consideration, contemplation, deliberation, reflection, meditation, thought, decision.

CANCER 30 A Daughter of the American Revolution. KEY-
WORD: *Inheritance*

a daughter of the Am. Revolution

THEME: *A Standard Bearer.* This symbol speaks to established tradition and to a lack of sympathy with anything that threatens it. The image of a Daughter of the American Revolution cautions against resistance to change, and it stresses the importance of holding only to those ways of going that have proved their value. The emphasis here is on integrity and the courage to live an exemplary life in faithfulness to the highest ideals of humankind. Positive: At its highest this symbol represents a charismatic ability to inspire individuals to work together toward common goals within the framework of eternal values. Negative: Arrogance, tyranny or simple haughtiness.

TODAY: The accent is on tradition and precedent. Protect those things that have proven their worth.

Opportunity: Your greatest advantage lies in being conservative or moderate at this time. Understatement works best.

Risk: Guard against resisting change out of a misguided loyalty to the past. Don't fool yourself into believing that tenure or length of time with any project or group equates to superiority. Quality ever trumps quantity.

STEPPING STONES: Tradition, heritage, background, standards, values, ideals, patriotism, moderation, conservatism, preservation, commitment, dedication, resistance to change, pride.

Leo

♌

LEO 1 A case of apoplexy. KEYWORD: *Irresistibility*

[handwritten: a case of apoplexy]

THEME: *Determination*. This symbol speaks to potentiality full to bursting, and to a pressing need to find suitable outlets for self-expression. The image of a case of apoplexy describes an individual who has been suddenly struck with paralysis and loss of consciousness as a result of pressure on the brain. This is another of the reversed symbols, and it dramatizes what can happen when an individual's desire to do as he pleases is frustrated and he is unable to find positive ways to release the buildup of his tension. On a practical level, this symbol can represent burnout. The emphasis here is on man's basic need to express himself freely and avoid limitation and restraint. Leo 1 was described in the 1931 mimeograph version of these symbols as "the first and key symbol of the three-hundred-sixty, first of twenty-four that more properly if less conveniently identify the spans or activity hours, or King Man himself." Positive: At its highest, this symbol represents creative genius effectively expressed and applied in daily living. Negative: Demandingness and self-centered insensitivity to the burdens placed on others as the result of an unwillingness to assume a fair share of responsibility.

TODAY: The accent is on frustration and tension. There is a strong likelihood that the need to release pent-up thoughts and emotions will result in some individuals losing their composure and self-control

Opportunity: Your greatest advantage lies in finding productive and healthy ways to relieve stress.

Risk: Guard against burnout, or letting things go too long before doing something about them. Avoid making a fool of yourself by losing your temper or exploding as a result of your inability to make things go your way.

STEPPING STONES: Pressure, force, tension, stress, frustration, burnout, need for release, determination, compulsion, lack of self-control, loss of rationality, mobilization, explosiveness.

LEO 2 An epidemic of mumps. **KEYWORD:** *Infection*

An epidemic of mumps

THEME: *Opportunity for Expansion.* This symbol speaks to some one or more aspects of the self getting completely out of control, and to the tendency of man to want to escape or avoid facing reality when life gets unpleasant and there is no understanding of what needs to be done, or what is needed or required, to bring about a healing or restore health and organic integrity. The image of an epidemic of mumps suggests a situation that affects not only individual but group functioning. The emphasis in this reversed symbol is on a temporary inability to continue in some present wished-for activity and a need to understand that while momentum has been restricted in one direction it has opened up the opportunity for expansion in another. Here is a call to realize that there is a reason for everything in life that happens. The task at hand is to comprehend the higher purpose or interest being served by the limitation. Positive: At its highest, this symbol represents self-expansion and dramatization of some unique aspect of self as the means for a constructive contribution to each phase of living. Negative: Highlighting inadequacies in order to escape experience and avoid responsibility.

TODAY: The accent is on dis-ease and momentum. Things could get out of control or become unstoppable within a particular group. Healing may be needed.

Opportunity: Your greatest advantage lies in understanding the greater purpose being served by a difficult drama that is being played out. Be sensitive to the opportunities being revealed.

Risk: Guard against the temptation to downgrade your abilities and know-how in order to avoid responsibility. Running away from experience will only create greater problems.

STEPPING STONES: Contagiousness, infection, transmission, expansion, momentum, outbreak, increase, upsurge, eruption, outburst, disease, affliction, malady, disorder, sickness.

LEO 3 A woman having her hair bobbed. KEYWORD: *Decision*

A woman having her hair bobbed

THEME: *The Courage to Change.* This symbol speaks to the fact that individuals are free to make choices, change, and free themselves from bondage to outworn habits and unprofitable ways of living. The image of a woman having her hair bobbed or cut short symbolizes independent thinking, modernization, and a desire to fit into the immediate social milieu and be part of what is current and "in." The emphasis is on self-examination, the avoidance of crystallization, and a willingness to examine the self and take whatever steps are necessary to facilitate personal growth. The transformation implied in this image is sudden, rather than gradual, and the implication here is of a sudden realization that change is necessary. Positive: At its highest, this symbol represents the capacity to pull the self together and do whatever is necessary to move forward and accomplish a task or achieve a goal. Negative: Self-depreciation and feelings of inadequacy, or a complete lack of insight and inability to recognize self-worth or potential.

TODAY: The accent is on self-examination. The desire to belong or be a part of some significant activity could create a willingness on your part to make a personal sacrifice in order to achieve this goal. Change is indicated.

Opportunity: Your greatest advantage lies in breaking free from self-limiting thoughts and behaviors. Have the courage to do what needs to be done.

Risk: Guard against feeling sorry for yourself or resenting those who are doing what you would like to do. Don't blame others for your own failings or unwillingness to risk.

STEPPING STONES: Independence, freedom, self-expression, courage, change, modification, alteration, conversion, transformation, extremism, desire to fit in, aspiration.

LEO 4 A man formally dressed and a deer with its horns folded.
    KEYWORD: *Morale*

A man formally dressed and a deer with its horns folded

THEME: *Command.* This symbol speaks to stately or formal self-assertion that makes a dramatic or bold impact on the everyday world at large. The image of a man formally dressed and a deer with its horns folded symbolizes a submission of the lower habit nature to the higher intellectual nature. The deer in the 1931 mimeograph version of this symbol was described as "a lovely mounted moose head." The implication there was that the man's success in subduing his lower nature was memorialized, or commemorated, with a trophy or reward. Here formality symbolizes organization and the ordering of all lesser things to a higher purpose. Positive: At its highest, this symbol represents dignity, bearing, poise and presence, as well as a remarkable talent for gaining the respect of others. Negative: Attention-getting behavior or constant approval-seeking.

TODAY: The accent is on self-assertion and getting things to work for you. Situations may need to be more formally structured.

Opportunity: Your greatest advantage lies in taking command and maintaining your dignity and poise. Be decisive and consistent.

Risk: Guard against seeking approval for every decision you have to make. Don't let others control how you will live your life.

STEPPING STONES: Domination, power, control, command, mastery, authority, rulership, self-assertion, formality and overshadowing *or* submission, giving in, acceptance, subservience, obeisance, respect, reverence, obedience.

LEO 5 **Rock formations at the edge of a precipice. KEYWORD:** *Endurance*

THEME: *Character Building.* This symbol speaks to the manner in which various, interlacing events and involvements build up in crisis to the point where individuals recognize that there is a reality that must be dealt with, decisions to be made, and actions that must be taken. The image of rock formations at the edge of a precipice symbolizes sustainment in a hazardous situation. At the same time, there can be no sustainment for any individual who isn't willing to meet challenge and work through difficulty. Every change encountered or risk faced is an opportunity to discover some new aspect of self and build character. Positive: At its highest, this symbol represents inner calm, competency, and courage in the face of danger. Negative: Stubbornness and inflexibility or resistance to change.

TODAY: The accent is on courage and endurance. Your ability to maintain your place in the scheme of things may be challenged at this time.

Opportunity: Your greatest advantage lies in holding steady and refusing to give up. Decide what you want to achieve and persist until you get it.

Risk: Guard against refusing to change your mind or your course of action, even when you know you are wrong or headed for disaster. Don't cut off your nose to spite your face.

STEPPING STONES: Endurance, persistence, determination, resoluteness, tenaciousness, sustainment, courage, character, continuance, competency, reality, survival, stubbornness, challenge, caution, hazard, danger, risk.

LEO 6   An old-fashioned woman and an up-to-date girl. KEYWORD: *Contrast*

An old fashioned woman and a platter

THEME: *Something Old, Something New, Something Shared.* This symbol speaks to the function and purpose of role-play in the everyday world. The image of an old-fashioned woman and an up-to-date girl dramatizes opposites, and it emphasizes the importance of learning to cooperate and look at life from the reverse or flip side of things. Here conservatism, maturity, tradition and established values of the past are contrasted with liberalism, youth, innovation and formative values. The implication of competing impulses to both stand still and move forward (the Mars/Saturn effect) provides the stimulus for each side to look behind surface appearances for common ground on which to come together in mutual appreciation of what each side has to offer. Positive: At its highest, this symbol represents accomplishment through cooperation and creative use of the opinions and values of others. Negative: "In-your-face" self-assertion or fear of confrontation and change.

TODAY: The accent is on disparity and contradiction. The challenge is on finding ways to preserve those things of the past that have maintained their value while supporting whatever holds promise for the future.

Opportunity: Your greatest advantage lies in being sensitive to the feelings and needs of those who may be in conflict. Focus on commonly shared goals and ideals, and find ways to cooperate.

Risk: Guard against throwing the baby out with the bath by insisting on a complete purge or break with the past. It doesn't have to be "either/or."

STEPPING STONES: Contrast, difference, discrepancy, disparity, contradiction, conflict, disagreement, deviation, opposites, dissimilarity, distinction, divergence, variety, stimulation.

LEO 7 The constellations in the sky. KEYWORD: *Surety*

The constellations in the sky

THEME: *The Search for Meaning.* This symbol speaks to the futility of trying to determine the origin or cause of things in order to avoid dealing with them in the here and now. It also speaks to the fruitlessness of trying to avoid responsibility by blaming things on the cosmos or anything else external to self. The image of the constellations in the sky symbolizes the lure of lovelier realms beyond, and thus the ultimate quest for experience, but the suggestion here is that man's greatest fulfillment is to be found in mastering his inner space and understanding the significance of his own experience. The stars reflect or mirror events; they do not create them. Positive: At its highest, this symbol represents the ability to recognize and understand the significance of the patterns in life and align the self effectively with opportunity. Negative: Refusal to accept responsibility and attempts to avoid facing reality by retreating into the mysterious and unknown.

TODAY: The accent is on certainty and assurance. The message for today is that your answers lie within.

Opportunity: Your greatest advantage lies in paying attention to signature and synchronicity. Accept responsibility for your actions, learn from your mistakes and take pride in your accomplishments.

Risk: Guard against blaming God, the cosmos, fate, or others for your difficulties or suffering. Don't play the role of the helpless victim.

STEPPING STONES: Sureness, certainty, constancy, security, confirmation, lastingness, assurance, eternity, beauty, quest, inspiration, significance, predictability, pattern, astrology.

LEO 8 A Bolshevik propagandist. KEYWORD: *Leaven*

a Bolshevik propagandist

THEME: *Uprising.* This symbol speaks to the fire of passion, and to the hope that burns in men's hearts when they rise up against oppression or rally to some great cause. The image of a Bolshevik propagandist is another of the reversed symbols and it dramatizes protest and the dissemination of ideas and information that encourage change. The emphasis here is on selfless dedication to the welfare of a group, taken to the extreme by an actual incitement to riot or revolt and overthrow the established order. On a more practical level, this symbol applies to such historical figures and catalysts of change as Leon Trotsky, Martin Luther King, Nelson Mandela and Mikhail Gorbachev. Positive: At its highest, this symbol represents a special gift for raising the level of social consciousness by creating a vision of a new and better life, and the ability to make a positive difference in the world. Negative: Dissentiousness or constant complaining about every minor inconvenience.

TODAY: The accent is on propaganda and political controversy. A clash of ideals or a call for change is possible.

Opportunity: Your greatest advantage lies in refusing to align yourself with any but the most worthy causes. Seek the greatest good for the greatest number.

Risk: Guard against ranting and railing over every perceived injustice or letting yourself get talked into joining or supporting a movement or group that uses destructive means to accomplish their goals. Don't rely on hearsay. Check things out for yourself.

STEPPING STONES: Indoctrination, proselytizing, distortion, bias, rumor, gossip, hearsay, reporting, publishing, proclaiming, brainwashing, propaganda, revolution, political controversy, extremism, anarchy, insurrection, uprising.

LEO 9 Glass blowers. KEYWORD: *Deftness*

a glass blowers

THEME: *Creativity*. This symbol speaks to creativity and artistry, and to man's efforts to glorify his ideals and give them tangible expression. The image of glass blowers symbolizes imagination, skill and craftsmanship. It also alludes to a personal manifestation of the divine creation through the conscious outbreathing of individual life force. On a practical level, this delicate and airy image dramatizes the common desire of every individual to create something beautiful and distinctly unique. Positive: At its highest, this symbol represents artistic genius and an effective hands on approach to life. Negative: Gross exaggeration, or a twisting of facts and a tendency to distort reality.

TODAY: The accent is on imagination and artistry. Whether creating objects of art, or forming alliances or ideas, you will need to be clever and skillful in bringing your project to fruition.

Opportunity: Your greatest advantage lies in knowing what you want to accomplish before you start working. Use a light touch and move quickly to correct mistakes.

Risk: Guard against being too heavy-handed or twisting things out of proportion. Be careful not to embellish the facts or distort the truth.

STEPPING STONES: Creativity, expression, imagination, artistry, enthusiasm, manifestation, skill, craftsmanship, adroitness, expertise, ability, dexterity, adeptness, proficiency, cleverness, manipulation, aptness.

LEO 10   Early morning dew. KEYWORD: *Rejuvenation*

Early morning dew

THEME: *A New and Better Day*. This symbol speaks to the invigorating and refreshing energy and enthusiasm that accompany any renewal of effort or new cycle of experience, and to the cosmic assist given to all worthwhile struggle. The image of early morning dew alludes to the dawning of a new day or a fresh start. The dew that magically appears on the cold surface of the earth sometime during the night is actually the condensation of the previous day's warm atmospheric moisture, and its effect is to freshen and revitalize the fields and flowers. Implicit in this beautiful image is the idea that nature is blessing man's efforts. This symbol also alludes to the fact that an individual often receives the help he needs when he is facing the darkest moments of his soul. The seeker must learn to expect the unexpected. The emphasis in this degree is on cosmic sustainment and a refusal to recognize personal limitation. Positive: At its highest, this symbol represents a gift for finding the opportunity in every situation. Negative: Tendency to keep putting off decisions and actions until it's too late, and an inability to recognize the strength that lies within.

TODAY: The accent is on faith and guardian angels. You may receive unexpected help or be given a fresh start today. Expect a miracle.

Opportunity: Your greatest advantage lies in refusing to acknowledge defeat. Try to look at the bright side of the situation and see what tomorrow brings.

Risk: Guard against losing hope or giving up too soon. Avoid thinking in terms of limitation or lack. Don't create a self-fulfilling prophesy.

STEPPING STONES: Rejuvenation, renewal, revival, restoration, revitalization, invigoration, stimulation, energy, strength, refreshment, fortification, support, blessing, favor, grace, endowment, bestowal, fresh start, purity.

LEO 11   Children on a swing in a huge oak tree. KEYWORD: *Delight*

Children on a swing beneath a huge oak tree

THEME: *Background as Sustainment.* This symbol speaks to the satisfaction experienced by the individual who is able to live his life as he wishes. It also speaks to the physical and social support that sustains him while he does this. The 1931 mimeograph version of children on a swing in a huge oak tree expanded the meaning of this image by adding that the activity was taking place in the rising heat of the noonday sun and that the shelter of the tree "provided the real contribution of background to growth." The image of children on a swing in a huge oak tree thus emphasizes facilitation and assistance. The implication is that but for the shade of the tree and its swing, the play would have ceased. The oak tree is an archetypal symbol of knowledge, and its pairing with a children's swing suggests that learning can be fun. The tree in this image also symbolizes the overshadowing of universal life, and the inference is that as each individual accepts this universal overshadowing, his personal understanding of his place in the overall scheme of things is heightened and enhanced. Positive: At its highest, this symbol represents enthusiasm, boundless energy, and an eagerness to experience all of life. Negative: Misguided pride in taking life easy and avoiding commitments.

TODAY: The accent is on enjoyment. The rhythm is lighter, happier and carefree. The universe supports you when you make every effort to act responsibly.

Opportunity: Your greatest advantage lies in being yourself. Establish your own unique rhythms and faithfully maintain them. Know when to advance and when to retreat.

Risk: Guard against taking pride in your ability to get out of work or commitments. Don't expect others to pick you up every time you fall. Stand on your own two feet.

STEPPING STONES: Play, fun, recreation, diversion, delight, enthusiasm, enjoyment, amusement, entertainment, happiness, pleasure, protection, exercise, rhythm, learning, background as facilitation to growth.

LEO 12   An evening lawn party. KEYWORD: *Companionship*

An evening lawn party

THEME: *Feedback*. This symbol speaks to camaraderie, enjoyment and the mutual sharing of personal accomplishments with friends and neighbors in a relaxed, social environment. The image of an evening lawn party suggests celebration, relaxation and rejuvenation after a period of intense effort. The emphasis here is on interchange, feedback, recognition and appreciation for a job well done. On a practical level, this symbol is reflected in the celebrations that follow upon a graduation, career promotion or some other special achievement. Positive: At its highest, this symbol represents friendliness, an ability to work well with others and social maturity. Negative: Frivolousness and a tendency to live for the moment or avoid responsibility.

TODAY: The accent is on socializing and camaraderie. It's time to kick back and enjoy time with friends.

Opportunity: Your greatest advantage lies in expressing genuine appreciation for the achievements of others. Be encouraging and supportive. Let someone know when you think they have done a good job.

Risk: Guard against bragging or extolling your own virtues. Don't play the game of one-upmanship. It might bring you down instead.

STEPPING STONES: Camaraderie, companionship, association, affiliation, fraternization, celebration, mutual appreciation, interchange, sharing, socializing, gossip, superficialities, niceties, relaxation.

LEO 13   An old sea captain rocking. KEYWORD: *Retrospect*

An old sea captain rocking

THEME: *Historical Perspective.* This symbol speaks to retrospection, and to an ability to identify relevant turning points in life and predict the outcome of current events by reflecting on past experience or using historical perspective. The emphasis here is on the fact that history repeats itself and events occur in cycles. The image of an old sea captain rocking alludes to maturity and the stage of life when battles and adventures take place mostly in the mind. Thus, this symbol also refers to vicarious experience. Positive: At its highest, this symbol represents the ability to draw on whatever skills and resources have been developed in the past as they are needed in any present moment. Negative: Crystallization or being completely out of touch with the realities of the present as a result of living in the past.

TODAY: The accent is on maturity, reflection and reconstruction. You may be surprised, when looking back on some event in your life, that you now see it quite differently.

Opportunity: Your greatest advantage lies in drawing on your past experience to handle a present challenge.

Risk: Guard against withdrawing in order to avoid dealing with change or unknowns in the present. You may lose your place among your fellows if you refuse to adapt or learn new skills.

STEPPING STONES: Retirement, withdrawal, maturity, retrospection, nostalgia, reflection, remembrance, reminiscence, sentiment, longing contemplation, meditation, consideration, history, the past, contentment, rest.

LEO 14   The human soul awaiting opportunity for expression.
KEYWORD: *Ingenuousness*

The human soul
awaiting opportunity
for expression

THEME: *On the Verge of Experience*. This symbol speaks to anticipation, and to a childlike eagerness for new experience. The focus here is on innocence and the absence of mind-set, or prior conditioning. The image of the human soul awaiting opportunity for expression alludes to readiness, alertness and naive expectation. Positive: At its highest, this symbol represents an intuitive gift for knowing the right time and place to act and a willingness to give the whole of self to any effort. Negative: Fear of new experience as the result of an inability to think things through clearly or boredom and apathy.

TODAY: The accent is on anticipation. You may find yourself standing back waiting for just the right time to get involved or show someone what you can do.

Opportunity: Your greatest advantage lies in knowing when to act. Use your intuition and be alert to the signatures that tell you it's time to make your move.

Risk: Guard against procrastinating or missing your chance because you're afraid to make a decision. Don't hide your light under a bushel too long.

STEPPING STONES: Expectation, anticipation, eagerness, aspiration, potential, promise, initiation, beginnings, genesis, inception, new experience, sensitivity, ingenuous, openness, trust, naïveté, innocence, gullibility.

LEO 15   A pageant. KEYWORD: *Demonstration*

a pageant

THEME: *A Moment of Glory.* This symbol speaks to pride in accomplishment, and to the public display of the fruits of a cooperative group effort. The image of a pageant conceptualizes that magical moment of celebration and fellowship when every individual who has played even a minor role in a project feels himself whole and at one with every other member of the team. The emphasis in this symbol is on group excellence and the dramatic articulation of social ideals. Positive: At its highest, this symbol represents self-esteem as the result of having made a worthwhile and valuable contribution to the common good and welfare of a group. Negative: Bragging and boasting or crude exhibitionism and pushiness.

TODAY: The accent is on accomplishment through group effort. Genuine fellowship is created as people learn to appreciate each other's differences and work together in harmony.

Opportunity: Your greatest advantage lies in encouraging everyone to take some part in achieving a common goal. Be supportive and willing to overlook minor mistakes while people are learning and developing their skills.

Risk: Guard against letting perfectionism or your desire to win overcome your obligation to your fellows. Don't brush aside or exclude those whose abilities or knowledge don't meet your standards.

STEPPING STONES: Public display, glory, exhibition, demonstration, manifestation, revelation, illustration, drama, ceremony, parade, procession, exhibition, extravaganza, articulation, fellowship, group effort, exaltation.

LEO 16   Sunshine just after a storm. KEYWORD: *Recovery*

Sunshine just after a storm

THEME: *Bounceback.* This symbol speaks to recuperation, and to the ability of individuals to reenter life fit and refreshed after major stress and strain. The image of sunshine just after a storm speaks to healing and rebirth. The storm is seen here as a process of cleansing and purging. Times of upset and turbulence are the necessary means for clearing away whatever stands in the way of healthy growth and functioning. The emphasis here is on recovery and reconstruction. Positive: At its highest, this symbol represents an exceptional ability to hold steady through turmoil and confusion and not lose sight of the higher purpose in all things. Negative: Emotionalism and a tendency to fly off the handle or get upset over every little thing.

TODAY: The accent is on recuperation, restoration and healing. Freedom and happiness follow limitation and sorrow.

Opportunity: Your greatest advantage lies in using stress productively. Stay centered and look for the silver lining in the clouds.

Risk: Guard against letting yourself get thrown off balance by disappointment or loss. Don't rain on someone's else's parade or dampen their enthusiasm and joy with your bad mood.

STEPPING STONES: Recovery, recuperation, relief, improvement, restoration, healing, reestablishment, renewal, revival, rebirth, cleansing, purging, clearance, health.

LEO 17   A nonvested church choir. KEYWORD: *Communion*

A non-vested church choir

THEME: *Cooperation.* This symbol speaks to the value of informal or unregimented group experience in learning cooperation and respect for personality. The image of a nonvested church choir alludes to fellowship and a sense of community. The suggestion here is that group functioning, in the absence of official rules and regulations, is an exercise in learning self-discipline and respect for the rights, contributions and idiosyncrasies of others. Positive: At its highest, this symbol represents joy in working with others who share a common passion. Negative: Competitiveness or attempts to curry favor by telling others what they want to hear.

TODAY: The accent is on volunteerism and informal group activities.

Opportunity: Your greatest advantage lies in learning to respect and appreciate difference. Praise others for the efforts they make and see what happens.

Risk: Guard against trying to make yourself look more important than others by doing things to stand out, or deliberately calling attention to yourself. The attention you get may not be what you had in mind.

STEPPING STONES: Community, fellowship, cooperation, harmony, friendship, rapport, informality, volunteerism, lack of regimentation, group experience, respect for personality.

LEO 18   A teacher of chemistry. KEYWORD: *Instruction*

a teacher of chemistry

THEME: *Experimentation*. This symbol speaks to trying to solve the deeper mysteries of life, and to man's insatiable desire to understand, predict and control the world in which he lives. The image of a teacher of chemistry alludes to education, experimentation and the creative use of scientific principles for everyday problem solving. The suggestion here is that man must take responsibility for whatever he creates. Positive: At its highest, this symbol represents extraordinary organizational and intellectual skills and a simple delight in testing the practical workability of every new concept or idea. Negative: Closed-mindedness or a rigid insistence on "going by the book" and staying with the safe and known.

TODAY: The accent is on scientific principles and education. Solving complex issues could occupy a lot of your time.

Opportunity: Your greatest advantage lies in testing things out and deciding for yourself. Experiment and find the right tools for the job. Remember that a master key unlocks more than one door.

Risk: Guard against guaranteeing failure by using the same approach, time after time, even when it isn't working.

STEPPING STONES: Education, learning, mastership, advice, guidance, leadership, instruction, training, insight, perception, discernment, acumen, discrimination, problem-solving, creativity, experimentation, scientific principles.

LEO 19   A houseboat party. KEYWORD: *Congeniality*

a house boat party

THEME: *Celebration*. This symbol speaks to creative resourcefulness, and to finding clever and imaginative ways to relax and enjoy life before beginning some new cycle of effort. The image of a houseboat party suggests laughter, good times and merriment. The closed setting alludes to the technique of intensifying or building up power by keeping things private and protected until enough energy is generated to accomplish an objective. The emphasis in this symbol is on light-hearted fellowship as it becomes the means for cultivating the inspiration and enthusiasm through which all accomplishment of enduring value is achieved. The suggestion here is that with a little ingenuity, any ordinary or commonplace experience can become an adventure in building or refining personal skills and knowledge. At it highest, this symbol represents a unique talent for motivating others and creating plussage in any group, and the ability to finesse a cooperative response from the cosmos in every worthwhile endeavor. Negative: Self-pampering and a complete disregard for the needs of others.

TODAY: The accent is on finesse. A catalytic intensification of creativity and inspiration is building as the result of holding back and containing or keeping things private.

Opportunity: Your greatest advantage lies in finding clever ways to turn even the most ordinary or routine occasion into a special and exciting event. Be gracious and encouraging.

Risk: Guard against self-indulgence, or considering only your own wants and needs. Don't rationalize your selfishness and tell yourself that you deserve more and better than everyone else merely because you want it.

STEPPING STONES: Celebration, party, gathering, fun, creativity, jubilation, excitement, enjoyment, revelry, festivity, merriment, entertainment, amusement, delight, diversion.

LEO 20   The Zuni sun worshipers. KEYWORD: *Fidelity*

THEME: *Respect for Tradition.* This symbol speaks to self-strengthening, faithfulness to higher source and the preservation of those values that have stood the test of time, even as new ones are forming. The image of the Zuni sun worshipers depicts an ancient ritual of homage, or paying respect to authority, designed to assure the continuing approval of personal or community activities. The emphasis in this degree is on loyalty. The implication here is that the individual who decides to break completely with established custom or tradition will soon find himself outside of the group. Positive: At its highest, this symbol represents self-confidence and certainty as the result of a full and complete understanding of the illimitability of resource to be found in both situation and background. Negative: Ritualistic behavior or obsession with the appearance of things.

TODAY: The accent is on loyalty. Respect for tradition and ceremonies that celebrate important values of society are emphasized today.

Opportunity: Your greatest advantage lies in following established customs and procedures. Honor the source of your sustainment.

Risk: Guard against losing touch with or failing to understand the underlying meaning of things. Try not to judge by appearance or take things too literally.

STEPPING STONES: Ritual, ceremony, rite, natural forces, strength, loyalty, faithfulness, allegiance, homage, respect, tradition, custom, assurance, sustainment, protection.

LEO 21   Chickens intoxicated. KEYWORD: *Accentuation*

Chickens not intoxicated

THEME: *Making Use of What You Have.* This symbol speaks to the dangers inherent in using anything alien or unnatural to self for stimulation or excitement. The reversed symbolism in the image of chickens intoxicated highlights this message by dramatizing the consequences of attempting to raise the level of consciousness or achieve spiritual results through artificial means or unconventional techniques. The image of chickens intoxicated places the emphasis on transforming stumbling blocks into stepping stones. What cannot be eliminated from the self must be used and glorified. Limitations are to be utilized creatively rather than relied upon to justify personal failures and deficiencies. The suggestion here is that handicaps and restrictions are opportunities and challenges that lead to accomplishment and bring potential into manifestation. Positive: At its highest, this symbol represents a remarkable talent for finding creative ways to overcome obstacles in even the most difficult situations. Negative: Lack of initiative and over-reliance on external stimulation to get the self moving.

TODAY: The accent is on unpredictability and a loss of self-control. Things may be unusually out of the ordinary today.

Opportunity: Your greatest advantage lies in realizing that your personal limitations are also your opportunities. Make them work for you. If you can't lose them, use them.

Risk: Guard against trying to solve your problems by running away from them. Beware of the dangers in bizarre practices and artificial solutions.

STEPPING STONES: Intemperance, abandonment, lack of control, debauchery, excess, hedonism, immoderation, excess, overindulgence, dissipation, licentiousness, inebriation, recklessness, craziness, profligacy, self-indulgence, sensualism, imprudence, capriciousness, carelessness, foolhardiness, indiscretion.

LEO 22   A carrier pigeon. KEYWORD: *Enlightenment*

a carrier pigeon

THEME: *A Message Received.* This symbol speaks to communication, and to learning what needs to be known in order to handle any new situation or crisis. The image of a carrier pigeon symbolizes the process of sending and receiving information. The emphasis in this symbol is on the development of intuition, or a highly refined sensitivity to those things that ordinarily might escape notice or be missed. On a practical level, this symbol is operational when answers magically appear, precisely at the moment they are needed, or the individual finds himself at the right time and place to discover just what he is looking for. In a broad sense, this image epitomizes telepathy. It also alludes to karma. Positive: At its highest, this symbol represents psychic sensitivity or highly developed mental faculties and a remarkable ability to understand the higher meaning of things and events. Negative: Gossip and an inability to sense when to keep quiet.

TODAY: The accent is on communication. Important news and messages that you have been waiting for may arrive today.

Opportunity: Your greatest advantage lies in keeping your eyes and ears open. Pay attention. Be sensitive to subtleties of expression and nonverbal cues.

Risk: Guard against the temptation to gossip or breach a confidence. Know when to keep quiet.

STEPPING STONES: Messenger, courier, liaison, communication, announcement, news, gossip, rumor, report, information, learning, understanding, intuition, telepathy, mental faculties, messages.

LEO 23   **A bareback rider. KEYWORD:** *Audacity*

A bone back rider

THEME: *Daring to Do.* This symbol speaks to a conscious mastery of experience, and to a capacity for seizing the advantage in any situation that offers opportunity for self-advancement. The image of a bareback rider symbolizes mastery of the lower animal or sense nature, and the implication here is of an ability to maintain self-composure and perform at peak even in the most unstable situations. This symbol also alludes to drama and self-marketing, or skill in showcasing personal talents and achievements in the best light possible. Positive: At its highest, this symbol represents daring, fearlessness, pluck, and a relaxed, unruffled approach to problem-solving. Negative: Exhibitionism or a tendency to be a show-off.

TODAY: The accent is on risk-taking and adventure. Some individual may make a bold or unexpected move that surprises everyone.

Opportunity: Your greatest advantage lies in promoting your skills and talents. Nothing ventured, nothing gained. Show what you can do.

Risk: Guard against exaggerating your abilities. Don't promise more than you can deliver.

STEPPING STONES: Daring, fearlessness, exhibition, performance, act, demonstration, display, dramatics, mastery, spunk, pluck, boldness, adventurousness, achievement, accomplishment, courage.

LEO 24   An untidy, unkempt man. KEYWORD: *Imperturbability*

An untidy unkempt man

THEME: *Judging by Appearance.* This symbol speaks to inner reality, and to total immersion in some self-exalted task or goal. The image of an untidy, unkempt man is another of the reversed or negative symbols and it alludes to the indifference to physical comfort, outer appearance and opinions of others that often accompanies an obsession with a mission. The suggestion here is that whatever the individual has brought to center in his person from the outer world will be refined, developed and poured back for the benefit of those who will accept and use it. The earliest description of this image described the figure as a "yogi of transcendent powers" thereby alluding to the spiritual quality of this particular degree. Positive: At its highest, this symbol indicates unflustered finesse in handling all practical matters and a wisdom born of experience. Negative: Self-obsession or slovenliness and irresponsible self-neglect.

TODAY: The accent is on indifference to criticism. Outer appearances are ignored as the focus turns inward.

Opportunity: Your greatest advantage lies in doing what has to be done without being concerned about what others think about it.

Risk: Guard against jeopardizing your health by becoming so over-involved in your projects that you forget to take care of your basic needs. Don't push yourself beyond your limits.

STEPPING STONES: Inner-directedness, self-sufficiency, independence, confidence, self-assurance, self-reliance, carelessness, neglect, indifference, self-absorption, insensitivity, self-possession, impassivity.

LEO 25   A large camel crossing the desert. KEYWORD: *Adequacy*

a large camel crossing the desert

THEME: *Endurance.* This symbol speaks to courage, personal endurance, and the ability to overcome outer limitations and come out on top of things. Here is a fearlessness based on experience and the ability to survive hardships. On a practical level, this may take the form of unrelenting persistence and a refusal to give up until every possible means to achieve a goal has been exhausted. This is a "do-it-yourself" degree. The image of a large camel crossing the desert suggests self-sufficiency, or that whatever is needed for survival lies within the individual himself. The desert symbolizes an environment that gives little in the way of sustainment and therefore this symbol implies a lack of outer assistance or cooperation. The camel is a beast of burden, and there is also a caution here to resist taking on the problems of others to the detriment of self. Positive: At its highest, this symbol represents tenacious perseverance, a tireless giving of self and a remarkable ability to overcome difficulties. Negative: Callous indifference to the needs of others or excessive self-indulgence.

TODAY: The accent is on endurance. Your ability to keep going in the face of hardship and limitation may be tested today.

Opportunity: Your greatest advantage lies in taking things one step at a time and keeping your eye on the goal ahead. Believe in yourself. You can do it.

Risk: Guard against riding roughshod over others in the process of trying to accomplish your own goals. On the other hand, don't overburden yourself by taking on the responsibilities and problems of others.

STEPPING STONES: Endurance, survival, fortitude, stamina, determination, self-containment, self-mobilization, persistence, perseverance, self-sufficiency, independence, self-reliance.

LEO 26   A rainbow. KEYWORD: *Significance*

a rainbow

THEME: *Hope*. This symbol speaks to the universal awareness that comes to those individuals who work toward the achievement of enduring goals. It also speaks to divine cooperation and the opening of the cosmic treasure chest to all who are trying to bring their highest visions to fruition. The image of a rainbow is the traditional symbol of hope, and it dramatizes God's covenant with man or His promise that those who remain faithful will never be destroyed or abandoned. Positive: At its highest, this symbol represents the application of spiritual principles to every phase of living. Negative: Gullibility and magical thinking.

TODAY: The accent is on inspiration and reassurance. You may receive a sign today that provides the guidance you've been looking for. A turning point is indicated.

Opportunity: Your greatest advantage lies in finding the hidden promise in even the worst of situations. Nurture the highest potential wherever you find it.

Risk: Guard against seeking magical solutions or placing your faith in omens and good luck charms in the hope of avoiding struggle and effort, or having to work for what you want.

STEPPING STONES: Hope, promise, aspiration, wish-fulfillment, encouragement, faith, inspiration, reassurance, potential, possibility, expectation, upliftment, motivation, signature, treasure, prospect, spiritual power.

LEO 27   Daybreak. KEYWORD: *Genesis*

Daybreak

THEME: *New Beginnings.* This symbol speaks to the dawn of new hope and to the fact that no situation or condition lasts forever. The image of daybreak offers symbolic assurance that no matter how chaotic or painful life can get, there will always be a new day, a better tomorrow and fresh opportunities. The emphasis here is on the necessity that individuals learn to understand the cycles in their lives as well as their place in them. On a practical level, this degree can represent a secret revealed, something hidden coming to light or the end of a long period of mourning or depression. Positive: At its highest, this symbol represents the continual unfolding of the meaning of life and significance of experience through the process of cyclic repetition at new and higher levels. Negative: Persistent dissatisfaction with any present moment and a firm belief that happiness is something only others find.

TODAY: The accent is on new beginnings. Forgiveness and second chances bring hope and encouragement.

Opportunity: Your greatest advantage lies in being willing to accept change and close the door to the past. Find the meaning in your experiences and move on.

Risk: Guard against harboring grudges or bringing the worst of the past into any present situation. Let go of whatever is holding you back or preventing you from getting on with your life.

STEPPING STONES: New beginning, hope, fresh start, commencement, genesis, inception, appearance, birth, infancy, advent, emergence, initiation, inauguration, debut, resurgence, potential, cycles of change.

LEO 28   Many little birds on the limb of a large tree.
KEYWORD: *Ramification*

THEME: *Rising Above the Petty*. This symbol speaks to rising above crisis and the petty things in life by focusing on the aesthetic and beautiful. Birds symbolize thoughts, communication, inspiration, and the spiritual and mental realms of being. Trees symbolize knowledge, stability and protection or security. Thus the image of many little birds on the limb of a large tree suggests a learning situation in which insight into the possible consequences of hasty decisions or emotional reactions to unforeseen events may be gained through group discussion and viewing things from a higher perspective. This degree also alludes to the importance of fellowship and cheerful, light-hearted repartee that lifts the spirits. At its highest this symbol represents the ability to bring all the skills and resources of self together when opportunity arises and effectively capitalize on the moment. Negative: Gossip and delight in creating confusion and problems in order to take the credit for solving them.

TODAY: The accent is on seeing things from a higher perspective. Talking things over with others may shed new light on some confusing situation.

Opportunity: Your greatest advantage lies in asking others for their opinions and listening to their ideas. Focus on the broader social implications of things rather than the consequences to any one individual.

Risk: Guard against letting too many cooks spoil the broth or losing yourself in a sea of confusing and trivial issues. Avoid the temptation to gossip or pass on juicy stories in order to get attention.

STEPPING STONES: Transcendence, aspiration, higher thought, happiness, lightness of heart, overtone, intimation, suggestion, connotation, insinuation, communication, discussion, chatter.

LEO 29   A mermaid. KEYWORD: *Importunity*

a mermaid

THEME: *Doing What Comes Naturally*. This symbol speaks to naïveté, and to a desire for self-fulfilling experience. The image of a mermaid alludes to a lack of sophistication, ingenuousness and unschooled innocence. It also suggests purity and a refusal to compromise the integrity of selfhood. The emphasis in this symbol is on the feminine element, or intuition, creativity and emotion. Positive: At its highest, this symbol represents a delicate sensitivity to the soul's inner stirrings and a tendency to do what comes naturally. Negative: Lack of self-refinement or simple crudeness.

TODAY: The accent is on a desire for experience that will help you build self-confidence and find your place in the world. You may find yourself a little gullible today.

Opportunity: Your greatest advantage lies in following your natural instincts. Trust your intuition regardless of what others may be telling you.

Risk: Guard against letting yourself be seduced by flattery or talked into something too quickly. Check things out before committing yourself.

STEPPING STONES: Eagerness, desire, natural instincts, determination, insistence, naïveté, lack of sophistication, ingenuousness, innocence, credulousness, gullibility.

LEO 30   An unsealed letter. KEYWORD: *Confidence*

An unsealed letter

THEME: *Trust.* This symbol speaks to respect for privacy, discretion, and faith in the basic honesty of others. The image of an unsealed letter was described in the 1931 mimeograph version of this degree as containing confidential information, and the suggestion here is that individuals generally are to be trusted unless or until that trust is betrayed. The emphasis in this symbol is on letting experience be the guide in any particular case. Suspicion is a state of mind that leads to pervasive fear and defensive behavior and should be avoided. Positive: At its highest, this symbol represents integrity and an ability to win the confidence and respect of others as a person who can be trusted. Negative: Inability to keep a secret or cleverness in leaking confidential information.

TODAY: The accent is on integrity. Confidential matters are emphasized.

Opportunity: Your greatest advantage lies in trusting others unless or until they actually betray that trust. Give others the same respect you expect from them.

Risk: Guard against invading someone's privacy or accidentally revealing something that should be kept private. Don't put anything in writing that you wouldn't want the whole world to know.

STEPPING STONES: Trust, integrity, honor, character, ethics, decency, honesty, morality, scruples, virtue, fidelity, nobility, reliability, respect, discretion, confidence, faith, openness.

Virgo

♍

VIRGO 1   A man's head. KEYWORD: *Character*

a man's head

THEME: *Integrity*. This symbol speaks to high character, distinction and personal integrity. The image of a man's head symbolizes intellectual and moral maturity and the ability to discern right from wrong. It also alludes to leadership and ambition. The implication here is that high character and maturity manifest outwardly in consistency, dependability and acceptance of responsibility for personal actions. The emphasis in this symbol is on being willing to pay the price demanded for the high rewards of life. Positive: At its highest, this symbol represents wisdom, conscientiousness, self-confidence and clearly defined objectives. Negative: Excessive pride or a tendency to bite off more than can be chewed.

TODAY: The accent is on integrity. Ethical issues may take the spotlight as they conflict with pride and ambition.

Opportunity: Your greatest advantage lies in having the courage to live up to your principles and accept responsibility for your acts and decisions.

Risk: Guard against sacrificing your principles in order to save face or achieve some goal at any cost. Pride goes before a fall.

STEPPING STONES: Maturity, integrity, morality, principles, ethics, standards, character, responsibility, ambition, pride, consciousness, vision, leadership, identity.

VIRGO 2   A large white cross upraised. KEYWORD: *Glorification*

a large white cross upraised

THEME: *Testimony.* This symbol speaks to loyalty, and to a willingness to testify openly to personal beliefs, even in the face of criticism or ridicule. The image of a large white cross upraised alludes to moral courage and a fearlessness that serves to inspire others to stand up for what they believe in and move toward higher expressions of their values and ideals. This symbol also emphasizes a sense of spiritual belonging as the greatest of all psychological needs. Positive: At its highest, this symbol represents a selfless dedication to improving the lives of others through some special service. Negative: Intolerance, closed-mindedness and arrogant dogmatism, or a tendency to proselytize and overrate the importance of personal causes.

TODAY: The accent is on inspiration and upliftment.

Opportunity: Your greatest advantage lies in having the courage and conviction to stand up for your beliefs, even when you are in the minority. Don't be afraid to testify to the wonders you have seen.

Risk: Guard against proselytizing or arguing that your way of life is the most correct and spiritually acceptable way to live, or that others are wrong in their beliefs. Avoid spending your time and energy on causes that you don't whole-heartedly believe in, just to please others.

STEPPING STONES: Testimony, confirmation, witnessing, declaration, statement, allegiance, glorification, exaltation, veneration, values, courage, fearlessness, service, stewardship, beliefs, religion, worship, spirituality.

VIRGO 3   Two angels bringing protection. KEYWORD: *Security*

Two angels bringing protection

THEME: *Invisible Assistance*. This symbol speaks to faith and divine intervention, or assistance from heavenly or invisible powers. The image of two angels bringing protection alludes to guardian angels or those spiritual beings who watch over and protect humankind. The implication in this symbol is that whenever man has reached the limits of his own resources, while yet continuing his efforts, he can expect some practical and tangible response to his prayers. Positive: At its highest, this symbol represents inner strength and an unwavering faith that assures success. Negative: Elitism, or claims to special privilege and entitlement.

TODAY: The accent is on protection. You may find yourself wondering how you got through some calamity or escaped suffering the consequences of your own foolishness.

Opportunity: Your greatest advantage lies in having faith that there is an ultimate good in all experience.

Risk: Guard against getting discouraged and giving up too soon on something you have worked hard to achieve. Help could be just around the corner.

STEPPING STONES: Protection, security, preservation, guardianship, sustainment, care, nurturance, aid, assistance, comfort, concern, vigilance, assurance, certainty, spiritual power, heaven, fulfillment.

VIRGO 4   A colored child playing with white children.
KEYWORD: *Intimacy*

[handwritten: a chocolate child playing with whites]

THEME: *Integration*. This symbol speaks to opportunities for endless varieties of relationships, and to respect for personality and the mutual appreciation of difference. The image of a colored child playing with white children focuses on social integration, but it also emphasizes the necessity that man learn to get along with himself as well as with others. Individuals often try to suppress or destroy those parts of themselves that they can't understand or appreciate and avoid or reject others who mirror these traits. The challenge here is to be able to recapture the sense of wonderment and exhilaration that children experience when they discover something unique or different and learn how to use it effectively. Every characteristic of man, and every individual, has a role to play in the overall scheme of things. Nothing is truly foreign except as it hasn't been experienced or its purpose yet recognized. Positive: At its highest, this symbol represents openness and receptivity to experiencing the unknown or unfamiliar and a keen understanding of the value of dissimilarity and variety. Negative: Prejudice and lack of self-integration.

TODAY: The accent is on integration. The emphasis is on cooperation and valuing the differences in others rather than attempting to artificially blur the lines of distinction or sacrifice individuality in order to achieve a surface harmony.

Opportunity: Your greatest advantage lies in finding ways to adjust to unfamiliar situations, and people whose ideas may be different from yours, without suppressing your own identity in the process. Be proud of who you are.

Risk: Guard against intolerance or failing to respect others' rights to form their own opinions and decide for themselves how to live their lives.

STEPPING STONES: Integration, openness, receptivity, acceptance, mutual appreciation, trust, respect, intimacy, friendship, understanding, tolerance, difference, dissimilarity, distinction, variety.

VIRGO 5   A man dreaming of fairies. KEYWORD: *Outlook*

A man dreaming of fairies

THEME: *The Magic of Vision*. This symbol speaks to imagination, inspiration, and the perception and consideration of possibilities. The image of a man dreaming of fairies alludes to magic, wish fulfillment and vision. As a man dreams, so shall he achieve. Positive: At its highest, this symbol represents the ability to influence others or move them to higher accomplishment by inspiring them to share their hopes and dreams and support each other as they work toward the fulfillment of their individual goals. Negative: Escapism and avoidance of effort and struggle through idle fantasy and wishful thinking.

TODAY: The accent is on vision and inspiration. Your creativity should be at its peak. Solutions to difficult problems may appear as if by magic.

Opportunity: Your greatest advantage lies in using your imagination. Let your mind flow. Be receptive.

Risk: Guard against rejecting new ideas simply because they don't fit your preconceived notions of the way things should be done. Don't tell yourself "it's impossible " or "it won't work" until you've tried it.

STEPPING STONES: Vision, imagination, inspiration, expectation, wish-fulfillment, hope, luck, magic, mysticism, enchantment, charm, perspective, fantasy, sorcery, supernatural, occult.

VIRGO 6   A merry-go-round. KEYWORD: *Diversion*

The a merry-go-round

THEME: *Cycles of Experience.* This symbol speaks to the repetition of cycles, and particularly to cycles of enjoyment. The image of a merry-go-round alludes to a time for fun. A play on the words describes a merry "go 'round," or a type of lighthearted repartee where differing points of view are dealt with in a friendly or joking manner. The symbolic inference to cycles points to a need for individuals to stop and assess where they are in any particular cycle of experience and know when a cycle is complete. The suggestion here is that if a situation is not released by the individual when the merry-go-round stops, then he will be stuck for another ride. It also alludes to the wisdom of not jumping off in the middle of a spin. Positive: At its highest, this symbol represents resourcefulness and the ability to make a game of it when dealing with unexpected challenges and emergencies. Negative: Going in circles or an inability to learn from experience.

TODAY: The accent is on starting new cycles of experience and finishing old ones. Life may seem more hectic than usual. A person from the past may suddenly come back into your life or you may have a deja vu experience in some new situation.

Opportunity: Your greatest advantage lies in keeping your sense of humor and nurturing the creative child within. Look for ways to enjoy the things you have to do. Make a game of it.

Risk: Guard against setting yourself up to repeat difficult experiences by refusing to profit from your mistakes the first time around. Be careful how you treat others. What goes around comes around.

STEPPING STONES: Cycles, going in circles, return, repetition, repartee, new opportunities, intensification, pleasure, enjoyment, play, fun, amusement, recreation, diversion.

VIRGO 7   A harem. KEYWORD: *Restraint*

a harem

THEME: *Retreat and Regroup*. This symbol speaks to tradeoffs, or giving up one advantage to gain another. The image of a harem symbolizes seclusion, restriction and a lack of freedom. It also emphasizes discipline, control, rules and regulations. Here is an allusion to an acceptance of regimentation as a means to avoid having to make decisions or act independently. In reality, individuals can learn and strengthen themselves in any group experience, even those that are endured rather than enjoyed. The mind and ideals can never be bound by physical limitations or restraints. Positive: At its highest, this symbol represents a refusal to acknowledge limitation as anything but opportunity. Negative: Cowardice and a preference for taking the easy way out, or lack of integrity and a willingness to sell the soul for a moment of pleasure.

TODAY: The accent is on restraint. You may feel held back or restricted in some way. Others may demand that rules and regulations be strictly observed.

Opportunity: Your greatest advantage lies in using any period of limitation to build up your strength. Make plans for the future and get your priorities in order. Identify what you can do and do it.

Risk: Guard against letting yourself become a doormat for others to walk on. Recognize the value of your services and don't let yourself be taken for granted. Try not to take the coward's way out by keeping quiet when you should speak up.

STEPPING STONES: Restraint, captivity, confinement, limitation, lack of freedom, servitude, seclusion, insulation, withdrawal, regimentation, discipline, feminine relationships, sexuality.

VIRGO 8   First dancing instruction. KEYWORD: *Assistance*

First dancing instruction

THEME: *Learning How to Do It*. This symbol speaks to self-perfection and learning through instruction. It also speaks to the importance of being able to function in a broad variety of social situations. The image of a first dancing instruction alludes to coordination, poise, gracefulness and flexibility as the skills necessary for successfully handling any situation when the going gets rough. It also emphasizes the importance of encouragement. The way to begin is to begin, and any beginning requires a willingness to risk failure and try again if the first attempt doesn't succeed. The key to mastery is practice, feedback, adjustment and determination, or a refusal to give up. Positive: At its highest, this symbol represents cooperation, competence, and an extraordinary talent for finessing the desired outcome in every difficult situation. Negative: Co-dependency and a willingness to accept a less than desired status quo rather than risk going it alone.

TODAY: The accent is on self-perfection and learning through trial and error. Encouragement is the key to achievement.

Opportunity: Your greatest advantage lies in finding the right teacher and putting the time and effort into reaching your goal. Be willing to accept constructive criticism. Admit your mistakes and correct them.

Risk: Guard against giving up too soon or telling yourself that less than your best is okay. Be careful not to step on someone's toes by trying to lead when you should be following.

STEPPING STONES: Self-perfection, refinement of skills, education, mentorship, learning, practice, rhythm, maneuvering, cooperation, assistance, demonstration, performance, coordination, flexibility, social grace, poise.

VIRGO 9   A man making a futurist drawing. KEYWORD: *Experiment*

a man making futurist drawing

THEME: *Personal Distinction.* This symbol speaks to personal distinctiveness, and to the fact that any genuine expression of individuality must be both original and unique. It also highlights the aesthetic or artistic side of life. The image of a man making a futurist drawing alludes to the difficulties that may be experienced by the individual who doesn't conform to the group's idea of what is acceptable or "normal" behavior—or who may indeed be odd, bizarre or eccentric. The danger for any person who attempts to carve out or establish a special niche for himself in the world is that he runs the risk of becoming so extreme or outrageous in his actions as to repulse or embarrass his fellows. Ultimately, he may find himself rejected and outside the group. The emphasis here is on developing a creative style that will stimulate others to discover and express their own uniqueness. Positive: At its highest, this symbol represents imaginative genius and a continuing expansion of awareness. Negative: Befuddlement or an inability to communicate ideas appropriately and effectively.

TODAY: The accent is on the unusual. Things may seem a bit offbeat or strange today and you might feel like you are trying to swim upstream against the flow of the river. Resistance to conformity and doing your own thing right now could upset others who like things comfortably predictable.

Opportunity: Your greatest advantage lies in expressing yourself creatively. Break the ice and do something different. Others may be waiting for just such an opportunity to follow suit.

Risk: Guard against offending community values and standards. Avoid mixups and mishaps by taking time to get organized. Find the correct balance between going too far and restraining yourself completely.

STEPPING STONES: Originality, uniqueness, imagination, creativity, vision, expression, revelation, prophecy, experimentation, talent, skill, artistry, aesthetics, abstraction, individualism, distinctiveness, symbolism.

VIRGO 10   **Two heads looking out and beyond the shadows.**
KEYWORD: *Intelligence*

Two heads looking out and beyond the shadows

THEME: *Objectivity.* This symbol speaks to transcendental comprehension, or the ability to see above and beyond superficial appearances and understand the higher significance and meaning of things and events. The image of two heads looking out and beyond the shadows alludes to stereoscopic vision, or looking at things from two points of view and combining the images perceived in order to get the effect of solidarity and depth. It also implies looking at things objectively, or using scientific reason to integrate various concepts and ideas and formulate basic principles for effective and productive living. Positive: At its highest, this symbol represents the ability to see both sides of an issue and a special gift for creating harmony out of chaos by helping others find common or shared values and goals. Negative: A self divided within or distorted perceptions and a tendency to filter facts and information through personal feelings and prejudices.

TODAY: The accent is on perspective. Things that have been foggy or obscure should become clearer. A compromise or meeting of the minds on some sharply divided issue is likely.

Opportunity: Your greatest advantage lies in looking at things from both sides. Ask others for their opinions and weigh your options before making an important decision.

Risk: Guard against getting yourself into a no-win situation by refusing to look at things from the other fellow's point of view, or refusing to negotiate. Don't look too far afield for an answer that might be right under your nose.

STEPPING STONES: Perspective, perception, comprehension, balance, objectivity, seeing both sides of an issue, three-dimensional thinking, precognition, clairvoyance, duality, duplication, double-vision, marriage of the minds, agreement.

VIRGO 11   A boy molded in his mother's aspiration for him.
KEYWORD: *Exaction*

a boy molded in his mother's aspiration for him

THEME: *Shaping the Future.* This symbol speaks to personal immortality, or staying alive in the memory of others, through genetics, the passing down of possessions, or a succession of achievements through a family line. The image of a boy molded in his mother's aspiration for him alludes to influence, or the power of persons and things to affect each other. The emphasis in this degree is on the ability of ideals to sustain themselves and find fertile soil for their continuance. Positive: At its highest, this symbol represents distinguished achievement as the result of a conscious fulfillment of personal potential. Negative: Going through motions to make things look good, or satisfaction with superficial appearances.

TODAY: The accent is on overshadowing. You may feel pressured to conform to the expectations of others or follow precedent in some important matter.

Opportunity: Your greatest advantage lies in thinking for yourself and breaking free of restrictive influences that affect your ability to achieve your own goals.

Risk: Guard against sacrificing your integrity and self-esteem by trying to please everybody. Don't let others do your thinking for you.

STEPPING STONES: Shaping, conformity, influence, overshadowing, brainwashing, behavior modification, obedience, submission, succession, heredity, exaction, definition, requirements.

VIRGO 12   **A bride with her veil snatched away.** KEYWORD: *Invitation*

A bride with her veil snatched away

THEME: *A Moment of Truth.* This symbol speaks to discovery and accountability, or to a moment of truth and a demand that some prior claim or assertion now be proved. The image of a bride with her veil snatched away may be better understood in countries where the groom is not permitted to see his bride's face until after the wedding ceremony. The inference here is that this degree reflects a time of reckoning or for bringing things out in the open for all to see and judge. This symbol also suggests that once a conscious choice or commitment is made, the individual should allow that experience to run its course and refrain from prematurely opting out before he has given himself the opportunity to profit from it. Positive: At its highest, this symbol represents integrity, a total giving of self, and faithfulness to commitments. Negative: Moral weakness or a misguided sense of honor and self-respect.

TODAY: The accent is on discovery. Something that was hidden may come to light today. The truth will be revealed.

Opportunity: Your greatest advantage lies in verifying things for yourself. Check out all claims made before making purchases or relying on representations.

Risk: Guard against impatience or ripping the chrysalis from the cocoon too soon. Try not to invade someone's privacy or unmask them in public. Respect the dignity of even the least of your fellows.

STEPPING STONES: Revelation, moment of truth, proof, unveiling, exposure, uncovering, disclosure, divulgence, publishing, discovery, accountability.

VIRGO 13   A strong hand supplanting political hysteria. KEY-WORD: *Power*

A strong hand supplanting political hysteria

THEME: *Taking the Reins.* This symbol speaks to power and leadership as it is demonstrated by those rare individuals who command the respect of their fellows by bringing about stability and order when chaos and confusion are winning the upper hand. The image of a strong hand supplanting political hysteria symbolizes direct intervention at a point of crisis, or where things have reached a boiling point after a long period of administrative incompetency. The suggestion here is that weak or ineffective leadership eventually results in confusion, fear and anarchy. Positive: At its highest, this symbol represents exceptional administrative skill, keen judgment and outstanding leadership. Negative: Indecision and weakness, or abdication of personal responsibility by refusing to make decisions or take a stand on anything.

TODAY: The accent is on leadership and decisiveness. You may have to take the bull by the horns to rescue a situation that is getting out of hand.

Opportunity: Your greatest advantage lies in doing something about it. It's time to get involved. Set your objective. Act with confidence and be firm.

Risk: Guard against hitting the panic button or faltering in the face of a crisis. Don't vacillate or appear weak. You may lose the confidence of those who depend on you.

STEPPING STONES: Leadership, mastery, authority, command, control, administration, superiority, supremacy, domination, management, supervision, domination, order, regulation, strength, force, power, repression, restriction.

VIRGO 14   A family tree. KEYWORD: *Gentility*

a family tree

THEME: *Background as Influence*. This symbol speaks to cultural heritage, origins and traditions as a driving force that leads individuals to cherish and build on, or reject and attempt to destroy, their own personal roots. The image of a family tree emphasizes background and the historical development of any present situation. On a practical level, when this degree is involved, the implication is that the real issue in any current social crisis are not those being expressed on the surface. Rather they are deeper ones involving traditions, old alliances and threatened relationships. Implicit in this image is the idea that each man is unique, and that those who are bound in their relationships by common experiences, blood lines or allegiances will still, at times, find themselves at odds with each other as they work through their experiences together in the practical and everyday world. Positive: At its highest, this symbol represents faithfulness to source while yet fulfilling the promise of an individual and unique destiny. Negative: Misconceptions concerning biological or social heritage, or feelings of alienation and a sense of rootlessness.

TODAY: The accent is on heritage. Genealogy and questions about family roots could arise today. Tracing the origin and history of some object or issue could be time consuming.

Opportunity: Your greatest advantage lies in getting to the bottom of whatever is bothering you. Ask questions and don't be misled by glib answers or slight-of-hand coverups.

Risk: Guard against trying to be something or someone you aren't. Be yourself and play your strong suit.

STEPPING STONES: Heritage, ancestry, roots, origins, source, genes, tradition, background, derivation, culture, history, lineage, endowment, legacy, reputation, influence, guidance.

VIRGO 15   An ornamental handkerchief. KEYWORD: *Gracefulness*

An ornamental handkerchief

THEME: *Noblesse Oblige*. This symbol speaks to gentleness and refinement, and to man's desire to lift himself above the ordinary to more transcendent and aesthetic realms of existence. The image of an ornamental handkerchief was described in the 1931 mimeograph version of these symbols as "of finest linen" and lying "folded near milady's mirror by a bottle of rare perfume." Thus the emphasis is feminine and on grace, elegance, dignity and cultivation. The handkerchief and perfume both symbolize romance and are delicate reminders of civility, honor and spirituality. The implication here is of a longing for all that is fine, beautiful and lovely. The suggestion inherent in this image is that the real value of a thing lies in its significance, or meaning, and what it inspires men to do. Positive: At its highest, this symbol represents gentility, graciousness and charm. Negative: Ostentatiousness and overconcern with the frivolous and petty.

TODAY: The accent is on gentility and refinement. Manners will be important and crudeness in any form will not be tolerated.

Opportunity: Your greatest advantage lies in being gracious. Watch your tongue and maintain your dignity and poise. Using your charm brings special rewards.

Risk: Guard against putting on airs or holding yourself out to be socially or spiritually superior to your fellows. You might get elegantly put in your place.

STEPPING STONES: Refinement, delicacy, loveliness, noblesse oblige, chivalry, gentility, gracefulness, elegance, charm, graciousness, dignity, cultivation, aristocracy, culture, spirituality.

VIRGO 16   An orangutan. KEYWORD: *Dexterity*

THEME: *Primitive Urges.* This symbol speaks to raw and primitive energy that can be refined and put to higher use. The word orangutan is of Malay origin, and it means "man of the forest" or "woodsman." It describes a large and powerful orange-colored ape that is native to Borneo and Sumatra. The image of an orangutan alludes to the id, or that part of the psyche that is regarded as the reservoir of the libido and the source of instinctive energy and impulses. This powerful force is necessary to the survival of man and is usually mobilized during emergencies and crises. The emphasis here is on the necessity that individuals learn to use their reason and judgment to keep primitive impulses under control and channel their energies in more productive ways. Positive: At its highest, this symbol represents a do-it-yourself approach to life and an ability to get down to the basics and rise effectively and appropriately to any occasion. Negative: Rationalizing the use of brutality and violence to accomplish selfish ends.

TODAY: The accent is on impulsiveness. You may find it harder than usual to keep yourself from acting immediately on your thoughts and ideas. Juggling priorities could be especially challenging.

Opportunity: Your greatest advantage lies in using your head. Think about consequences before you act. Find constructive outlets for your energy.

Risk: Guard against getting carried away by your emotions. Try not to get all worked up over a situation that may take care of itself if you just leave it alone and wait a little bit.

STEPPING STONES: Primitive, crude, raw, unrefined, animalistic, uncivilized, atavistic, uncultivated, unsophisticated, id, libido, unconscious desires, natural resources, dexterity, agility, adroitness, deftness.

VIRGO 17   A volcano in eruption. KEYWORD: *Explosion*

a volcano in eruption

THEME: *A Dramatic Outburst.* This symbol speaks to outburst and to the unleashing of energy as the result of a blind determination to survive. The image of a volcano in eruption graphically dramatizes a powerful and volatile display of force that goes beyond normal or expected boundaries due to a massive buildup of internal pressure. On a practical level, this symbol can describe a volatile and angry outburst, uncontrollable weeping, heart attack or stroke or hysterical laughter. The emphasis in this degree is on a need to bring the self back to its normal condition. The implication here is that the externalization or outpouring is self-preserving in that it allows the internal pressure that might destroy its source to be released. This outburst can also represent birth pangs and genesis, or a bringing to the surface of previously hidden or unknown potential. Positive: At its highest, this symbol represents creative passion and a refusal to live a tepid existence or tiptoe through life. Negative: Explosive temper tantrums and inflammatory tirades or a complete lack of self-control and inability to conform to socially accepted conduct or behavior.

TODAY: The accent is on explosiveness. This could turn out to be an unforgettable day. Tension that has been building could climax in a crisis with everyone running for cover.

Opportunity: Your greatest advantage lies in counting to ten—or higher if necessary. Stay out of what doesn't concern you and try to protect what does.

Risk: Guard against adding fuel to the fire. Avoid the temptation to interfere in a process that needs to run its course.

STEPPING STONES: Explosion, outburst, release, expansion, excess, outpouring, spillover, discharge, flare-up, crisis, destruction, violence, temper, blow-up, loss of emotional control.

VIRGO 18   An ouija board. KEYWORD: *Acumen*

an ouija board

THEME: *Extrasensory Perception.* This symbol speaks to divination, and to the ability to anticipate the future by using practical reason to understand the meaning and significance of signs and signatures. The image of an ouija board focuses on the planchette or the pointing device that is lightly touched by the parties and used to convey and record messages from invisible to visible realms. The planchette symbolizes the mind or consciousness. The emphasis here is on rational divination, or the development of a sensitivity to potential as it is discovered in the practical and everyday world, and on the ability to make sense of what is perceived. Positive: At its highest, this symbol represents highly refined intuition or psychic sensitivity and extraordinary insight that is used to advantage in mastering the everyday challenges of life. Negative: Superstitiousness or obsession with hidden meanings and an inability to recognize and comprehend the obvious.

TODAY: The accent is on communication and discernment. Answers to important questions may be found, and critical insights gained, by making connections and finding the patterns in events and things around you.

Opportunity: Your greatest advantage lies in being sensitive to the hidden messages in all things. Look for relevant signatures and meaningful convergences.

Risk: Guard against letting superstition ruin your day. Don't get so obsessed with hidden meanings that you fail to see the obvious.

STEPPING STONES: Psychism, channeling, communication, messages, telepathy, psychokinesis, divination, creative sensitivity, insight, perception, discernment, discrimination, acumen, articulation, signature.

VIRGO 19   A swimming race. KEYWORD: *Elimination*

a swimming race

THEME: *Competition*. This symbol speaks to the fact that at higher levels of existence there are no winners or losers. In the practical and everyday world, competition stimulates individuals to perfect and refine their unique skills and talents. The image of a swimming race also suggests that the individual who seeks to perfect and control only one part of himself will eventually divide himself from within. On a practical level, this symbol can indicate a race against time or a process of elimination to determine the best of a kind. Positive: At its highest, this symbol represents the ability to hone any personal skill or talent to perfection as needed. Negative: A win-at-all-cost philosophy and an inability to cooperate with others or establish the self in life in any meaningful way.

TODAY: The accent is on competition. Whether it's trying to beat time or win the game, you may find yourself scrambling to keep up with it all.

Opportunity: Your greatest advantage lies in making sure all the parts are in working order. Coordination and timing are important. Replacements may be necessary.

Risk: Guard against underestimating the time you need to complete some task or meet a deadline. Make sure you have everything you need before you start that important project.

STEPPING STONES: Competition, rivalry, conflict, challenge, contention, comparison, contest, process of elimination, skill, race, speed, urgency.

VIRGO 20   An automobile caravan. KEYWORD: *Variety*

An automobile caravan

THEME: *Group Adventure.* This symbol speaks to man's ability to broaden his horizons and find ways to make things easier for himself, and to his cleverness in motivating others by selling them on golden-opportunity ideas and creating expectations of high reward. The image of an automobile caravan implies mobilization or forward movement, and it alludes to team effort, a spirit of adventure and a willingness to endure hardship to reach a common goal. It also suggests the concept of safety in numbers. Positive: At its highest, this symbol represents a special gift for enriching and enhancing the potential of any experience and for making every group project an unforgettable and memorable adventure. Negative: Discontent and wanderlust, or an inability to sit still in one place for long.

TODAY: The accent is on mobilization and adventure. This could be the day you finally decide to start things rolling or get moving on some new project.

Opportunity: Your greatest advantage lies in involving others in your game plan. Encourage them to be part of the process. Look for ways to make difficult tasks enjoyable.

Risk: Guard against letting yourself drift aimlessly. Don't lose your opportunity by refusing to make commitments. The path of least resistance can be a slippery slope to loss of self-respect or outright failure.

STEPPING STONES: Progress, mobilization, travel, journey, migration, excursion, adventure, safety in numbers, group activity, following the leader, gypsies.

VIRGO 21 **A girls' basketball team. KEYWORD:** ***Expression***

a girls' basket ball team

THEME: *Team Spirit*. This symbol speaks to teamwork, or to everyone working together doing what each does best in a shared division of labor. It also speaks to the endless number of opportunities that exist for an individual to make his own niche in the world in some special area. The image of a girls' basketball team emphasizes cooperation, and it alludes to the fact that life is a game in which everyone can be a winner when they pool their resources and work together toward common goals. Positive: At its highest, this symbol represents self-fulfillment in group work, flexibility and skill in making quick and effective adjustments to the unexpected twists and turns of life. Negative: Preference for going along with the group rather than have to voice an opinion or act independently.

TODAY: The accent is on teamwork. Pooling resources can be the solution to accomplishing a difficult task. Enthusiasm runs high.

Opportunity: Your greatest advantage lies in choosing the right person for the job. Have a plan and stick to it.

Risk: Guard against going along with the crowd because you're afraid to say no. You might find yourself headed for a wall.

STEPPING STONES: Team spirit, ambition, division of labor, group effort, cooperation, coordination, sportsmanship, skill, common goals, games of life, flexibility.

VIRGO 22 **A royal coat of arms. KEYWORD:** ***Prerogative***

a royal coat of arms

THEME: *The Rights of Privilege*. This symbol speaks to the fact that there is a reason and purpose for everything that exists. The image of a royal coat of arms symbolizes authority and certification, and it dramatizes the dignity to be found in following the traditions and customs that have been established by the elders and wise men of any society. This symbol also emphasizes inherited stewardship and the right to regulate and enforce the observance of those social rituals that strengthen and preserve a group's highest values and ideals. Positive: At its highest, this symbol represents the ability to solidify group unity and help others recognize their common purpose. Negative: Abuse of authority or manipulation and the use of devious means for controlling the unsuspecting and gullible.

TODAY: The accent is on inherited rights and privileges. Some group may assert their authority or pull rank based on their seniority.

Opportunity: Your greatest advantage lies in observing precedent and following established tradition. Be sensitive to the needs of others to maintain their dignity.

Risk: Guard against abusing privilege or violating social mores. Changing the rules or criticizing the way others have been doing things could meet with strong resistance and be resented.

STEPPING STONES: Heritage, tradition, family lineage, aristocracy, rulership, prerogative, privilege, license, right, authority, certification, tradition, stewardship, values, integrity, honor, group unity.

VIRGO 23   An animal trainer. KEYWORD: *Resoluteness*

An animal trainer

THEME: *Achieving Mastery*. This symbol speaks to self-discipline, and to the fact that man must break through his conditioning and develop his highest potential if he is to master his environment and gain control over his life. It also speaks to the necessity that an individual learn how to network, or capitalize on the various relationships of which he is a part, if he hopes to get his ideas across to others and achieve his goals. The image of an animal trainer symbolizes fearlessness, courage and dominance, and the implication here is that maintaining a position of authority requires an acute sensitivity to nonverbal cues and an ability to predict behavior based on a knowledge of individual or group habit patterns. Positive: At its highest, this symbol represents accomplishment through patience, determination and skill in handling the unexpected. Negative: Domineering and demanding personality or pretentious claims to greatness.

TODAY: The accent is on conditioning. Getting things under control could be the top priority of the day.

Opportunity: Your greatest advantage lies in being aware of the social, biological and physical relationships that exist in any project you are working on.

Risk: Guard against the temptation to save time by issuing orders rather than gaining the cooperation of others. In matters of accomplishment, be careful not to count your chickens before they hatch.

STEPPING STONES: Imposition, control, mastery, command, authority, superiority, domination, discipline, rulership, power, conditioning, determination, intention, resolution, fearlessness, courage.

VIRGO 24   Mary and her white lamb. KEYWORD: *Artlessness*

Mary and her white lamb

THEME: *Eternal Spring.* This symbol speaks to youthful perspective, or to seeing the world through the eyes of a child. The image of Mary and her white lamb symbolizes purity, innocence, trust, receptivity, and openness to experience. It also has religious undertones in its subtle allusion to Jesus and his mother. The 1953 commentary describes this image in terms of a "healthy approach to heaven through a child's wide-eyed expectations." The suggestion here is that adults have a responsibility to protect their own innocent expectations as well as those of children, as they are the earliest awakenings to potential. For the young child, anything and everything is possible and there are no limitations to realizing a dream or experiencing the wonders of life. On a practical level, this symbol asks the seeker to keep an open mind and expect the best. Positive: At its highest, this symbol represents a complete absence of ulterior motives and a naive creativity that captures men's hearts and lifts each relationship to its highest promise. Negative: Empty-headed and superficial approach to life or a complete inability to grow up and act responsibly.

TODAY: The accent is on purity and innocence. You may find yourself feeling more optimistic and inclined to trust others or take things at face value today.

Opportunity: Your greatest advantage lies in being open, receptive and sincere. Expecting the best from yourself and others brings positive results.

Risk: Guard against negative or suspicious thinking. Try not to project problems. At the same time, don't shirk your responsibilities or ignore what needs to be done.

STEPPING STONES: Innocence, purity, ingenuousness, sincerity, naïveté, gullibility, credulity, receptivity, openness, trust, genuineness, youth, Mary and Jesus, chastity.

VIRGO 25   A flag at half-mast. KEYWORD: *Respect*

a flag at half mast

THEME: *Reputation.* This symbol speaks to final judgments and to the fact that in the end our efforts will be applauded and rewarded, denounced and punished, or simply ignored on the basis of their ultimate worth or usefulness to our fellows. The image of a flag at half-mast is a symbol of mourning and respect. The emphasis is on public service. The highest values of society are created through humanitarian deeds and selfless acts, and the ultimate proof of immortality for any individual is high tribute and an honored place in history. The underlying theme of this symbol is reputation, or what is believed about a person. Positive: At its highest, this symbol represents universal respect and appreciation for outstanding civic achievements. Negative: Spotlight grabbing and self-serving attempts to take credit for the work of others or satisfaction with superficial appearances and making things look good.

TODAY: The accent is on honoring the contributions of some public figure. Today could also mark the end of an era in some manner. You might be feeling less than cheerful.

Opportunity: Your greatest advantage lies in guarding your reputation. Live up to your highest ideals.

Risk: Guard against feeling sorry for yourself or trying to elicit sympathy for your personal difficulties. Complaining about your lot in life can cause others to lose respect for you.

STEPPING STONES: Tribute, honor, respect, appreciation, reputation, public service, civic achievement, final judgment, mourning, loss, sorrow, death, endings, dissolution, departure, demise, extinction.

VIRGO 26   A boy with a censer. KEYWORD: *Rapture*

A boy with censer

a boy with censor
get this right

THEME: *Wonderment.* This symbol speaks to inspiration, and to the importance of taking the initiative and doing something if change is desired. The image of a boy with a censer shows action taken in the form of prayer and an outreaching to the highest power than can be petitioned or enlisted to help. The boy symbolizes the emerging masculine or active side of personhood as well as youthful innocence and faith. The censer is an ornamental container in which incense is burned as a symbolic sacrifice to God. The upward drifting smoke of the incense represents prayer as the aspiration of the heart for the highest spiritual good. In the 1931 mimeograph version of the Symbols, the boy was described as "rapt-eyed" and in a procession of priests who are automatons. That theme is continued in the 1953 version with the keyword "rapture," and the suggestion there is that hope, wonderment and a belief that all things are possible can easily be lost by the individual who overregulates his life through a misguided desire to avoid exerting mind and body. Positive: At its highest, this symbol represents an ability to find meaning and inspiration in even the smallest details of experience, as well as a life dedicated to living the highest ideals of humanity. Negative: Ritualistic behavior or lack of initiative and a dull, monotonous or habit-driven existence.

TODAY: The accent is on aspiration and appeals to higher authority.

Opportunity: Your greatest advantage lies in having faith that all things are possible. The journey of a thousand miles begins with a single step. Be willing to take it.

Risk: Guard against overregimenting your life or engaging in ritualistic and superstitious behavior. Going through the motions with your mind elsewhere will not get you the desired results.

STEPPING STONES: Initiative, outreach, aspiration, worship, prayer, petition, appeal to the Divine, invocation, benediction, consecration, supplication, adoration, holiness, spirituality, rapture, bliss, glorification.

VIRGO 27   Grande dames at tea. KEYWORD: *Aplomb*

grand dames at tea

THEME: *The Conclave.* This symbol speaks to maturity or the pinnacle of a cycle, and to a time for passing on the best of whatever will be of value to the next generation. The image of grande dames at tea depicts one of the oldest traditions of society, or a gathering of those elders and custodians of the most valuable assets of a group for the purpose of discussing what shall be done with them and how best to preserve them. In simple terms, this image describes a conclave. The emphasis here is on culture, dignity, formality, custom and propriety. It is a time for careful deliberation, thoughtful reflection and the practical projection of future needs. Positive: At its highest, this symbol represents conscientious administration of the property and affairs of a group and the capacity for using community resources to the greatest social advantage. Negative: Feelings of entitlement and the use of special privilege to achieve selfish ends.

TODAY: The accent is on passing the torch. Meetings and discussions are likely to center on choosing successors or transferring assets of some kind.

Opportunity: Your greatest advantage lies in thinking carefully and deliberately. Be sure you gather all the facts and get input from others before you make an important decision.

Risk: Guard against doing anything that could result in your being accused of self-dealing or using your position to obtain special privileges. Avoid conflicts of interest that could leave you open to censure or criticism.

STEPPING STONES: Aplomb, assurance, composure, poise, savoir-faire, dignity, formality, tradition, custom, propriety, grace, polish, culture, refinement, privilege, maturity, meeting, discussion, deliberation, stewardship, bequest, endowment, heritage, legacy.

VIRGO 28   A bald-headed man. KEYWORD: *Dominance*

THEME: *The Power of Personality*. This symbol speaks to the futility of trying to judge the value or power of things and people by title or superficial appearance, and to the necessity that each individual do more than simply look good or fill a chair at the table of life. The image of a bald-headed man was described in the 1931 mimeograph version of the Sabian symbols as "a bald-headed man in uniform completely dominating an assembly of men: diplomats, scientists and industrialists." The suggestion there was that despite the semblance of important standing in the world, outer rank is no match against the inner and "driving power of [a] real personality" who can create broad opportunities for enriching the lives of all of the people. Positive: At its highest, this symbol represents genuine or universally recognized and respected authority and exceptional self-mastery. Negative: Highly ingenious but perverse obsession with manipulating and dominating the lives of others.

TODAY: The accent is on the power of personality. The challenge is in finding a proper balance between being too heavy-handed and too soft in dealing with others.

Opportunity: Your greatest advantage lies in compelling respect by demonstrating self-mastery. Think before you act when emotional matters are involved.

Risk: Guard against overwhelming others with too many demands. Try to generate enthusiasm rather than force compliance.

STEPPING STONES: Authority, dominance, attainment, accomplishment, power, control, mastery, command, overshadowing, self-control, maturity, charisma, personality.

VIRGO 29   A man gaining secret knowledge from a paper he is reading. KEYWORD: *Discovery*

THEME: *Discovering Deeper Meaning*. This symbol speaks to the fact that the secrets of the universe remain hidden largely due to the world's insistence on maintaining a conservative and traditional approach to research and learning, and because men generally see only what they expect to see. It also alludes to the occult principle that information is given only when an individual has a genuine need to know. The image of a man gaining secret knowledge from a paper he is reading suggests that this individual has broken through his conditioned thinking and found the key to understanding the greater purpose and reality behind all things. On a practical level, this image indicates that a mystery has been solved. Positive: At its highest, this symbol represents ingenuity, imagination and dogged persistence. Negative: Tendency to miss seeing the obvious by getting lost in detail or suspiciousness and mistrust of whatever cannot be fully understood.

TODAY: The accent is on insight. You may unexpectedly find the answer you've been looking for in a book or letter.

Opportunity: Your greatest advantage lies in reading between the lines and paying careful attention to the way things are said. Breaks in pattern are special clues.

Risk: Guard against being too literal or failing to look at things from more than one perspective. Don't prematurely dismiss something as being of no value.

STEPPING STONES: Discovery, breakthrough, findings, detection, uncovering, acquisition, hidden wisdom, knowing, awareness, perception, insight, learning, espionage, undercover work, surveillance, invasion of privacy, intrusiveness.

VIRGO 30   A false call unheard in attention to immediate service.
KEYWORD: *Safeguard*

a false call / unheard / in
attention to immediate
service.

THEME: *A Higher Call to Duty.* This symbol speaks to responsibility, and to the fact that when an individual focuses on things of higher value and minds his own business he will seldom waste his time and energy on foolish distractions or lose his place in the immortal scheme of things. The image of a false call unheard in attention to immediate service dramatizes the principle of discrimination, or the ability to choose wisely. It also alludes to the fact that when an individual has found his true calling he knows where his duty lies and what he needs to do to get where he wants to go. Life and circumstances cooperate with the individual who creates a place for himself in the world. Positive: At its highest, this symbol represents integrity and self-fulfillment through accomplishing a special mission in life. Negative: Inability to separate the wheat from the chaff or indecision and a complete lack of discretion.

TODAY: The accent is on concentration and focus. Your time and attention are likely to be taken up trying to find solutions to pressing problems.

Opportunity: Your greatest advantage lies in prioritizing and putting first things first. Make a list and stick to it.

Risk: Guard against letting yourself get distracted or caught up in other people's problems. Don't put off until tomorrow what needs to be done today.

STEPPING STONES: Focus, concentration, discrimination, interest, dedication, devotion, commitment, stewardship, mission, responsibility, duty, competency, protection.

Libra

☐

LIBRA 1   A butterfly made perfect by a dart through it. KEY-
WORD: *Articulation*

*a butterfly made perfect
by a dart through it*

THEME: *Emergence.* This symbol speaks to a sudden and sharp awakening to the fact that individuals have the freedom to shape their own
destiny and make whatever they want of their lives. The image of a
butterfly made perfect by a dart through it suggests a piercing of consciousness and initiation, through sacrifice and pain, into a higher level of
understanding. The butterfly is a symbol of immortality or eternal and
unending existence. An analogy can be drawn here to the crucifixion of
Christ. The perfection of the butterfly alludes more to the completion of
a cycle than to any degree of excellence. The old dies and merges into
history. Life is born again in other forms. New potential waits to be
refined. Positive: At its highest, this symbol represents transformation
and change, and a rare ability to both perceive the underlying meaning
in endings and recognize the hidden opportunities in new beginnings.
Negative: Long-suffering martyrdom and witless fatalism.

TODAY: The accent is on initiation. A dramatic experience could make
you sharply aware of who you are at core.

Opportunity: Your greatest advantage lies in focusing on the reasons that
things come to an end, and on the potential that can be released or
uncovered through pain and suffering.

Risk: Guard against sacrificing yourself for all the wrong reasons or letting others mistreat you. Watch what you say. Words can wound.

STEPPING STONES: Awakening, awareness, emergence, transformation, significance freedom, self-expression, self-refinement, initiation, piercing of consciousness, sacrifice, pain, suffering, release.

LIBRA 2   The light of the sixth race transmuted to the seventh.
KEYWORD: *Threshold*

The light of the sixth race transmuted to the seventh

THEME: *Light on the Path.* This symbol speaks to the past projected into the future, or history as it reveals itself to a present generation in order to help them understand how they got to where they are and where they are headed if nothing happens to change the course of events. The image of the light of the sixth race transmuted to the seventh alludes to evolution, and it suggests organic transformation or a change in the appearance or form in which an ideal or vision will eventually manifest. Here is a call to stop for a moment and look at beginnings and the entire path behind in order to understand the original plan, the present situation as it relates to the overall scheme of this vision, and what yet needs to be done to fulfill the promise. This symbol can apply to individuals as well as society. The sixth race is described in the 1953 version of the Sabian symbols as a "modern and global society." The seventh race is defined as a "climactic manifestation," or the final, culminating and most forceful event in the progress of man. Positive: At its highest, this symbol represents broad, far-reaching vision and an enthusiastic commitment to bring the highest potential to fulfillment. Negative: Dissociation and loss of touch with reality or regressive thinking and an inability to deal with change or progress.

TODAY: The accent is on keeping a vision alive and bringing it forward on into the future. You may come to a clearer awareness of your mission or purpose today.

Opportunity: Your greatest advantage lies in stopping for a moment to assess where you've come from, or what you've been doing with your life, and asking yourself if you want to continue in the direction that this path has led you.

Risk: Guard against causing yourself to suffer unwanted consequences by failing to reflect on your experiences and how you came to have them. At the same time, try not to obsess over who caused what or spend all your time trying to nail down the genesis of everything that happens.

STEPPING STONES: Revelation, evolution, transformation, transmutation, passing the torch, historical progression, transmission, culmination, fulfillment of a vision.

LIBRA 3   The dawn of a new day, everything changed. KEY-
            WORD: *Innovation*

THEME: *Fresh Start*. This symbol speaks to transformation, and to a sudden awareness of change that has taken place behind the scenes or unnoticed. The image of the dawn of a new day, everything changed emphasizes the existence of unlimited potential waiting to be discovered and developed. The suggestion in this image is of a fresh start and opportunity to expand, unfold and glorify every aspect of the self. Here is a chance to start over again with hope and renewed vigor. Positive: At its highest, this symbol speaks to imaginative self-expression, a sense of adventure and a willingness to experiment or try new and novel techniques. Negative: Preference for the predictable and tried and true or a simple lack of awareness and an inability to recognize opportunity.

TODAY: The accent is on resourcefulness. You may find yourself scrambling to figure out how you're going to handle a situation that changed in the blink of an eye.

Opportunity: Your greatest advantage lies in being flexible and creative. Start gathering the resources and talent you're going to need in the days ahead.

Risk: Guard against trying to stop progress, prevent change or keep things the same forever. It can't be done.

STEPPING STONES: Transformation, change, new awareness, discovery, wiping the slate clean, fresh start, new beginnings, opportunity, potential, creation, originality, introduction.

LIBRA 4   **A group around a campfire. KEYWORD:** *Amiability*

a group around a campfire

THEME: *Fellowship.* This symbol speaks to a climactic experience in fellowship, or a sudden and deep feeling of unity and oneness with others. The image of a group around a campfire symbolizes illumination and the sharing of a common vision and purpose. The suggestion here is that a bonding of this sort can take place only when there is friendliness, respect for personality and freedom of choice. The greatest challenge for the members of any community will be found in learning how to cooperate and work together toward the achievement of group goals rather than in dramatizing and promoting personal agendas. Positive: At its highest, this symbol represents a unique talent for generating enthusiasm and optimism, and for creating and maintaining effective structures and systems that will facilitate the accomplishment of greater and broader objectives than any individual acting alone could hope to achieve.

Negative: Laziness, or a tendency to stand back and let others take the initiative and responsibility.

TODAY: The accent is on fellowship and inspiration. Personal differences are forgotten as people turn their attention to more important issues and common concerns.

Opportunity: Your greatest advantage lies in encouraging cooperation and being part of the process. Plan activities that everyone can enjoy and participate in.

Risk: Guard against depending on others to pick up your slack or do your work for you. Don't blame everything on others or criticize the way they do a job that you have refused to do.

STEPPING STONES: Fellowship, friendliness, sharing of experience, common purpose, vision quest, bonding.

LIBRA 5   A man teaching the true inner knowledge. KEY-
            WORD: *Affinity*

A man teaching the true inner knowledge

THEME: *Congruency*. This symbol speaks to the fact that nothing can destroy genuine inspiration, and that deeper insights can be communicated to others only as individuals reach out to their fellows and share common responsibilities in the practical and everyday world. The image of a man teaching the true inner knowledge symbolizes wisdom, and it alludes to a congruency between words spoken and actions taken. A man is what he does. The focus here is on self-integration and consistency, and a keen sensitivity to the highest potential of man and his world. Positive: At its highest, this symbol represents a natural gift for understanding and helping others come to a personal awareness of their own uniqueness and what they can individually achieve. Negative: Intellectual vanity or psychological manipulation of others.

TODAY: The accent is on enlightenment. You may find yourself looking for inspiring and encouraging words today. Metaphysical seminars or books may hold the key.

Opportunity: Your greatest advantage lies in listening carefully to what you hear and giving more credence to actions than words. Trust your intuition.

Risk: Guard against getting carried away with your own sense of importance. Try not to tell others what to do or sound "preachy." You can't know what is best for someone else.

STEPPING STONES: Wisdom, sharing knowledge, revelation, communication, inspiration, enlightenment, encouragement, instruction, discourse, education, explanation, indoctrination.

LIBRA 6   The ideals of a man abundantly crystallized. KEY-
           WORD: *Personification*

The ideals of a
man abundantly
crystallized

THEME: *Manifesting the Ideal*. This symbol speaks to a very concrete and outer manifestation of inner insights and realizations in the practical and everyday world. The image of the ideals of a man abundantly crystallized alludes to standards of excellence, beauty, and perfection taking definite form or shape. The suggestion here is that the function of ideals is to inspire men to take positive action when opportunity knocks, and that to rest satisfied in the mental construct of the ideal itself is the ultimate escape. Man comes to be what he is as a result of the ideals he forms and his ability to live up to them, and he draws to himself the experiences he needs to refine them. Positive: At its highest, this symbol represents a unique ability to develop all potential to its highest expression through creative resourcefulness and uninhibited imagination.

Negative: Failure to rise above the level of mediocrity as the result of an uninspired complacency or the avoidance of commitments and a preference for keeping the status quo.

TODAY: The accent is on seeing your ideals manifested concretely. You may receive proof or verification that something you believed in and hoped was true really is.

Opportunity: Your greatest advantage lies in holding fast to your dreams. Expect the best and be willing to work for what you want.

Risk: Guard against losing faith and becoming bitter.

STEPPING STONES: Substantiation, manifestation, realization, appearance, disclosure, display, reality, demonstration, embodiment, emergence, evidence, verification, documentation, proof, exhibition, incarnation, representation.

LIBRA 7   A woman feeding chickens and protecting them from the hawks. KEYWORD: *Shrewdness*

THEME: *Balancing Opposite Forces.* This symbol speaks to maintaining a proper balance between opposing forces by protecting the weak while preserving the strong. The image of a woman feeding chickens and protecting them from the hawks emphasizes the importance of supporting and developing that which is of present value while holding in reserve that which doesn't sustain, and may even harm, immediate objectives. The focus here is on discrimination and the ability to use good judgment. The challenge in any situation is to be able to tell the difference between the chickens and the hawks. Positive: At its highest, this symbol represents keen administrative skills and an ability to determine the most appropriate response in any given situation. Negative: Confusion and bungling or inability to separate the wheat from the chaff and make competent decisions.

TODAY: The accent is on protecting what you value. Your possessions or something you are responsible for could be in jeopardy.

Opportunity: Your greatest advantage lies in being vigilant and alert to sudden changes in others. Look for breaks in patterns—things that happen when they shouldn't or don't happen when they should.

Risk: Guard against taking things for granted or neglecting your responsibilities. Don't promise more than you can deliver.

STEPPING STONES: Protection, preservation, precaution, nurturance, administration, guardianship, stewardship, care, artfulness, cleverness, discernment, vigilance, watchfulness, discrimination.

LIBRA 8   A blazing fireplace in a deserted home. KEYWORD: *Guardianship*

a blazing fireplace in a deserted home

THEME: *Matters of the Heart.* This symbol speaks to loyalty, hope, passion and invisible sustainment. The image of a blazing fireplace in a deserted home alludes to the tendency of people and things to continue doing what they have been used to doing, even when there is no immediate need to do it. On the one hand, this symbol may refer to a fruitless expenditure of energy as the result of habit or a blind refusal to release and let go. On the other, it may reveal a tenacious clinging to hope or an indomitable will to live and survive. Individuals passionately support those things in which they see themselves reflected and confirmed. The emphasis here is on feelings, emotions and sentiment. The implication is that decisions associated with this degree tend to be made with the heart rather than the head. Positive: At its highest, this symbol represents a remarkable talent for achieving goals through effective emotional appeals that stir the passions. Negative: Neglect of duty and abandonment of responsibility or a simple refusal to acknowledge the obvious and act accordingly.

TODAY: The accent is on faithfulness. Refuge and security take top priority. You may find yourself revisiting your early childhood memories.

Opportunity: Your greatest advantage lies in making people feel welcome and cared about. Be consistent and protect the things you value.

Risk: Guard against clinging to the past or foolishly wasting your time and energy on dead issues. Release whatever is holding you back from your own progress.

STEPPING STONES: Loyalty, dedication, commitment, allegiance, constancy, devotion, faithfulness, service, stewardship, passion, spirit within, refusal to give up hope.

LIBRA 9   Three old masters hanging in an art gallery.
               KEYWORD: *Accord*

THEME: *Self-Integration.* This symbol speaks to man's capacity to understand his world and the universe through his own personal experience. The image of three old masters hanging in an art gallery alludes to the three souls in Plato's scheme—mind or intellect, feeling or emotion, and habit or instinct. The three paintings hang together as a set or unified creative expression. The suggestion here is that the fulfillment of all individual potential is achieved through effective self-integration or the harmonious blending and cooperative functioning of mind, body and spirit. The masters symbolize the past and our heritage. The implication is that we are irrevocably linked to Source and our roots, and that by standing on the shoulders of the giants who came before us we revitalize that heritage and carry it forward with our own individual accomplishments. Positive: At its highest, this symbol represents a special gift for healing conflict and dissension, and for bringing diverse people together in harmony by emphasizing mutual goals and objectives. Negative: Refusal to let go of outworn habits and traditions or selfish insistence on having one's own way, even at the expense of sacrificing the good of the whole or the best interest of the group.

TODAY: The accent is on learning how to get along with others and solve your own problems.

Opportunity: Your greatest advantage lies in recognizing that there can be more than one winner, and being willing to share the limelight with others.

Risk: Guard against trying to be a crowd pleaser or basing your decisions on your opinion of how things have always been done. You could be wrong or the technique may not work in this particular situation.

STEPPING STONES: Unity, affinity, compatibility, relationship, harmony, integration, heritage, the past, excellence, creative expression, fine arts, values, appreciation of excellence.

LIBRA 10   A canoe approaching safety through dangerous waters. KEYWORD: *Competency*

A canoe approaching safety through dangerous waters

THEME: *Proficiency.* This symbol speaks to risk-taking and to personal involvement. It is only through direct participation in life that personal skills can be improved and experience made real. The image of a canoe approaching safety through dangerous waters suggests the survival of a crisis or serious predicament. The emphasis here is on fortitude, competence, endurance, and a refusal to give up or stop trying until a goal is reached. Positive: At its highest, this symbol represents a genius for determining the right course of action or thing to do to bring any difficult situation to the desired or most successful conclusion. Negative: Foolish risk-taking, recklessness and a preference for living dangerously or naive dependence on luck and a tendency to leap before looking.

TODAY: The accent is on surviving crisis. You may need all your perseverance and skills to get through some challenging situation.

Opportunity: Your greatest advantage lies in choosing the right course of action. Know the potential hazards of any undertaking before you begin. Make sure you're equipped to handle them.

Risk: Guard against depending on luck or others to rescue you from your own foolishness. Avoid taking risks you don't have to take if you're not prepared to lose as well as win.

STEPPING STONES: Skillfulness, risk-taking, adventure, survival, fortitude, courage, endurance, stamina, competence, proficiency, adeptness, mastery.

LIBRA 11   A professor peering over his glasses. KEYWORD: *Specialization*

THEME: *Scholarship*. This symbol speaks to the excellence, pride and self-confidence required of any individual who seeks to establish and maintain a position of authority for himself. The image of a professor peering over his glasses dramatizes the process of education. The implication here is that men tend to sharpen and refine their skills and knowledge in those areas that promise the greatest rewards, or that gain them the highest respect, esteem and admiration of their fellows. The emphasis here is on the ability to stimulate learning and on the transfer of information and techniques to the next generation. Positive: At its highest, this symbol represents mastership in some unique field or a special gift for teaching. Negative: Intellectual intimidation or a simple delight in making others feel incompetent or inferior.

TODAY: The accent is on skill and knowledge. Expert advice may be sought to answer some perplexing question.

Opportunity: Your greatest advantage lies in sticking with what you like and are good at. Let others handle the rest.

Risk: Guard against the temptation to give advice on matters in which you have little experience or knowledge. Try not to be a know-it-all or give the impression that you have all the answers. Don't make others feel small by belittling their lack of knowledge or criticizing them in front of others.

STEPPING STONES: Knowledge, wisdom, specialization, skill, proficiency, know-how, expertise, self-refinement, mastery, instruction, responsibility.

LIBRA 12   Miners emerging from a mine. KEYWORD: *Escape*

Miners emerging from a mine

THEME: *Plumbing the Depths.* This symbol speaks to taking a break and returning to normal living after a period of restraint and restriction or deep involvement in some particular situation. The image of miners emerging from a mine alludes to investigation, or digging beneath the surface of things. It can also refer to psychological exploration, or plumbing the depths of selfhood. The implication here is that an answer or solution to a difficult question or problem is being sought and that time out is being taken to clear the mind, look at things from a different perspective, and rest. The emphasis is on determination and a willingness to persist, even in the face of the most unpleasant of circumstances, in order to accomplish a goal or bring matters to a successful conclusion.

Positive: At its highest, this symbol represents ingenuity, fortitude and extraordinary resourcefulness. Negative: Lack of ambition and a complete failure to live up to personal promise, or a tendency to accept defeat too easily.

TODAY: The accent is on curiosity and persistence. You may have to dig deeper for answers.

Opportunity: Your greatest advantage lies in investigating all leads and digging for answers. Be willing to get your hands dirty or give up some of your leisure and social time to get the job done.

Risk: Guard against staying silent when you should speak up or trying to keep a low profile in order to escape notice or avoid responsibility. You might, instead, look very conspicuous.

STEPPING STONES: Reentrance, emergence, reappearance, completion, taking a break, completion, escape, evacuation, exodus, endurance, exploration, investigation, curiosity, psychological exploration, labor, work.

LIBRA 13   Children blowing soap bubbles. KEYWORD: *Enchantment*

Children blowing soap bubbles

THEME: *The Art of Play.* This symbol speaks to the beauty and pleasure that can be discovered in even the most unpromising of relationships and circumstances when the mind is free from all prejudice and preconceptions. The image of children blowing soap bubbles symbolizes playfulness, amusement, and delight in innocent or frivolous pastimes. The emphasis here is on imagination and an enjoyment of the lighter side of life. The challenge in this degree is in being able to distinguish the difference between childlike and childish behavior. Positive: At its highest, this symbol represents creativity, charm, and a talent for adding sparkle and wit to any situation. Negative: Refusal to grow up and accept responsibility, or difficulty functioning in the practical everyday world and a tendency to retreat to a world of fantasy and delusion when the going gets rough.

TODAY: The accent is on fun and entertainment. You may find it hard to keep your mind on your work today.

Opportunity: Your greatest advantage lies in using your imagination. Take a fresh look at situations and people you have been taking for granted. Find at least one new and exciting thing to do that you weren't aware of before. Allow yourself to enjoy.

Risk: Guard against failing to take a crisis seriously. Don't fiddle while Rome burns.

STEPPING STONES: Fun, play, amusement, enjoyment, delight, imagination, fantasy, charm, euphoria, magic, innocence, childish, childlike.

LIBRA 14   A noon siesta. KEYWORD: *Recuperation*

a noon siesta

THEME: *Taking It Easy.* This symbol speaks to unconscious attunement with the universe, and to the achievement of a level of competence that permits occasional inattention to detail and duty without worrying that things will go wrong or fall apart. The image of a noon siesta suggests rest and relaxation in natural and rhythmic sequence with work and responsibility. Implicit in this image is the idea that success has its rewards and that it is important to live a well-balanced life. Positive: At its highest, this symbol represents extraordinary skill in organizing and managing the daily affairs of living. Negative: Apathy and boredom or laziness and neglect of responsibility.

TODAY: The accent is on living a balanced life and taking care of your health. You may need time to rebuild your energy or take a mental break from things.

Opportunity: Your greatest advantage lies in balancing work with pleasure. Learn to pace yourself. Slow down and relax.

Risk: Guard against feeling guilty if you aren't being productive twenty-four hours a day. Don't neglect your physical and psychological needs.

STEPPING STONES: Rest, relaxation, sleep, recuperation, recovery, healing, inner reorientation, intermission, leisure, time out, break, interlude, recess.

LIBRA 15   Circular paths. KEYWORD: *Congruity*

Circular paths

THEME: *Wheel of Life.* This symbol speaks to cycles, the repetition of experience, and self-rectification, or the process of returning to center for the purpose of reflection, self-assessment and inner realignment. The image of circular paths alludes to the fact that every journey and all things set in motion eventually run their course or come full circle and return to where they started. This image also suggests astrological cycles in that individuals often find themselves struggling and unable to see eye to eye with their fellows in the squares and oppositions of life—or facilitated, propelled and impacted with trines, sextiles and conjunctions. At its highest, this symbol represents the ability to self-correct or adjust when the need arises. Negative: Failure to learn from experience and a tendency to repeat the same mistakes over and over as a result of convoluted thinking and an inability to reason systematically and logically.

TODAY: The accent is on repetition. You could find yourself right back where you started, or having to do something over again.

Opportunity: Your greatest advantage lies in finishing what you start. If the journey is over, reflect on what you learned from it.

Risk: Guard against getting in a mental rut. Try not to repeat the same mistakes over and over again by refusing to change your approach. Think about what you're doing that isn't working.

STEPPING STONES: Repeating experience, going in circles, convoluted thinking, coming full circle, second chances, cycles, symmetry, fulfillment, completion.

LIBRA 16   A boat landing washed away. KEYWORD: *Respite*

a boat landing washed away

THEME: *The Opportunity in Loss.* This symbol speaks to superficial conflict, and to man's tendency to view the universe as unfriendly or even hostile when he is blocked or unable to establish and maintain the world about him according to his own personal desires. The image of a boat landing washed away is one of the negative or reversed symbols, and it shows nature attempting to restore herself to her pure and virginal condition. The challenge in this symbol lies in the opportunity to be creative and clever, or to develop alternatives and find new resources. There is also a suggestion in this symbol that whenever something has lost or outworn its usefulness, it will be swept away in order to make room for what is truly needed. Positive: At its highest, this symbol represents extraordinary competence and ingenuity, and a natural flair for making do in emergencies with brilliant stop-gap solutions. Negative: Self-defeating attitude, or a tendency to focus on all the reasons why something couldn't possibly work rather than giving it a try.

TODAY: The accent is on finding alternative solutions. You may be feeling cut off from things. Transportation problems are also possible.

Opportunity: Your greatest advantage lies in accepting loss as a signature that it's time to make a change. Open the door to new opportunity.

Risk: Guard against getting yourself upset and quitting every time things go wrong or you meet with frustration. Obstacles and loss aren't always bad omens or God's punishment.

STEPPING STONES: Opportunity through loss, reordering, return to natural condition, disappointment, frustration, handicap, challenge to start over, natural disaster, cleanup.

LIBRA 17   A retired sea captain. KEYWORD: *Relaxation*

A retired sea captain

THEME: *The Melody Lingers On*. This symbol speaks to satisfaction in a life well lived. It also speaks to mellowness, reflection, and to man's inclination to seek out those things, places and relationships that keep his most treasured memories vibrant and alive. The image of a retired sea captain alludes to that period of time, after completion of a cycle in living, when the significance and meaning of experience begin to fall in place, or become clear and understandable. The implication here is that the ability to relax and feel at ease depends on knowing that nothing important has been neglected or left undone. Positive: At its highest, this symbol represents self-confidence, pride and honor, and the ability to profit from experience. Negative: Tendency to live in the past, or to excuse all present lack of accomplishment by pointing the finger again and again to prior achievements in the old and glorious days of yore.

TODAY: The accent is on leisure and time to enjoy the fruits of your labor. You may find yourself reminiscing about the good old days or exchanging war stories with others who have had similar experiences.

Opportunity: Your greatest advantage lies in viewing your mistakes as learning experiences. Rethink the significance of your experiences constantly.

Risk: Guard against crying over spilled milk or agonizing over what could or might have been, if only . . . On the other hand, don't rest polluted in the spoils of your success.

STEPPING STONES: Completion, fulfillment, endings, reflection, reminiscence, relaxation, leisure, ease, freedom.

LIBRA 18   Two men placed under arrest. KEYWORD: *Consequence*

≙ *18*

a gang of robbers in hiding
Two men placed under arrest

THEME: *Restraint.* This symbol speaks to the inevitable consequences of antisocial behavior, and to the restraint and controls that eventually will be placed on the individual who is unable or unwilling to live in harmony with his fellows or within himself. The image of two men placed under arrest is one of the reversed or negative symbols and it emphasizes the importance of self-consistency or acting in accord with what is recognized as the self's best interest and what is right and proper in the circumstance. It also encourages individuals to be true to themselves and accept their limitations—not as any form of punishment but to help them direct the focus of their efforts to the achievement of their highest potential. Positive: At its highest, this symbol represents a remarkable ability to find the hidden and special opportunities in every restriction of life. Negative: Lack of self-control, or impulsive and inappropriate behavior.

*This image was originally designated as Libra 19; however it was changed to the present degree after Marc Jones verified his feeling with the ancient source of the images that a mistake had been made.

TODAY: The accent is on restraint and limitation. Repercussions and consequences may be felt today.

Opportunity: Your greatest advantage lies in following the rules and obeying the law. Use any period of restriction in one area to develop your skills in another.

Risk: Guard against getting involved in anything illegal or unethical. This is a period of almost instant karma. You won't get away with it.

STEPPING STONES: Restraint, consequences, repercussion, arrest, limitation, restriction, apprehension, curtailment, capture, detainment, detention, immobilization, interception.

LIBRA 19   A gang of robbers in hiding. KEYWORD: *Divergence*

≏ 19

A gang of robbers in hiding
Two men placed under arrest

THEME: *Covertness.* This symbol speaks to man's freedom to choose the manner in which he will satisfy his desires or obtain what he wants, even though that choice may violate social principles or cross the boundaries of the law and violate the rights of others. The image of a gang of robbers in hiding is another reversed symbol and it continues the emphasis of Libra 18 on antisocial behavior. But where the men in the preceding symbol have been apprehended or stopped, this gang of robbers still has the time and opportunity to change their minds. The implication here is that individuals usually try to hide their primitive instincts and destructive impulses from others and will often take the easy way out when they think they can get away with it, or not get caught. The emphasis in this symbol is on integrity, and on the need to earn rather than steal the rewards of life. Positive: At its highest, this symbol represents a strong desire for privacy and resistance to conformity. Negative: Mistrust and suspicion or deviousness, hidden agendas and a talent for manipulating situations from behind the scenes.

*This image was originally designated as Libra 18; however it was changed to the present degree after Marc Jones verified his feeling with the ancient source of the images that a mistake had been made.

TODAY: The accent is on the fear of being detected or getting caught. Medical diagnoses could be difficult at this time. Someone could be planning a sneak attack.

Opportunity: Your greatest advantage lies in being honest and doing the right thing. Stay alert to hidden danger. What you don't see can sometimes hurt you.

Risk: Guard against suspecting people of the worst without any evidence to support your suspicions. On the other hand, don't take foolish chances with your material assets, your health or your reputation.

STEPPING STONES: Hiding, seclusion, concealment, cover-up, fear of apprehension, sequestering, furtiveness, deviousness, law-breaking, anti-social acts, attempt to avoid consequences, fear of getting caught.

LIBRA 20   A Jewish rabbi. KEYWORD: *Heritage*

a Jewish Rabbi

THEME: *The Golden Thread.* This symbol speaks to effectiveness in helping others understand eternal or immortal values. The image of a Jewish rabbi symbolizes religious teachings, spiritual tradition and wisdom. The emphasis here is on responsibility to a group, and the implication is that such a responsibility requires social maturity and a harmonious blend of both masculine and feminine qualities, or strength and assertiveness in equal proportion to gentleness and nurturance. The suggestion in this degree is that any individual or group dedicated to the highest ideals can become a channel or instrument for the aspirations of all humankind. Positive: At its highest, this symbol represents extraordinary insight, vision, and a determination to build on the achievements of the giants of the past. Negative: Egocentricity and intellectual smugness, or an attitude of being better than everyone else.

TODAY: The accent is on religion and tradition. Spiritual solutions may be sought as practical or secular methods fail to resolve a serious problem.

Opportunity: Your greatest advantage lies in being of service. Prayer and meditation, in conjunction with hands-on help, can work miracles.

Risk: Guard against being condescending, or trying to give the impression that you are somehow superior or better than others. Teach, don't preach.

STEPPING STONES: Wisdom, knowledge, maturity, tradition, heritage, roots, culture, religion, ritual, minister, clergy, spiritual guidance.

LIBRA 21   A crowd upon the beach. **KEYWORD**: *Exhilaration*

A crowd upon the beach

THEME: *Going With the Flow*. This symbol speaks to relaxation, enjoyment, and going with the mood of the moment. The image of a crowd upon the beach alludes to recreation and fellowship. The rhythmic ebb and flow of the ocean symbolizes naturalness, spontaneity, and the release of tension. The suggestion here is that social interchange creates opportunities to discover and express new facets of the self. Positive: At its highest, this symbol represents a positive and friendly outlook on life, and the ability to go with the flow of things. Negative: Self-centeredness or feelings of entitlement and a refusal to give of self.

TODAY: The accent is on letting your hair down and releasing your inhibitions. It might be difficult to keep your mind on your work today.

Opportunity: Your greatest advantage lies in being friendly and sociable. Relax the rules and enjoy the results.

Risk: Guard against overregimenting your life or trying to control everything and everyone around you. Don't expect others to open up to you if you're not willing to share yourself with them.

STEPPING STONES: Lack of inhibition, light-heartedness, relaxation, enjoyment, recreation, naturalness, spontaneity, going with the flow, friendliness.

LIBRA 22   A child giving birds a drink at a fountain. KEY-
WORD: *Solicitude*

a child giving birds a drink at a fountain

THEME: *Facilitation*. This symbol speaks to an unshakeable trust in the
basic friendliness of the universe, and to a delight in discovering that the
world is a place of unlimited opportunity waiting to be explored. The
image of a child giving birds a drink at a fountain symbolizes helpfulness,
care, and concern for others. The emphasis is on sympathy and little acts
of kindness through which personal ideals can be tested, refined and
expressed. The suggestion here is that happiness is found more in giving
and reaching out to others than in receiving and gathering in to self.
Positive: At its highest, this symbol represents a deeply held belief in the
essential goodness of all living things and a genuine joy in sharing.
Negative: Superficiality and false charity, or concern with appearances
and self-serving efforts to make things look good.

TODAY: The accent is on friendliness and helpfulness. You're likely to
be feeling especially sympathetic and generous toward those less fortunate
than yourself.

Opportunity: Your greatest advantage lies in performing random acts of
kindness. Make this day special by surprising a stranger with a gift. You
never know how far the results will spread.

Risk: Guard against trying to buy friendship by doing too much for
others or inundating them with what you think they need. Don't be a
doormat or invite others to take advantage of you by failing to put a
value on your services.

STEPPING STONES: Helpfulness, naïveté, friendliness, responsibility,
care, attention, concern, consideration, kindness, benevolence, charity,
sympathy, trust, sharing.

LIBRA 23   Chanticleer. KEYWORD: *Fervor*

Chanticleer

THEME: *The Cock of the Walk*. This symbol speaks to self-image, or an individual's mental picture of who he is, and to self-acclaim, or a demand that others recognize and acknowledge this self-perception. The image of Chanticleer, the rooster who dramatically heralds the dawn with a loud and boisterous crow, symbolizes enthusiasm, assertiveness, ambition and pride in having a definite purpose and role to play in society. The suggestion here is that there are benefits to be gained by drawing attention to those things that are important or special in the overall scheme of things. On a practical level, this image can signify a wake-up call or indicate that something needs to be attended to. Positive: At its highest, this symbol represents self-confidence, competency, and a convincing air of authority that gains a loyal following. Negative: Arrogance and cockiness, or obnoxious attempts to elevate the self through grandiloquent, high-sounding rhetoric.

TODAY: The accent is on ego and self-affirmation. Bold and dramatic means are likely to be used to get a message across or gain the attention of others.

Opportunity: Your greatest advantage lies in speaking up for what you want and saying what's on your mind. Pay attention to early warning signals that something may be wrong or out of order.

Risk: Guard against exaggerating or overstating your case. Being too loud and aggressive can work against you.

STEPPING STONES: Self-confidence, pride, ambition, conceit, cockiness, assertiveness, enthusiasm, zeal, ardor, passion, boisterousness, wake-up call, alarm.

LIBRA 24   A third wing on the left side of a butterfly. KEY-
WORD: *Distinctiveness*

a third wing on the
left side of a butterfly

THEME: *Uniqueness*. This symbol speaks to the fact that there is
unlimited potential in man and his world. When an individual respects
and capitalizes on his own uniqueness, and is sensitive to every opportunity that presents itself, then there is no limit to what he can achieve. The
image of a third wing on the left side of a butterfly is a powerful symbol
of originality, extraordinary differentiation and distinctiveness. Here is
a plussage that rises above the ordinary. The suggestion here is that every
mutation, aberration or deviation from the norm has its own special
contribution to make to experience. Positive: At its highest, this symbol
represents creativity, uniqueness and a special genius for recognizing the
latent opportunity in even the most seemingly unpromising or hopeless
situations. Negative: Obsession with the bizarre and abnormal or an
inability to recognize the true value of things.

TODAY: The accent is on things that are unique or one of a kind.
Something that may appear to be defective, at first glance, may turn out
to be extremely valuable.

Opportunity: Your greatest advantage lies in capitalizing on peculiarities.
Identify what makes a thing different and use that feature to create an
attractive asset.

Risk: Guard against rejecting things that don't measure up to your
standards of perfection. On the other hand, don't overvalue a thing on
the simple basis of its rarity.

STEPPING STONES: Unique, original, distinctive, different, exceptional, remarkable, extraordinary, peculiar, anomalous, mutant, aberrant,
deviant.

LIBRA 25   Information in the symbol of an autumn leaf. KEY-
            WORD: *Tact*

THEME: *Revelation*. This symbol speaks to imagination and to an ability to understand the subtle messages in all things and events through a sensitivity to pattern. The image of information in the symbol of an autumn leaf emphasizes the importance of observation and paying attention to detail. The suggestion here is that intelligence is basically the capacity to understand how things can be used to achieve desired ends and benefit the self and others. The emphasis in this degree is on understanding the mutual and necessary interdependence of man and his world. Positive: At its highest, this symbol represents adaptability, intuition, a natural ability to see beyond surface appearances and comprehend the ultimate meaning and purpose of things, and an unwavering commitment to the highest good in all situations. Negative: Tendency to get lost in inconsequential detail or lose perspective in foolish flights of fancy.

TODAY: The accent is on interpretation. Translating information from one medium or language to another may require your time and attention.

Opportunity: Your greatest advantage lies in focusing on your objective and being diplomatic in getting your message across.

Risk: Guard against believing that because something is difficult to understand that it is more important or has more value. Avoid confusing others with irrelevant details or talking about things they can't relate to or have no interest in.

STEPPING STONES: Meaning, significance, revelation, message, sensitiveness, intuition, understanding, imagination, secret codes.

LIBRA 26   An eagle and a large white dove turning one into the other. KEYWORD: *Adeptness*

An eagle and a large
white dove turning one
into the other

THEME: *The Airborne Chameleon.* This symbol speaks to adeptness and flexibility, and to the capacity to adapt to change and handle each different situation on its own terms. The image of an eagle and a large white dove turning one into the other reflects creativity, imagination, and resourcefulness at its best. The emphasis here is on personal responsibility for the course of events in every situation in which the individual participates, and on the complete frustration that an individual can experience when all his efforts to make a situation conform to some ideal of perfection fail. Implicit in this symbol is the idea that man is in charge of his life only to the extent that he acts in his own best interest and remains true to self. On a practical level, this image alludes to fluctuation, and alternating between extremes such as war and peace or aggressive and passive behavior. The eagle and dove also symbolize the head and heart, and thus this image can allude to vacillating back and forth between intellectual and emotional responses. Positive: At its highest, this symbol represents a highly-developed sense of appropriateness, and intuitive skill in resolving conflict and strife. Negative: Indecisiveness or unfaithfulness and betrayal.

TODAY: The accent is on instability and unpredictability. Just when you think things have been decided, and matters put to rest, the situation may change.

Opportunity: Your greatest advantage lies in being able to adapt smoothly. Stay flexible and try to go with the flow. Address issues as they arise, but wait until the dust settles before making long-term plans.

Risk: Guard against allowing yourself to get upset when you can't control things or situations. Don't get caught unprepared for a sudden change in affairs.

STEPPING STONES: Agility, skill, versatility, flexibility, transformation, indecision, inconsistency, vacillation, war and peace, head and heart, fluctuation, change.

LIBRA 27   An airplane hovering overhead. KEYWORD: *Reflection*

an airplane hovering over head

THEME: *Rising Above It All.* This symbol speaks to the development of high standards and ideals, and to the achievement of immortality through imagination and creative resourcefulness. The image of an airplane hovering overhead symbolizes transcendence, achievement, higher perspective, and the ability to understand cause-and-effect relationships as the result of a mastery of experience. It can also indicate detachment, tranquility and a preference for serene and peaceful surroundings. On a practical level, this degree suggests surveillance. Positive: At its highest, this symbol represents psychological insight and a talent for maintaining poise and objectivity. Negative: Loss of touch with reality and flights of fancy, or mind wandering and a refusal to take things seriously.

TODAY: The accent is on the broad overview. This is a time for looking at the whole picture rather than focusing on the details.

Opportunity: Your greatest advantage lies in stepping back and analyzing how you got where you are. Try to see your life in terms of cause and effect, especially your own part in it all.

Risk: Guard against taking off at the wrong time and leaving situations to resolve themselves, or function effectively without supervision. Don't wait too long to make an important decision.

STEPPING STONES: Perspective, overview, transcendence, surveillance, poise, contemplation, viewpoint, reflection, study, deliberation, consideration, examination.

LIBRA 28   **A man in the midst of brightening influences.** KEYWORD: *Responsiveness*

A man in the
midst of brightening
brightening   influences

THEME: *Moving Toward the Light At the End Of the Tunnel.* This symbol speaks to the basic friendliness of life when it is understood and accepted on its own terms. The image of a man in the midst of brightening influences symbolizes an awakening, or a change in the way circumstances are viewed rather than any actual or outer change in conditions. The emphasis is on mood and expectation, and on the fact that success is the result of keeping a forward movement toward the light at the end of the tunnel and refusing to give up in discouragement. The suggestion here is that attitude creates and sustains circumstance. Life is what the individual decides to make of it. Positive: At its highest, this symbol represents optimism, attunement with all of life and an unshakeable faith in the higher purpose of all experience. Negative: Self-defeat through inertia and brooding or a tendency to engage in magical thinking and hope that things will improve without effort.

TODAY: The accent is on a positive turn of events. Something you see or hear today could give you new hope. Things are looking up.

Opportunity: Your greatest advantage lies in staying the course and keeping your eye on the goal ahead. Give it a little more time and sustain yourself in the interim by focusing on the positive.

Risk: Guard against giving up too soon. You could lose everything you have worked for.

STEPPING STONES: Hope, expectation, optimism, encouragement, reassurance, confidence, motivation, promise, anticipation, ambition, inspiration, turn for the better.

LIBRA 29   **Humanity seeking to bridge the span of knowledge.**
             KEYWORD: *Rationality*

THEME: *Bridging the Gap.* This symbol speaks to the fact that man has the capacity to make himself a channel for the wisdom that sustains and supports the world in which he lives. The image of humanity seeking to bridge the span of knowledge symbolizes a desire to understand and achieve something significant—or to learn, to know and to do. Implicit in this image is the importance of recognizing the illimitable number of opportunities and areas of specialization in which an individual can successfully concentrate his efforts and find self-fulfillment. The emphasis in this degree is on building self-confidence through the testing and proving of ideas. Positive: At its highest, this symbol represents inventiveness and a unique talent for finding new and productive uses for things. Negative: Dissatisfaction due to a pervasive feeling that no matter what is accomplished, it isn't good enough.

TODAY: The accent is on logic and planning. Finding ways to link things that are now separate and apart could be quite challenging.

Opportunity: Your greatest advantage lies in using reason to solve immediate problems. Pool your resources and make it a group effort.

Risk: Guard against thinking you can solve everything by yourself. Don't let your pride stand in the way of asking for help.

STEPPING STONES: Outreach, networking, linking, connection, merger, union, channels, understanding, reason, thought, intellect.

LIBRA 30   **Three mounds of knowledge on a philosopher's head.**
             KEYWORD: *Prescience*

Three mounds of knowledge on a philosopher's head

THEME: *The Prophet.* This symbol speaks to the fact that life is as life is made to be, and when man understands this principle of cosmic order he can see it at work in his life and use it to direct his affairs. The image of three mounds of knowledge on a philosopher's head challenges the seeker to develop his physical, emotional and intellectual faculties (or his skills, allegiances and ideals) in equal measure. In so doing, he comes to comprehend the basic workings of cause and effect and the interrelatedness of all things. Thus he is able to anticipate or predict the future. Positive: At its highest, this symbol represents prophetic genius, psychological wholeness and self-integration. Negative: Excessive reliance on intellectual solutions at the expense of spiritual or humanitarian concerns.

TODAY: The accent is on intuition and insight. You may have a startling realization that causes you to make a change of some kind in the way you have been doing something.

Opportunity: Your greatest advantage lies in using more than one tool or technique to accomplish your goal. Pay special attention to things that seem out of the ordinary. A change is being forecast that you need to prepare for.

Risk: Guard against missing an important message by focusing too narrowly in one direction. Don't rationalize away your psychic perceptions.

STEPPING STONES: Well-roundedness, self-integration, wisdom, vision, foresight, perception, judgment, precognition, clairvoyance, prophetic genius.

Scorpio

♏

SCORPIO 1   A sight-seeing bus. KEYWORD: *Friendliness*

a sight-seeing bus

THEME: *Window-Shopping*. This symbol speaks to open-mindedness, inquisitiveness, and naive curiosity. The image of a sight-seeing bus alludes to a broadening of experience through vicarious participation in the affairs of others, without the usual obligations and responsibilities. It also suggests camaraderie, fellowship and the sharing of personal insights and viewpoints. The emphasis here is on the development of compassion and empathy, and learning that there are many different ways to live and express things. Positive: At its highest, this symbol represents objectivity and an absence of mind-set that makes it possible for the seeker to avoid getting entangled in conflict and controversy while, at the same time, recognizing the opportunities that arise therein. Negative: Irresponsibility, voyeurism and opportunism, or a tendency to take advantage of others and try to get by with the least amount of effort possible.

TODAY: The accent is on learning more about other people and places and sharing experiences.

Opportunity: Your greatest advantage lies in looking out and beyond your immediate environment for ideas you might be able to use to make your life more productive and enjoyable. Visit some place that you haven't been to before.

Risk: Guard against judging others for the way they handle situations that you haven't experienced. Don't be too nosey. You could get a door shut in your face.

STEPPING STONES: Curiosity, interest, voyeurism, inquisitiveness, window-shopping, camaraderie, friendliness, travel, tourism adventure.

SCORPIO 2   A broken bottle and spilled perfume. KEYWORD: *Permeation*

a broken bottle and spilled perfume

THEME: *The Lingering Fragrance.* This symbol speaks to the indelible impression man leaves on his fellows when he pours the full essence of himself into his every experience and permeates the world with the fragrance of his soul. The image of a broken bottle and spilled perfume is one of the reversed or negative symbols, and it alludes to some great sacrifice in which an individual fulfills his potential in an extraordinary way and, in the process, leaves behind a persisting and poignant reminder of himself and his immortal contribution. Here in this image is nobility and a never-to-be-forgotten quality of greatness. Positive: At its highest, this symbol represents integrity, or a refusal to compromise or betray the self and its principles. Negative: Melancholia or a tragic and senseless waste of every resource of self.

TODAY: The accent is on impressions left behind. You may find yourself thinking about a loved one from the past or someone who sacrificed to make a difference in the world.

Opportunity: Your greatest advantage lies in pouring your creative efforts into your own special project. Use your own ideas and put your own unique stamp on your work.

Risk: Guard against trying to fit yourself into someone else's mold. Don't overextend yourself. Your energy could be at a low point.

STEPPING STONES: Remembrance, essence, saturation, impact, release, outflow, emptying, loss, endings, death, disappointment, dissipation, evaporation.

SCORPIO 3   A house-raising. KEYWORD: *Helpfulness*

a house raising

THEME: *Building Community*. This symbol speaks to cooperation, altruism, and neighborly outreach. The image of a house-raising is an event that was more common in rural, frontier America but it carries the essence of joy in fellowship and working together to build a community. The emphasis here is on relationships, shared experience, group effort, and the comfort of knowing that the support of others is available in times of crisis and need. Positive: At its highest, this symbol represents community leadership and a special genius for inspiring volunteerism by making work look fun. Negative: Difficulty in sharing responsibility and working well with others, or simple wilfulness and insistence on having one's own way.

TODAY: The accent is on teamwork. Activities center around community and family projects.

Opportunity: Your greatest advantage lies in improving your home and neighborhood. Planning a party around some major task could get you the help you need.

Risk: Guard against thinking you can do everything yourself, without any assistance. Refusing to cooperate or answer a call for help can have repercussions. One hand washes the other.

STEPPING STONES: Building community, new home, neighborliness, cooperation, teamwork, collaboration, assistance, helpfulness, support, friendship.

SCORPIO 4   A youth holding a lighted candle. **KEYWORD:** *Reliance*

a youth holding a lighted candle

THEME: *Illumination*. This symbol speaks to enlightenment, and to an expansion of consciousness that brings an awareness of the ultimate sacredness of all life, or the fact that the divine spirit flows equally through all. The image of a youth holding a lighted candle symbolizes illumination, transcendental vision, insight, and the ability to see beyond the superficial appearance of things. The emphasis here is on discernment and the search for higher meaning and significance in every experience. Implicit in this symbol is a childlike faith that lifts the soul and fills the heart with hope and inspiration. Positive: At its highest, this symbol represents spiritual sensitivity, an unwavering trust in the essential good and purpose to be found in all experience, and a special gift for helping others see things more clearly. Negative: Impractical solutions to the problems of life, or simple witlessness and lack of sound judgment.

TODAY: The accent is on illumination. Answers you have been seeking may come in a quiet moment of reflection.

Opportunity: Your greatest advantage lies in spending time alone to still your mind and open yourself to receive higher guidance. Listen to the voice within.

Risk: Guard against the dangers inherent in ignoring the practical realities of life. Learn to distinguish the difference between illusion and illumination. Be careful of fires.

STEPPING STONES: Vision, inspiration, clarification, enlightenment, guidance, assistance, way-shower, illumination, radiance, bliss, spirit, faith, good, discernment.

SCORPIO 5   A massive, rocky shore. KEYWORD: *Stabilization*

a massive rocky shore

THEME: *A Firm Foundation.* This symbol speaks to the reassuring effect that solid and lasting or permanent things have on the lives of men. The image of a massive, rocky shore symbolizes hardiness, durability, and safe harbor or security. The shore itself alludes to water and emotions. The suggestion here is that inner strength, or psychological fitness, is the foundation and basis of a stable outer life. On a practical level, this symbol can refer to the rock-of-Gibraltar or pillar-of-strength qualities found in those individuals who are recognized for their ability to stay calm and collected in even the most challenging or volatile of situations. Positive: At its highest, this symbol represents strength of character, dependability and persistence. Negative: Dogmatism, stubbornness and resistance to change.

TODAY: The accent is on security. You could be looking for something solid and dependable to hold on to today.

Opportunity: Your greatest advantage lies in being pragmatic and practical. Make sure all your foundations are stable. Focus on the physical.

Risk: Guard against being uncompromising and stubborn, or refusing to cooperate. It's better to bend than be broken.

STEPPING STONES: Foundation, dependability, reliability, sustainment, firmness, stability, endurance, permanence, strength, conservativeness, stubbornness.

SCORPIO 6   A gold rush. KEYWORD: *Ambition*

a gold rush

THEME: *Seizing Opportunities*. This symbol speaks to resourcefulness, or the ability to take creative advantage of what is at hand when a need or opportunity arises. The image of a gold rush dramatizes ambition and a willingness to make personal sacrifices, or endure temporary hardships, in order to gain the greater rewards ahead. The emphasis in this symbol is on the necessity that men learn to think intelligently, or use their heads and exercise their initiative to overcome limitations. The suggestion here is that when individuals focus on their assets and capabilities, rather than on their deficiencies and problems, then their situations will improve. Positive: At its highest, this symbol represents optimism and a natural gift for spotting opportunity and bringing out the best and highest potential of every situation. Negative: Opportunism and greed or lack of discrimination and an inability to recognize the true value of things.

TODAY: The accent is on eagerness. News about an exciting new opportunity may cause a flurry of activity by those hoping to cash in.

Opportunity: Your greatest advantage lies in preparing yourself adequately before you take off on some new venture. Be sure the reward you seek is worth the price you might have to pay to get it.

Risk: Guard against being taken in by easy-money schemes. If it looks too good to be true, it probably is.

STEPPING STONES: Initiative, eagerness, ambition, aspiration, greed, avarice, desire, frenzy, treasure hunting, opportunism, adventure, competition.

SCORPIO 7   Deep-sea divers. KEYWORD: *Involvement*

THEME: *Exploration*. This symbol speaks to the rejection of superficial experience, a desire for deep and enduring relationships, and a tendency to saturate or immerse the self totally in everything of current interest. The image of deep-sea divers alludes to an unshakeable determination to investigate or explore every opportunity, unravel every unsolved mystery, and get directly to the bottom of things. The emphasis in this symbol is on self-improvement and perfection through subjecting the self to life's more challenging tests. On a practical level, this image can refer to psychological analysis, research, getting below the surface, and all undertakings that plumb the depths of man's existence. Positive: At its highest, this symbol represents extraordinary psychological insight and a dogged refusal to accept anything at face value or leave any stone unturned in a search. Negative: Snooping and prying, or reclusiveness and social withdrawal.

TODAY: The accent is investigation and exploration. Expect to have to dig deep for what you want. Motivation plays a big part in some strange occurrence. An underwater adventure could make the news.

Opportunity: Your greatest advantage lies in being persistent. Look behind the scenes or beneath the surface for your answers. Check things out before acting on what you hear.

Risk: Guard against getting in over your head or taking on more than you can handle. Don't try to get away with anything today.

STEPPING STONES: Exploration, investigation, research, psychological analysis, saturation, immersion, taking the plunge, jumping in, getting involved.

SCORPIO 8   The moon shining across a lake. KEYWORD: *Rapport*

The moon shining across a lake

THEME: *Moon Magic.* This symbol speaks to magic, transformation, inspiration, and the healing power of romance. The image of the moon shining across a lake alludes to mystical experience, and it portrays a quiet beauty that softens the heart and lifts the soul to shimmering realms of loveliness. There is also a suggestion of regression in this symbol as the moon reflects the light of the sun which, in turn, is reflected by the lake. Thus, this reflection of a reflection can symbolize the past, memory, reverie, nostalgia and the unconscious. On a practical level this symbol can indicate being caught up in the mood of the moment or temporarily transcending everyday problems through a shift in consciousness to gentler and more peaceful or mellow thoughts. Positive: At its highest, this symbol represents tranquility, serenity, and a special gift for finding imaginative solutions to the problems of life. Negative: Tendency to speak in vague and nebulous terms as a way of avoiding commitment, or taking a stand, or a simple, pipe-dreaming, head-in-the-clouds witlessness.

TODAY: The accent is on romance and reconciliation. You may be feeling especially nostalgic and reflective. Emotional appeals are particularly effective. This is a day of magic.

Opportunity: Your greatest advantage lies in going with the flow and following your heart. Take time for reflection. Light a candle and set the mood.

Risk: Guard against letting yourself get depressed over what could have been or what is now over. Make room in your life for what could be if you'd let it.

STEPPING STONES: Reflection, contemplation, serenity, the past, memory, reverie, nostalgia, melancholia, romance, yearning, desire, inspiration, magic-mirror, mystery, the unconscious, psychological realignment.

SCORPIO 9   Dental work. KEYWORD: *Practicality*

Dental work

THEME: *Staying in Shape.* This symbol speaks to maintaining health at all levels, whether physical, emotional or spiritual. The image of dental work symbolizes repair, rehabilitation, reconditioning and restoration. Teeth are related to speech, and thus this image can also refer to the prevention of gossip or loose talk and miscommunications. The emphasis here is on personal excellence and fitness, and on taking proper care of possessions. Positive: At its highest, this symbol represents a "Mr. Fixit," or inventiveness and mechanical ability. Negative: Tendency to let things drift into a state of disrepair before taking action or overconcern with surface appearances and making things look good.

TODAY: The accent is on repair. Health concerns and fixing things that are broken or not working could occupy your time.

Opportunity: Your greatest advantage lies in taking care of first things first. Prioritize. Be practical. Get your checkups.

Risk: Guard against waiting until things break down completely before taking action. Watch what you say. A careless word could be regretted.

STEPPING STONES: Repair, rehabilitation, maintenance, corrective measures, restoration, health, speech, preventing gossip, improvement of appearance.

SCORPIO 10 A fellowship supper. KEYWORD: *Fraternity*

a fellowship supper

THEME: *Mutual Support.* This symbol speaks to friendship, and to a coming together of individuals in mutual support and appreciation. The image of a fellowship dinner dramatizes the ancient ritual of communion, or the tradition of breaking bread together that symbolizes unity and oneness and a common bond and purpose. The emphasis here is on a sense of community and companionship at the most basic social level. Positive: At its highest, this symbol represents a dedication of personal skills and talents to the achievement of a group objective. Negative: Clan-consciousness, or a refusal to act independently and a failure to rise above the most primitive levels of functioning.

TODAY: The accent is on intimate gatherings with close friends. Activities center around reinforcing bonds with those who share mutual hopes and dreams.

Opportunity: Your greatest advantage lies in nurturing and renewing relationships with those who mean the most to you.

Risk: Guard against becoming too group dependent, or constantly seeking the approval of others before you do anything. Avoid nurturing mediocrity by insisting that everyone conform to a common group standard. Encourage independent thinking.

STEPPING STONES: Community, human services, brotherhood, fraternity, camaraderie, companionship, friendship, association, togetherness, mutual support, communion, common bond.

SCORPIO 11 A drowning man rescued. KEYWORD: *Safety*

a drowning man rescued

THEME: *Sink or Swim.* This symbol speaks to a tremendous love of life, and to a desire to reexperience those moments that have been the most memorable and pleasurable. The emphasis here is on living life to the fullest and having the courage to continue on toward goals, even when it seems there is no chance to succeed. The image of a drowning man rescued suggests unexpected assistance in an emergency or crisis. The implication here is that when an individual keeps his faith and refuses to be beaten by life, even an apparent tragedy or stroke of bad luck can turn out to be a fortuitous event through which he eventually profits. On a practical level, this image can symbolize a rescue from a situation where someone is "in over his head" or where, through some accident of chance, a seemingly enjoyable or ordinary undertaking takes a perilous turn. This image might also reflect a situation where a person risks his own life or position to save another. **Positive:** At its highest, this symbol represents an ability to survive the most challenging situations of life as the result of a refusal to give up or accept defeat. **Negative:** Foolish risk-taking or putting others at risk through irresponsible actions.

TODAY: The accent is on survival. You could receive unexpected help at the twelfth hour, or just when you had nearly given up.

Opportunity: Your greatest advantage lies in holding on until help arrives. Keep your mind's eye on what you still hope to achieve and what means the most to you.

Risk: Guard against abandoning hope and quitting in despair. Don't lose your composure and cause yourself unnecessary harm by making it hard for others to help you. Cooperate.

STEPPING STONES: Emergency, survival, rescue, assistance, support, sustainment, help, deliverance, salvation, extrication, liberation, recovery.

SCORPIO 12 An embassy ball. KEYWORD: *Display*

An embassy ball

THEME: *Formal Maneuvers.* This symbol speaks to social ritual at its highest, and to the opportunity it brings each individual to recognize for himself whether or not his perceptions and the hopes and expectations that first moved him to pledge or affiliate himself with a particular organization or cause have been realized or met. The image of an embassy ball is associated with politics and governments. The dance alludes to the intricate steps and fancy footwork that must be learned in any effective social maneuvering. Implicit in this symbol is a dramatization of values. Here the political process of a group is exposed as either a means to encourage and develop personal excellence among all its members or a tool to exploit the skills and resources of the weak and disenfranchised. The emphasis in this symbol is on revelation through theatrical exaggeration and the chance to see things as they really are. Positive: At its highest, this symbol represents a natural poise and grace that facilitates group integrity and stability. Negative: Arrogance and class-consciousness or use of Machiavellian tactics to achieve desired ends.

TODAY: The accent is on lavish show and formality. Activities center on special events that require you to look and perform at your best.

Opportunity: Your greatest advantage lies in following the lead of those in the know. Let the others speak and act first and then make your move.

Risk: Guard against committing a faux pas by failing to adequately inform yourself beforehand on the proper protocol or custom for some important social ritual or occasion.

STEPPING STONES: Formality, dance, grandeur, social drama, politics, exhibition, show, pomp, ostentation, ceremony, splendor, pageantry, affectation, maneuvering.

SCORPIO 13 An inventor experimenting. KEYWORD: *Cleverness*

An inventor experimenting

THEME: *The Willingness to Try Again and Again.* This symbol speaks to the sheer pleasure and exhilaration to be found in intellectual and creative achievements. The image of an inventor experimenting dramatizes imagination, ingenuity, and the knotty process of trial-and-error testing. The emphasis in this symbol is on personal resourcefulness, a determination to succeed, and the will to keep trying—even in the face of persistent failure. The suggestion here is that there is a special niche or place in life for everyone. The challenge is in finding it. Positive: At its highest, this symbol represents originality, inspiration, and success when it's least expected. Negative: Time wasting and disorganization or eccentricity and a preference for the garish and bizarre.

TODAY: The accent is on creativity and resourcefulness. You may find yourself making do with what you have or cleverly substituting for something you need but don't have.

Opportunity: Your greatest advantage lies in trying different approaches until you find the one that works. Use your imagination and wit and develop your own techniques.

Risk: Guard against ruining a good thing by making one too many changes. Avoid trying to be different for the sake of attracting attention. You could get your wish and be sorry.

STEPPING STONES: Trial and error, imagination, creativity, inventiveness, ingenuity, wit, resourcefulness, innovation, determination, cleverness, originality.

SCORPIO 14 Telephone linemen at work. **KEYWORD:** *Attachment*

Telephone linemen at work

THEME: *Connecting.* This symbol speaks to networking, communication, and the establishment of relationships. The image of telephone linemen at work also refers to the process of linking people, places and experiences, transcending time and space, and overcoming impediments to the free flow of information. The 1953 commentary on this degree alludes to the relationship between higher and lower elements, or the necessity that the higher protect the lower while the lesser serves the needs of the greater. Positive: At its highest, this symbol represents a special genius for finding novel solutions for complex problems. Negative: Well-intentioned busybodiness, or a tendency to meddle in the affairs of others.

TODAY: The accent is on networking, linking, and expanding human relationships.

Opportunity: Your greatest advantage lies in repairing broken lines of communication and verifying that communications you sent were actually received.

Risk: Guard against interfering and meddling, or sticking your nose in where it doesn't belong. Don't try to patch up what doesn't belong to you or isn't your business.

STEPPING STONES: Communication, linking, repair, connection, association, joining, bridging gaps, union, relationships, ties, nexus.

SCORPIO 15 Children playing around five mounds of sand.
          KEYWORD: *Naïveté*

Children playing around
five mounds of sand

THEME: *Halcyon Days.* This symbol speaks to the formative stages of social consciousness, and to the earliest efforts to develop personal competence. The image of children playing around five mounds of sand alludes to time and the five senses, and it symbolizes playfulness, creativity, self-expression and spontaneity. It also refers to the psychological aspect of interpersonal relationships, or learning how to stimulate interest and work cooperatively with others. The emphasis here is on ingenuity and learning how to get the most out of the potential in any experience. Positive: At its highest, this symbol represents a childlike eagerness to find the special gifts waiting to be discovered in the continual process of self-unfoldment, and a genuine delight in learning how to do new things. Negative: Aimlessness and lack of a sense of direction or purpose in life.

TODAY: The accent is on learning and the five senses. Activities center around creative exploration.

Opportunity: Your greatest advantage lies in forming your own impressions. Judge from your own experiences. Do your own thinking.

Risk: Guard against letting your physical desires overcome your better judgment. Be careful about going overboard when you're having a good time. Learn when to stop or say no.

STEPPING STONES: Social development, self-expression, self-discovery, creativity, spontaneity, five senses, playfulness, innocence.

SCORPIO 16 A girl's face breaking into a smile. KEYWORD: *Acquiescence*

a girl's face breaking into a smile

THEME: *Sunshine*. This symbol speaks to genuineness of character, self-revelation, and "being who you are." The image of a girl's face breaking into a smile reflects happiness and pleasure. The emphasis in this symbol is on appreciation and the magical effect of charm, personality and friendliness. Here also is positive response, or cooperation. Positive: At its highest, this symbol represents self-fulfillment through the simple things in life. Negative: A tendency to give in too easily or a simple failure to recognize what is not in the self's best interest.

TODAY: The accent is on friendliness. People are more open and willing to communicate. You may meet someone again that you haven't seen for a long time. A new friendship could begin today.

Opportunity: Your greatest advantage lies in being yourself and being honest in your communications with others.

Risk: Guard against trying to please others at the expense of your own welfare. Don't put yourself in a compromising situation by failing to say no before it's too late to turn back.

STEPPING STONES: Happiness, surprise, delight, friendliness, self-revelation, giving in, capitulation, compliance, agreement, concession, consent, surrender.

SCORPIO 17 A woman the father of her own child. KEYWORD: *Nucleation*

a woman the father of her own child

THEME: *The Perfect Blend.* This symbol speaks to man's struggle to meet his practical obligations in the everyday world while, at the same time, longing to find higher meaning in his life or live on more transcendent levels. In simple terms, here is an awareness of what is and what yet could be. The image of a woman the father of her own child is a symbol of creativity, self-sufficiency and independence. In cabalistic terms, this symbol describes the integration of the feminine and masculine, or spiritual and material natures, and the blending of head and heart, or reason and emotion. On a practical level, this symbol can describe those periods in an individual's life when his time is taken up with job, family and other practical responsibilities and he feels he is not living up to his full potential. Implicit in this symbol is inner harmony, personal strength and a certain "do-it-yourself" quality. Positive: At its highest, this symbol represents an extraordinary capacity for accomplishment and the ability to find significance and purpose in the everyday obligations of life. Negative: Willfulness and a refusal to cooperate with others.

TODAY: The accent is on independence and creativity. You could be feeling that it's time to take charge of your life or take matters into your own hands.

Opportunity: Your greatest advantage lies in doing what you feel is best for yourself. Decide what you want to achieve and start gathering what you need to do it.

Risk: Guard against burning all your bridges behind you by offending or cutting yourself off from those who can help you. Don't bite the hand that feeds you.

STEPPING STONES: Creation, birth, formation of new life, do-it-yourself attitude, independence, self-sufficiency, pulling things together, self-integration.

SCORPIO 18 A woods rich in autumn coloring. KEYWORD: *Fulfillment*

a woods rich in autumn coloring

THEME: *Harvest Time.* This symbol speaks to life cycles, and to the bounty of nature. The image of a woods rich in autumn coloring dramatizes the culmination point of a cycle, a time of harvest and reward, and the fulfillment of a promise. The emphasis in this symbol is on patience, timing and the process of natural unfoldment. More often than not, individuals fail to see the potential excellence or beauty of things in their earliest stages of development. On a practical level, this symbol speaks to the importance of avoiding hasty judgments, or jumping to conclusions, and knowing when the time is ripe to take action. Unto everything there is a season. Positive: At its highest, this symbol represents maturity and success. Negative: Poor sense of timing or sheer wastefulness.

TODAY: The accent is on completion and the fulfillment of a promise. Something you have worked hard to achieve may come to fruition today.

Opportunity: Your greatest advantage lies in appreciating the beauty of the moment. Take time to relax and enjoy the simple things of life. Pay attention to timing.

Risk: Guard against trying to force things to a conclusion too soon. On the other hand, don't expect things to turn out the way you want if you neglect them.

STEPPING STONES: Maturity, harvest, fruition, reward, manifestation, achievement, completion, accomplishment, realization, actualization, attainment, gratification, consummation, satisfaction.

SCORPIO 19 A parrot listening and then talking. KEYWORD: *Conventionality*

a parrot, listening and then talking

THEME: *Regurgitation*. This symbol speaks to the learning process, and to the effect of mind-set on perception and behavior. The image of a parrot talking symbolizes repetition and mimicry, or imitation. As such it alludes to a primitive level of intelligence, a lack of discrimination, and the absence of creativity. The emphasis here is on developing a sensitivity to sources of information and the credibility and motivations of those who are doing the speaking or writing. Individuals create and project their own reality out of experience, and the suggestion here is to refuse to accept another's reality as your own, or let others do your thinking for you. On a practical level, this symbol can point to a need to be more circumspect in regard to what is being said and who might be listening. It also alludes to the value of thinking things through and hearing everything out before jumping to conclusions, forming opinions or speaking. Positive: At its highest, this symbol represents practicality and the ability to use whatever is immediately available to accomplish a task at hand. Negative: Gossip and copying others or a complete lack of originality.

TODAY: The accent is on imitation. Whether the issue is gossip, interpreting for someone with a communication problem or efforts to learn and retain information, repeating what's heard is the focus of activity today.

Opportunity: Your greatest advantage lies in being discreet and investigating the sources of information your receive. Make sure you have a story straight before passing it on to others or acting on the basis of what you hear or read.

Risk: Guard against setting bad examples for others to follow. Monkey see, monkey do. Be careful of what you say and how you say it. Don't jump to conclusions.

STEPPING STONES: Gossip, mimicking, copying, imitation, impersonation, repetition, regurgitation, practice, learning, lack of discrimination, absence of creativity.

SCORPIO 20 A woman drawing two dark curtains aside.
KEYWORD: *Daring*

a woman drawing two dark curtains aside

THEME: *Moving Forward.* This symbol speaks to clairvoyance, psychological insight, and to the perception of higher values or a greater reality. The image of a woman drawing two dark curtains aside alludes to a piercing of the veil or investigation of that which is unknown and beyond the normal realm of the senses. The emphasis here is on daring, and a willingness to risk the secure and known in order to open the self to new experience. On a practical level, this symbol can indicate the confrontation of some issue that an individual has avoided facing or the discovery of something that has been hidden from awareness. It can also indicate emergence from self-imposed seclusion or recovery from a depression. Positive: At its highest, this symbol represents curiosity, inquisitiveness, a sense of adventure, and a refusal to be conquered by fear. Negative: Exhibitionism or intrusion into the affairs of others.

TODAY: The accent is on investigation. You may find the courage you need to face something you've been dreading. Secrets may be revealed today.

Opportunity: Your greatest advantage lies in making yourself aware of what's going on in the outside world. On the other hand, protect yourself from intruders or those who may be trying to pry into your affairs.

Risk: Guard against exposing yourself to criticism by revealing too much. Don't open Pandora's box by bringing attention to something that's better left alone at this time.

STEPPING STONES: Investigation, curiosity, courage, risk, exposure, coming out, readiness, openness, piercing the veil, clairvoyance, psychological insight.

SCORPIO 21 A soldier derelict in duty. KEYWORD: *Deviation*

A soldier derelict in duty

THEME: *Termination is Cooperation.* This symbol speaks to living with the consequences of decisions and, in particular, to the consequences of impulsiveness, or the failure to think things through thoroughly before acting. The image of a soldier derelict in his duty is one of the reversed or negative symbols, and it dramatizes the dilemma faced by the individual who makes a commitment in the hope of achieving some personal goal and discovers too late that he has made a mistake. Instead of fulfilling his dream he is living a nightmare or compromising his own integrity. The implication here is that man basically moves toward his highest good and will not continue for long in any direction that frustrates him or fails to bring him happiness. Positive: At its highest, this symbol represents the ability to find cooperative means for resolving problems and a willingness to accept responsibility for mistakes. Negative: Irresponsibility and selfishness.

TODAY: The accent is on negligence. You may find yourself dealing with the repercussions of someone failing to do what they promised to do.

Opportunity: Your greatest advantage lies in resigning responsibly from any situation or position that holds no promise or potential for you. Tie up loose ends before you leave.

Risk: Guard against letting yourself get carried away by emotion or desire in the middle of an important job. The consequences could be greater than you are prepared to face.

STEPPING STONES: Delinquency, carelessness, omission, oversight, disregard, failure, inefficiency, inattention, incompetence, malfeasance, indifference, thoughtlessness, wrongdoing, negligence.

SCORPIO 22 Hunters starting out for ducks. KEYWORD: *Enterprise*

THEME: *The Shortest Path to the Goal.* This symbol speaks to directness, aims and goals, and to a mission or strong sense of purpose. The image of hunters starting out for ducks emphasizes initiative, ambition and aggression. It also suggests a lack of restriction or freedom from physical and psychological pressure. On a practical level, this symbol can indicate a team approach to meeting objectives. Positive: At its highest, this symbol represents an enterprising, do-it-yourself quality and the ability to relieve stress and tension in healthy, productive ways. Negative: Overkill or ruthless opportunism.

TODAY: The accent is on accomplishing objectives. You may be unusually determined to reach some goal today or put an end to something.

Opportunity: Your greatest advantage lies in sticking to your guns and letting nothing deter you. Make sure you start on time.

Risk: Guard against failing to take aim before you fire or you might hit the wrong target. Don't forget that words can also wound.

STEPPING STONES: Ambition, aggression, force, aspiration, enthusiasm, expectation, initiative, diligence, purpose, goal-orientation, enterprise.

SCORPIO 23 A bunny metamorphosed into a fairy. KEYWORD: *Transition*

a bunny metamorphosed into a fairy

THEME: *The Magic of Imagination.* This symbol speaks to creativity, imagination, and personal meanings. The image of a bunny metamorphosed into a fairy suggests enchantment, magic and the transformation of reality through supernatural powers of the mind. Implicit in this symbol is the ability of every individual to enhance his enjoyment of life by changing the way he views the world in which he lives. Positive: At its highest, this symbol represents personal growth and development through the power of positive thinking and creative visualization. Negative: Dissociation or escape from reality through unhealthy fantasies and delusions.

TODAY: The accent is on transformation and change. You could be shocked or surprised by something that happens today.

Opportunity: Your greatest advantage lies in looking for the highest and best in others. Find the hidden promise in all things and nurture it. Think in terms of possibilities.

Risk: Guard against preferring bizarre or fantastic explanations over a truth you're afraid to face. Confront your fears and deal with them.

STEPPING STONES: Transformation, enchantment, magic, trickery, change, conversion, flux, alteration, transmutation.

SCORPIO 24 Crowds coming down the mountain to listen to one
man. KEYWORD: *Appeal*

THEME: *Spiritual Leadership*. This symbol speaks to an intuitive
recognition of wisdom, and to intellectual or spiritual authority. The
image of crowds coming down the mountain to listen to one man focuses
on the effect of inspiration, and it alludes to the necessity that spiritual
guidance or instruction be presented in down-to-earth terms, or have
relevancy and practical application in the lives of people, before it will be
understood or followed. The emphasis in this symbol is on the importance of relating to others in terms of their individual experiences and
needs. Positive: At its highest, this symbol represents charisma and charm
or the ability to inspire others to action through the spoken word.
Negative: Gullibility and indiscrimination, or an inability to think
independently.

TODAY: The accent is on a desire to know. You may be willing to go
to extraordinary lengths to obtain the information you want in the form
you want it.

Opportunity: Your greatest advantage lies in keeping your message clear
and simple. Know your audience and talk to them in terms they
understand. Be practical.

Risk: Guard against trying to impress others with your knowledge. Don't
talk over their heads or make things too complicated.

STEPPING STONES: Leadership, wisdom, attraction, charisma,
fascination, charm, magnetism, interest, opportunity, recognition.

SCORPIO 25 An X ray. KEYWORD: *Investigation*

an X-Ray

THEME: *Second Sight.* This symbol speaks to the ability to see through superficialities and penetrate to the true nature or heart of a matter. The image of an X-ray focuses on exploration, inquiry, research and examination. It also alludes to physical fitness and the necessity that individuals act responsibly and maintain their health so that they can function independently and pull their own weight in the world. On a more symbolic level, this image can indicate an investigation or search for truth. Here is a call to look a little deeper and not accept anything at face value. Things may not be what they appear to be. Positive: At its highest, this symbol represents a deep and penetrating mind and the ability to see through sham and pretense. Negative: Sensitivity to criticism or intrusiveness and a refusal to respect the privacy of others.

TODAY: The accent is on seeing through things. It will be hard to pull the wool over people's eyes today.

Opportunity: Your greatest advantage lies in checking things out. Pay particular attention to foundations, structures and health. Investigate thoroughly.

Risk: Guard against believing everything you're told. Ask questions and consult other sources of information.

STEPPING STONES: Penetration, scrutiny, investigation, inquiry, research, inspection, analysis, exploration, examination, perception, revelation, diagnosis.

SCORPIO 26 Indians making camp. KEYWORD: *Extemporization*

Indians making camp

THEME: *Resourcefulness.* This symbol speaks to self-establishment, and to man's skill in finding or obtaining everything needed to function competently wherever he finds himself. The image of Indians making camp is a symbol of adaptability and resourcefulness, or being able to make do with whatever is immediately at hand. On a practical level, this image can indicate a fresh start in a new place. There is a suggestion here that an individual is where he is in life as the result of his choices, or what he has accepted and rejected in the past. Self-fulfillment here becomes a matter of discovering what you are good at and doing it. Positive: At its highest, this symbol represents versatility, innovation, and a pioneering spirit of adventure. Negative: Avoidance of struggle and a blind acceptance of whatever happens in life as destined or fated.

TODAY: The accent is on setting things up and getting started. Activities focus on preparation and making sure you have what you need.

Opportunity: Your greatest advantage lies in being practical. Choose the useful over the aesthetic or pretty.

Risk: Guard against spending so much time getting ready that there is no time left to enjoy what you're preparing for. Trying to make everything perfect is usually an exercise in futility. Be willing to make do with what you have.

STEPPING STONES: Settlement, establishment, new foundations, organization, community, resourcefulness, making do, improvisation, innovation, adaptability.

SCORPIO 27 A military band on the march. KEYWORD: *Intrepidity*

A military band on the march

THEME: *Bravado.* This symbol speaks to ambition, and to a desire to achieve fame or distinction. The image of a military band on the march depicts a dramatic show of strength and it alludes to fearlessness and the assertive or aggressive side of man. Here is mobilization, a marshaling of resources, and a colorful display of self-confidence and pride. On a practical level, this symbol can indicate bluffing, or an attempt to impress others with a power that may not actually exist. Positive: At its highest, this symbol represents a talent for organization, or pulling loose ends together and bringing order out of chaos. Negative: Exhibitionism or a tendency to exaggerate and engage in loud or outrageous behavior as a means for gaining attention.

TODAY: The accent is on assertiveness. You may hear a lot of noise and bragging about capabilities and power today.

Opportunity: Your greatest advantage lies in making your point with panache and drama. Stand up for what you believe in.

Risk: Guard against tooting your own horn or telling others how wonderful and competent you are. If it's not already evident, you're in trouble.

STEPPING STONES: Mobilization, organization, fearlessness, assertiveness, show of strength, power, bravery, courage, exhibition, marshaling resources, self-confidence, pride.

SCORPIO 28 The king of the fairies approaching his domain.
KEYWORD: *Allegiance*

THEME: *The Kingdom Within*. This symbol speaks to the fact that richness in life is an inner state of satisfaction that is achieved through the fulfillment of individual potential rather than the possession of worldly goods or fame. The image of the king of fairies approaching his domain symbolizes the attainment of a position of recognized authority. The suggestion in this symbol is that it is what a person is rather than who he knows that brings respect. Here, creative visualization becomes a magical power that can be used to conform the outer world to an inner reality.

Positive: At its highest, this symbol represents a natural gift for recognizing the highest potential possible in a situation and the ability to achieve it. Negative: Selfishness and feelings of entitlement, or demands for special privilege.

TODAY: The accent is on creative visualization. Wishes can come true today in strange and wonderful ways.

Opportunity: Your greatest advantage lies in acknowledging that you have created the situation you are in. Think about where you want to be five years from now and hold that image. Use the magic power of your mind to create yourself anew.

Risk: Guard against putting yourself above others or demanding privileges you haven't earned. Don't expect special treatment.

STEPPING STONES: Leadership, rulership, mastery, administration, authority, command, control, domination, dominion, government, management, supervision, supremacy, superiority.

SCORPIO 29 An Indian squaw pleading to the chief for the lives of her children. KEYWORD: *Effectiveness*

An Indian Squaw pleading to the Chief for the lives of her children

THEME: *Balancing Interests*. This symbol speaks to the fact that individuals must sometimes sacrifice or subordinate their personal needs and desires to those of the group, and that the group in turn has an obligation to safeguard the welfare of all of its members. The image of an Indian squaw pleading to the chief for the lives of her children illustrates such a balancing of the interests of the group against those of the individuals. On a practical level, this symbol can refer to advocacy on behalf of the disenfranchised, a request for a favor or an appeal to final authority. Positive: At its highest, this symbol represents eloquence and a gift for persuasive speech or discrimination and the ability to prioritize matters effectively. Negative: Sycophantic pandering or a simple inability to understand the difference between being useful and being used.

TODAY: The accent is on intercession. Appeals made on behalf of those who have no voice or power may take the spotlight today.

Opportunity: Your greatest advantage lies in speaking out against injustice and being willing to do what is necessary to protect the interests of all concerned.

Risk: Guard against being used by those who are unwilling to take the risk of speaking up for themselves. Be careful not to get yourself caught in the middle of someone else's personal war.

STEPPING STONES: Supplication, begging, intercession, petition, prayer, plea, advocacy, appeal, invocation, request.

SCORPIO 30 The Halloween jester. KEYWORD: *Spontaneousness*

The Halloween Jester

THEME: *The Magic of Merriment*. This symbol speaks to light-hearted fun, and freedom from rules and regulations. The image of a Halloween jester focuses on humor and playfulness as an antidote to stress or spiritual crystallization. The emphasis here is on spontaneity, enthusiasm, and an experimental or unstructured approach to living that creates magic in the most unexpected ways. In the Middle Ages, the jester was a professional fool whose job was to amuse the king or ruler with jokes and pranks, or comical tricks, and divert him from anger, worry or depression. On a practical level, this symbol says it's time to lighten up and break pattern or let your hair down and have a good time. Positive: At its highest, this symbol represents a contagiously creative and spontaneous way of thinking and living that inspires others. Negative: Lawlessness and refusal to conform to common standards of social conduct or a tendency to send mixed messages and create mass confusion.

TODAY: The accent is on diversion and comedy. Someone may try to hide the truth or throw up a smoke screen by clowning around and making jokes or diverting attention from the real issue at hand.

Opportunity: Your greatest advantage lies in keeping your sense of humor. Relax the rules and do what comes naturally.

Risk: Guard against ridiculing or making fun of others. There is a fine line between laughing at or with someone. Make sure you know where it is.

STEPPING STONES: Humor, joking, clowning around, punning, foolishness, playfulness, wittiness, tricks, pranks, ridicule, mockery, drama, spontaneity, diversion, amusement, creativity.

Sagittarius

♐

SAGITTARIUS 1   A Grand Army of the Republic campfire.
                 KEYWORD: *Reminiscence*

a g a. R. Camp fire

THEME: *The Reunion.* This symbol speaks to an appreciation of the value in all experience, and to a recognition of the principle that any present well-being is dependent on having taken right action in the past. The image of a Grand Army of the Republic campfire depicts a reunion of elderly soldiers reminiscing about "the good old days," or reliving the past, and it reflects camaraderie and a common bond developed out of group effort and shared experience. The emphasis here is on the inner strength that derives from not placing either negative or positive value on experience during any immediate crisis. On a practical level, this symbol is about doing your best. Positive: At its highest, this symbol represents group support and the ability to unite individuals by helping them see their common goals and interests. Negative: Resting on laurels or a glorification of the past as an excuse for failing to accomplish anything meaningful or significant in the present.

TODAY: The accent is on reunion. You may find yourself sharing stories with friends and family and reminiscing about the way things used to be.

Opportunity: Your greatest advantage lies in finding inspiration from your reflections on the past that will lead you forward to even more fulfilling experiences.

Risk: Guard against losing sight of the roads yet untraveled or letting yourself rest satisfied on prior achievements.

STEPPING STONES: War stories, the past, camaraderie, remembrance, recollection, reflection, reminiscence, enduring friendships, shared experiences, revivification.

SAGITTARIUS 2   The ocean covered with whitecaps. KEY-WORD: *Irrepressibility*

The ocean covered with white caps

THEME: *Spirit-Stirred Consciousness.* This symbol speaks to the bountiful response of the universe to an individual's expectations, in terms of giving him whatever he needs in life. The image of the ocean covered with whitecaps captures the idea of spirit-stirred consciousness. Implicit in this image is a certain restlessness of the soul and anticipation of the vast potential and opportunity lying just beyond. The emphasis in this symbol is on the necessity for channeling or directing the energy of this restlessness toward the accomplishment of worthwhile goals. The insight to be gained here is that an individual flourishes and becomes successful as he is inspired from within himself to fulfill his own higher potential, rather than allow himself to be pushed or prodded by others to pacify their own needs. On a practical level, this image symbolizes excitement, eagerness, passion and enthusiasm. Positive: At its highest, this symbol represents resourcefulness and an effervescent anticipation of the opportunities and challenges of everyday life. Negative: Nervousness and restlessness or a tendency to fret and stew over trivial matters.

TODAY: The accent is on activity. You could be feeling especially restless today. Something may be brewing that you should find out more about.

Opportunity: Your greatest advantage lies in channeling your energy into concrete goals. Write down the ideas that come to you today. Think before you act on that impulse.

Risk: Guard against flitting from one half-finished project to another. Try not to let yourself get distracted at some critical moment.

STEPPING STONES: Activity, restlessness, turbulence, excitement, eagerness, enthusiasm, stirring of consciousness, quickening, spiritual actuation, mobilization, animation, flux.

SAGITTARIUS 3   Two men playing chess. KEYWORD: *Ability*

Two men playing chess

THEME: *Battle of the Minds.* This symbol speaks to extraordinary competency, and to mastery as it is achieved through mental discipline, imagination, and the ability to profit or learn from experience. The image of two men playing chess dramatizes intellectual competition, and it highlights the importance of strategy and long-range planning. Here is a necessity for patience, sustained concentration, and the ability to predict the moves of the other fellow and think before acting. Here also is an emphasis on being able to respond effectively and forcefully when the unexpected occurs. The goal in chess is to limit the king, or highest authority figure, by blocking every move he could possibly make. The suggestion here is that a potential loss of freedom is at stake. Positive: At its highest, this symbol represents unusual intelligence, keen insight, and a love of mental challenge. Negative: Psychological one-upmanship or a lack of cooperation.

TODAY: The accent is on strategy and planning your moves wisely before you make them.

Opportunity: Your greatest advantage lies in knowing the habits and behavior patterns of those you are dealing with. Be willing to make short-term sacrifices for long-term gain. Have a plan.

Risk: Guard against leaving yourself wide open to attack or letting yourself be rushed into making a foolish mistake. Don't hurt your chances of success by exposing your hand too soon.

STEPPING STONES: Strategy, tactics, competition, rivalry, contest, schemes, tournament, long-range planning, study, mental acuity, concentration, focus, mastery.

SAGITTARIUS 4   **A little child learning to walk. KEYWORD:** *Individuality*

a little child learning to walk

THEME: *Gaining Independence.* This symbol speaks to encouragement as it relates to the development of personal skills and character and facilitates the socialization process. The image of a little child learning to walk alludes to trial-and-error efforts, practice, and a desire to function independently. Here is man at the beginning of his pilgrimage. The emphasis here is on allowing others enough elbow room, time, and opportunity to make and rectify their own mistakes while, at the same time, supporting their efforts without doing the job for them or preventing them from experiencing the consequences of their choices. Positive: At its highest, this symbol represents a do-it-yourself philosophy that leads to high competency and success. Negative: Excessive dependence on others, or fear of risk and failure and a refusal to take chances or try anything new.

TODAY: The accent is on practice. You could find yourself in some new situation that requires you to struggle on your own until you can stand independently.

Opportunity: Your greatest advantage lies in being willing to pick yourself up and try again. Lean on the familiar and ask for help when you need it.

Risk: Guard against being so afraid of making a mistake or suffering even minor hurt or pain that you would rather give up than forge ahead to achieve your goal.

STEPPING STONES: Effort, initiative, mobilization, trial and error, experimentation, struggle, rehearsal, practice, growing up, development of skills, individuation.

SAGITTARIUS 5   An old owl up in a tree. KEYWORD: *Normality*

An old owl up in a tree

THEME: *The Wisdom of Self-Restraint.* This symbol speaks to stability, and to the importance of staying centered in broadly-accepted and universal values. The image of an old owl up in a tree symbolizes wisdom, emotional detachment and self-control. The emphasis here is on dignity, self-respect and knowing when to keep silent. On a practical level, this symbol can indicate social withdrawal, or a preference for spending time alone. Positive: At its highest, this degree represents maturity, discrimination, wisdom and confidence. Negative: Haughtiness, or a delight in putting others down and making them look small, foolish or ignorant.

TODAY: The accent is on self-restraint. You may have to bite your tongue or hold back in order to avoid getting drawn into a situation that you don't want to be in or shouldn't get involved with.

Opportunity: Your greatest advantage lies in letting others solve their own problems and minding your own business. Silence is golden at this time.

Risk: Guard against pretending you have all the answers when you don't. You may be asked to give them.

STEPPING STONES: Wisdom, perspective, detachment, watchfulness, silence, observation, self-restraint, wait-and-see approach, maturity, discrimination, self-respect.

SAGITTARIUS 6   A game of cricket. KEYWORD: *Sportsmanship*

a game of cricket

THEME: *Let the Means Justify the Ends*. This symbol speaks to competition and challenge, and to man's compelling need to improve himself, or do and be his best. Here is a passion for perfection and a burning desire for success and recognition. The image of a game of cricket alludes to moral integrity and to playing fair, or by the rules, and it emphasizes the fact that ultimately it is the process, or means taken to achieve an objective, and not the outcome or final result of the effort that counts in the eternal scheme of things. Positive: At its highest, this symbol represents personal excellence, integrity and a strength of character that rejects any win-at-all-cost approach to playing the games of life. Negative: Misrepresentation or Machiavellian tactics.

TODAY: The accent is on being fair and playing by the rules.

Opportunity: Your greatest advantage lies in being consistent and acting with integrity. Do it the right way, even if it's the hard way.

Risk: Guard against taking on projects that offer little challenge or competing only with those whose skills are far below yours in order to guarantee success or an easy win. It's a delusion that others will see through, even if you don't.

STEPPING STONES: Refinement, propriety, decorum, etiquette, sportsmanship, playing by the rules, ethics, morals, scruples, integrity, fairness.

SAGITTARIUS 7   Cupid knocking at the door. KEYWORD: *Allurement*

Cupid knocking at the door

THEME: *The Glory of Love.* This symbol speaks to romance, and to the fact that life is always presenting opportunities for new and fulfilling relationships. The image of cupid knocking on the door symbolizes a call or an invitation to experience that quickens the heart and soul. The emphasis in this symbol is on the willingness of an individual to change his attitudes and behaviors or even his style of living, if necessary, in order to attract those kinds of relationships that will bring him happiness and help him come alive and grow. Positive: At its highest, this symbol represents idealism, sentimentality and a need to be passionately involved in meaningful projects and intimate relationships. Negative: Lack of self-restraint or a tendency to put the self first in relationships with others.

TODAY: The accent is on romance. You may receive an invitation that requires you to make a change of some kind before you can accept it.

Opportunity: Your greatest advantage lies in being willing to put disappointment behind you when things don't work out. Make needed self-improvements and prepare yourself for that next opportunity.

Risk: Guard against accepting the first offer that comes along out of a fear that this may be the only chance you'll get. You may miss a later one that's more to your liking.

STEPPING STONES: Romance, opportunity, enticement, seduction, inducement, attraction, temptation, quickening, invitation, allurement.

SAGITTARIUS 8   Rocks and things forming therein. KEY-
                  WORD: *Composition*

THEME: *Building on Firm Foundations.* This symbol speaks to stability. Here is the necessity that each individual build his personal foundations in life from the elements of his own unique experiences. The image of rocks and things forming therein alludes to the shaping of individual character and to the fact that an individual must be firmly in control of his circumstances if he hopes to establish a permanent place for himself in the overall scheme of things. Here is a call to make the most of heritage, roots, and natural skills and talents. Positive: At its highest, this symbol represents strength of character and ingenuity, or the ability to bring all the right elements together to effect a desired change. Negative: Confusion, or an inability to organize facts and thoughts clearly and effectively.

TODAY: The accent is on creating stability. You may find yourself trying to figure out how to put the pieces of some situation together in order to get things under control.

Opportunity: Your greatest advantage lies in making sure you understand what you're working with and what potential it has.

Risk: Guard against waiting too long to take action, or refusing to acknowledge the reality of something you would rather not face, until the situation gets completely out of hand.

STEPPING STONES: Foundations, stability, character formation, building, construction, establishment, development, groundwork, underpinnings, creation, composition, pattern.

SAGITTARIUS 9   A mother with her children on stairs. KEY-
                   WORD: *Education*

A mother with her children on stairs

THEME: *The Teacher*. This symbol speaks to training, guidance, nurturance, and the development of a social conscience. The image of a mother with her children on stairs dramatizes the process of education through the use of inspiration, encouragement, and keen sensitivity to what is needed in order to help each individual or group grow to independence and full maturity. Here is a call to higher service that demands genuine caring, the ability to lead by example and the capacity to distinguish the difference between what is being demanded and what is actually needed in any particular situation. Positive: At its highest, this symbol represents a natural talent for finding effective solutions to unique problems and for helping others become self-sufficient. Negative: Immature and childish behavior or a refusal to grow up and accept personal responsibility.

TODAY: The accent is on giving assistance. Activities today are likely to center on encouraging and teaching others to do for themselves in the future while, at the same time, helping them with their immediate needs.

Opportunity: Your greatest advantage lies in being patient with those who are learning. Be willing to give a little of your time and effort to work with your fellows who are struggling in unfamiliar situations.

Risk: Guard against doing everything for others or trying to prevent them from suffering though a learning period. Don't be an enabler for those who don't wish to take responsibility for themselves.

STEPPING STONES: Supervision, guardianship, assistance, guidance, watchfulness, vigilance, care, protection, education, training, instruction, encouragement, inspiration.

SAGITTARIUS 10   A golden-haired goddess of opportunity.
KEYWORD: *Reward*

a golden haired goddess
of opportunity

THEME: *Looking Beyond Surface Appearances.* This symbol speaks to the rewards guaranteed to the individual who is independent, self-reliant and willing to work hard for what he wants. The image of a golden-haired goddess of opportunity alludes to the individual who follows his own dreams, creates his own good fortune, and refuses to prejudge a situation or accept anything at face value. The emphasis in this symbol is on keeping an open and unconditioned mind. The individual who believes that bread can be made only from wheat might easily starve in a field of rye. Implicit in this symbol is the principle that every organism possesses the secret of its own survival, and that self-knowledge is the ultimate key to success. Positive: At its highest, this symbol represents self-confidence and an incredible sense of timing, or a knack for being in the right place at the right time. Negative: Opportunism or wild-goose chasing.

TODAY: The accent is on being in the right place at the right time to catch the brass ring. Luck plays an important role today.

Opportunity: Your greatest advantage lies in putting forth the effort to reap the benefits of the opportunities you are given. Be willing to continue in a course you know is right for you, even if you have to go it alone.

Risk: Guard against expecting others to carry you or cater to your whims. Don't lose your enthusiasm or abandon your goals just because you aren't continually receiving a pat on the back.

STEPPING STONES: Good fortune, luck, reward, subsidy, benefit, protection, prosperity, compensation, remuneration, restitution, reimbursement.

SAGITTARIUS 11   The lamp of physical enlightenment at the left temple. KEYWORD: *Reconciliation*

THEME: *Approximation*. This symbol speaks to the entrance or descent of soul into matter for the purpose of obtaining spiritual growth through physical experience. The image of the lamp of physical enlightenment at the left temple suggests the dawning light of realization. This concept is portrayed in modern times by various artistic depictions of a light bulb going off above an individual's head. Implicit in this symbol is the importance of being able to adapt and make adjustments. The focus here is on insight as it is gained through social feedback and the consequences of individual experimentation with self-expression. Positive: At its highest, this symbol represents the ability to learn quickly from mistakes and build on success. Negative: Confusion and lack of direction or an inability to understand the basic relationship between cause and effect.

TODAY: The accent is on understanding. You could have an "Aha!" experience as the result of trying something for the first time or realizing why something you keep doing the same way isn't working.

Opportunity: Your greatest advantage lies in analyzing the results of your actions in terms of how close they come to moving you toward your goals. Be willing to experiment and make changes.

Risk: Guard against focusing too much on *what* happens rather than on *why* it happens. Don't close your mind to the meaning of an unusual convergence.

STEPPING STONES: Enlightenment, illumination, awareness, understanding, insight, knowledge, comprehension, discernment, perception, clarification, elucidation, discrimination, realization, discovery.

SAGITTARIUS 12   A flag that turns into an eagle that crows.
KEYWORD: *Adjustment*

a flag that turns into an eagle that crows

THEME: *Transformation.* This symbol speaks to the struggle every individual experiences in trying to maintain his identity as a member of a social group, on the one hand, and as a unique individual on the other. The image of a flag that turns into an eagle that crows alludes to individuation, or the process by which individuals in society become differentiated from each other. In general, people seek the comfort of predictability in their relationships. Therefore, when an individual is perceived by his fellows to be changing to a degree that demands a reciprocal change in the way they will be required to relate to him, then that individual will usually meet with strong resistance or outright rejection. It is in man's struggle to express himself freely, while adapting to the demands and expectations of others, that he comes to understand and define himself. Positive: At its highest, this symbol represents a special talent for being able to express the self genuinely at all times while maintaining the respect and admiration of others. Negative: Irrational opinions or a tendency to make statements that have no basis in fact.

TODAY: The accent is on speaking out. You could be surprised when someone suddenly voices an opinion that differs sharply from the rest of the group.

Opportunity: Your greatest advantage lies in having the courage to speak your truth, even if it doesn't meet with applause, and in being sensitive to the rights of others to do the same.

Risk: Guard against bragging about your exploits or exaggerating your facts. Try not to forget that all of those who aren't with you aren't necessarily against you.

STEPPING STONES: Growth, individuation, finding your own way, adjustment, balancing loyalties, assertiveness, independence, alteration, transformation, conversion, change, mutation, shift, modification.

SAGITTARIUS 13   A widow's past brought to light. KEYWORD: *Rectification*

A widow's past brought to light

THEME: *Forgiveness*. This symbol speaks to the fact that when suffering becomes public knowledge, everyone is affected. The image of a widow's past brought to light is one of the reversed symbols, but it emphasizes the process of learning from past mistakes and the readiness of others to understand, forgive and support their fellows. Through the process of sharing his agony the individual experiences a healing of the soul, and those who hear him are encouraged to heal themselves through a similar sharing. Here is a turning point in psychological survival with the realization that no consequences attached to revealing a secret or imperfection could be worse than continuing to endure pain alone. Positive: At its highest, this symbol represents the willingness to admit error, the courage to accept consequences, and the capacity for self-forgiveness. Negative: Denial and refusal to admit fault.

TODAY: The accent is on revelation. A painful secret may be shared today.

Opportunity: Your greatest advantage lies in being willing to acknowledge your mistakes and trust others to understand and forgive.

Risk: Guard against being insensitive, or becoming so involved with your own concerns that you fail to recognize the suffering and needs of your fellows.

STEPPING STONES: Revelation, self-confrontation, embarrassment, emotional pain, crisis, catharsis, release, reconciliation, self-integration, self-correction, learning from mistakes.

SAGITTARIUS 14   The Pyramids and the Sphinx. KEYWORD: *Certification*

The pyramids + the sphinx

THEME: *Building on the Past.* This symbol speaks to immortality, and to physical or material evidence of the race's creative genius. It also testifies to the ability of future generations to survive and build even more magnificent realities on the foundations of the past. The image of the pyramids and the sphinx symbolizes higher wisdom and knowledge. The three faces of the pyramid symbolize the threefold principle of creation while the enigmatic sphinx alludes to the eternal mysteries. The emphasis in this degree is on man's need to have tangible or visible proof that he can make his mark on the world. Positive: At its highest, this symbol represents a fertile imagination and a special talent for putting novel ideas to practical use. Negative: Foolish efforts to look important.

TODAY: The accent is on finding inspiration in ordinary things and everyday experience.

Opportunity: Your greatest advantage lies in using your imagination and ingenuity to make your own mark on the world. Build continuously on prior achievements.

Risk: Guard against the temptation to imitate others rather than make the effort to create something original or be yourself. Don't be fooled into believing that more or bigger is better.

STEPPING STONES: Immortality, survival, the past, accomplishment, achievement, testimony, evidence, proof, imagination, higher knowledge, Egyptian, mystery.

SAGITTARIUS 15   The ground hog looking for its shadow.
KEYWORD: *Reassurance*

The ground hog looking for its shadow

THEME: *Checking Things Out.* This symbol speaks to intuition, a keen sensitivity to signatures and signs of change, and highly developed investigative skills. The image of a ground hog looking for its shadow alludes to a practical testing of the waters, or a sampling of conditions in order to determine whether or how to proceed. Implicit in this symbol is an attempt to divine the future or discern predictable patterns. The emphasis here is on flexibility, and the willingness to make whatever changes are required in order to accomplish objectives. At its highest, this symbol represents a natural gift for knowing how to handle difficult or challenging situations. Negative: Uncertainty and a lack of self-confidence.

TODAY: The accent is on investigation. You would be wise to play it safe and check things out before you decide what to do. Knowing what you don't know is the key to your survival.

Opportunity: Your greatest advantage lies in being willing to adapt and find the advantage in the situation at hand.

Risk: Guard against being a scaredy-cat, or letting yourself be ruled by your fears. Life on the run isn't fun.

STEPPING STONES: Curiosity, inquisitiveness, investigation, apprehension, concern, interest, self-protection, tentativeness, sensitivity to cues, prognostication, prediction.

SAGITTARIUS 16   Sea gulls watching a ship. KEYWORD: *Alertness*

Sea gulls watching a ship

THEME: *Staying Alert to Opportunity.* This symbol speaks to an assertion of rights to the fruits and privileges of life. The image of seagulls watching a ship symbolizes vigilance, a state of heightened alertness, and a time of waiting for the right opportunity or moment to act. Implicit in this symbol is the idea that value is in the eye of the beholder, or that one man's trash is another man's treasure. Here also is illustration of the concept of "finders-keepers," or that whatever has been abandoned or rejected is free for the taking. Positive: At its highest, this symbol represents a sharp eye for spotting opportunity and the ability to move swiftly to seize the prize. Negative: Lack of clearly defined goals or vague hopes of getting something for nothing.

TODAY: The accent is on waiting for the right opportunity to seize the victory.

Opportunity: Your greatest advantage lies in keeping your eye on what you want and being prepared to move quickly to claim it.

Risk: Guard against becoming a freeloader or being willing to accept the table crumbs you can get without cost or effort rather than work for a full meal. Try not to miss your chance for success by falling asleep at the switch or failing to pay attention when you should.

STEPPING STONES: Surveillance, vigilance, anticipation, expectation, alertness to opportunity, readiness, watchfulness, attentiveness.

SAGITTARIUS 17   An Easter sunrise service. KEYWORD: *Rebirth*

THEME: *Upliftment.* This symbol speaks to spiritual fellowship and higher values. The image of an Easter sunrise service symbolizes hope, rebirth and transcendence, or a rising above physical limitation. Here, a community is shown coming together to celebrate the resurrection of Christ in a ceremony that adds beauty and meaning to the lives of all participants. The suggestion here is that the human race is lifted as individuals work together toward their common and more enduring goals rather than compete with each other for personal gain. On a practical level, this image alludes to the old adage that it is always darkest before the dawn. Positive: At its highest, this symbol represents new beginnings and the ability to survive even the most difficult situations by drawing strength from higher Source. Negative: Inability to recognize the underlying significance in rituals and traditions.

TODAY: The accent is on celebration and renewal. Something you may have thought was over and gone may renew itself or come back into your life.

Opportunity: Your greatest advantage lies in keeping your attitude positive and cheerful.

Risk: Guard against being a harbinger of gloom or bringing others down by talking about how bad or hopeless everything is.

STEPPING STONES: Resurrection, spiritual renewal, rebirth, restoration, revitalization, religious celebration, hope, transcendence.

SAGITTARIUS 18   Tiny children in sunbonnets. KEYWORD: *Innocence*

Tiny children in sun bonnets

THEME: *Health and Well-Being*. This symbol speaks to self-protection, and to psychological health and fitness. The image of tiny children in sunbonnets alludes to the need to live a properly balanced life, and it emphasizes the importance of socialization and participation in normal everyday activities. The implication is that spending too much time alone or concentrating too intently on one thing for too long can lead to ineffectiveness, frustration, and narrow thinking or an inability to recognize the obvious. The suggestion here is to lighten up, take a break, and do something fun and relaxing. Positive: At its highest, this symbol represents the prevention of self-crystallization and ill-health by continually exploring and experimenting with the potentials of self and capitalizing on the opportunities that arise. Negative: Solipsism, or a self-centered and childish insistence on having one's own way and a self-defeating refusal to cooperate with others.

TODAY: The accent is on well-being. Activities today may center on protecting the weak and innocent from harm.

Opportunity: Your greatest advantage lies in maintaining a sensible balance between spending too much time alone and being a social butterfly.

Risk: Guard against demanding that others cater to your every whim or protect you from your own foolishness. Try not to be a crybaby or whine about your lot in life.

STEPPING STONES: Self-protection, shielding, covering, safeguarding, screening, health, well-being, socialization, innocence, play, youth, simplicity.

SAGITTARIUS 19   Pelicans moving their habitat. KEYWORD:
Frontier

THEME: *Migration.* This symbol speaks to self-sufficiency, or to individual character as whole and complete within itself and with every personal skill or talent available to be called into action as needed. The image of pelicans moving their habitat dramatizes the need for individuals to move on to new experience when any present situation becomes unrewarding, or when all available resources and opportunities have been exhausted. The emphasis here is on having the courage to make needed changes, try something new, and challenge the self to higher accomplishments. Positive: At its highest, this symbol represents ingenuity, resourcefulness and adaptability. Negative: Inflexibility and an inability to cooperate or get along well with others.

TODAY: The accent is on starting over. Activities may center on reestablishing yourself in some way.

Opportunity: Your greatest advantage lies in being prepared to set yourself up again if things don't work out where you're at. Sharpen your skills. Get rid of excess baggage.

Risk: Guard against letting yourself get caught unprepared by a surprise ending or sudden termination. Pay attention to changes going on around you.

STEPPING STONES: Reestablishment, starting over, move, journey, travel, change of residence, emigration, new experience, resourcefulness, reorientation, adaptation, change.

SAGITTARIUS 20   **Men cutting through ice.** KEYWORD: *Procurement*

Men cutting through ice

THEME: *The Grasshopper and the Ants.* This symbol speaks to the skill men have for understanding their environment, and to their ability to utilize natural resources and processes for their own benefit. The image of men cutting through ice emphasizes cooperation, organization and joint effort. The ice in this image was described in the 1931 mimeograph version as "summer ice" that would be needed for cooling purposes in the next season. At that time ice boxes were being used to refrigerate and preserve food; thus there is the implication that thinking ahead and planning for the future is a critical factor in survival. There is also the suggestion that the achievements of any civilization are largely dependent on the availability of both environmental and personal resources, and on man's ability to make the best use of both. On a practical level, this image can refer to "breaking the ice," or removing the barriers that separate individuals from one another. Positive: At its highest, this symbol represents a remarkable ability to turn stumbling blocks into stepping stones to higher achievements. Negative: Tendency to do things the hard way and overlook obvious solutions.

TODAY: The accent is on looking ahead to future needs. It's time to take stock of what you're going to need about six months from now and start making arrangements to get everything in order.

Opportunity: Your greatest advantage lies in anticipating obstacles and planning ways to get around them before they arise. If you need to make your project a joint effort, start listing the skills needed to make it successful and get your team lined up.

Risk: Guard against making it hard for yourself by waiting until the last minute to get things done. Take care not to procrastinate too long.

STEPPING STONES: Preparation, long-range planning, foresight, group effort, resourcefulness, procurement, breaking the ice, socialization.

SAGITTARIUS 21   A child and a dog with borrowed eyeglasses.
KEYWORD: *Examination*

A child and a dog with borrowed eye-glasses

THEME: *Scrutiny*. This symbol speaks to the absence of any clear lines of separation between lower and higher life forms or levels of competency, and to the opportunities that this absence of clear division provides for curing and supplementing individual deficiencies. The image of a child and a dog with borrowed eye glasses alludes to borrowed perspective, or an attempt to see things more clearly and experience the world through the eyes of another. Thus it symbolizes curiosity, role-play, and a desire for personal growth and higher knowledge. Ultimately, each person creates his reality through his own unique mode of perception and then acts out of it. Positive: At its highest, this symbol represents resourcefulness in using every possible means to find new opportunity. Negative: Failure to see the obvious and lack of objectivity.

TODAY: The accent is on ambition and improving your status in the world. You may find yourself struggling to gain more control over your life.

Opportunity: Your greatest advantage lies in obtaining the experience you need to get the position you want. Take it one step at a time. Volunteer to take on a project or ask for an apprenticeship where you would like to be.

Risk: Guard against looking at life through rose-colored glasses, or only seeing what you want to see. A biased perspective could cause you to miss something you should be paying attention to.

STEPPING STONES: Role-play, pretense, disguise, ambition, seeing things through the eyes of another, perspective, vision, inspection, scrutiny, exploration, examination.

SAGITTARIUS 22   A Chinese laundry. KEYWORD: *Seclusion*

A chinese laundry

THEME: *Self-sufficiency.* This symbol speaks to self-refinement through behind-the-scenes activities, and to a total involvement in some special interest that could result in social isolation. The image of a Chinese laundry emphasizes a willingness to sacrifice immediate rewards for long-term goals. The 1953 commentary on this symbol states that this involvement may be through "unsuspected or even generally unaccepted activities"; however, this image may only indicate that the community views this activity as strange, alien, or odd in some manner. On a practical level, this symbol can refer to the scientist, researcher, explorer, writer, and others who often work alone. Positive: At its highest, this symbol represents poise, dignity, and the ability to function competently and independently in any situation. Negative: Workaholic or feelings of inferiority.

TODAY: The accent is on being able to sustain yourself in unfamiliar situations. You may need to learn new skills.

Opportunity: Your greatest advantage lies in finding others who share your interests and concerns. Be willing to face possible rejection by those who fear anything or anyone different from themselves.

Risk: Guard against worrying about what others think of you. Try not to let criticism get you down or cause you to lose faith in yourself.

STEPPING STONES: Social isolation, solitude, unfamiliar situations, self-refinement, cleanup, labor, hard work, self-sustainment, responsibility, specialization, long-term goals.

SAGITTARIUS 23   Immigrants entering. KEYWORD: *Entrance*

Immigrants entering

THEME: *Trying Something New.* This symbol speaks to the recognition of opportunity, and to a willingness to risk, or leave the safe and familiar in the hope of finding greater freedom and meaning in life. The image of immigrants entering dramatizes the importance of being able to let go and detach from any situation that offers no further potential for growth or creative expression and reestablish the self in friendlier surroundings. On a practical level, this image symbolizes new beginnings and new experience in unfamiliar territory. The suggestion here is that a trial-and-error period of learning and orientation is just around the corner. Positive: At its highest, this symbol represents adaptability and the courage to start over when any present situation proves unprofitable or unworkable. Negative: Giving up too easily or a "grass is greener on the other side of the fence" philosophy.

TODAY: The accent is on closing the door to the past and opening wide the gateway to the future. You may sense that it's time to pull up roots and make a change.

Opportunity: Your greatest advantage lies in finding the environment that offers the greatest support for your potential. Be willing to endure some hardships while reestablishing yourself.

Risk: Guard against chasing will-o-the-wisps. Don't give up what you have of value for an unknown that simply sounds or appears to be better.

STEPPING STONES: Influx, pioneering, foreigners, strangers, arrival, reestablishment, resettlement, uprooting, reorientation, entrance, courage, hope, aspiration.

SAGITTARIUS 24   **A bluebird standing at the door of the house.**
                  KEYWORD: *Fortune*

a blue bird standing at the door of the house

THEME: *Providence.* This symbol speaks to the dangers of missing the rewards in experience by failing to recognize or pay attention to them when they arrive. This degree also stresses the importance of possessing a proper sense of self-worth. Life tends to give men what they believe they have the right to receive. The image of a bluebird standing at the door of the house symbolizes happiness, good fortune and luck. The emphasis here is on the need to stay alert and be ready to respond when opportunity knocks. On a practical level, this translates to listening and watching for propitious signs and signatures, and recognizing fortuitous convergences. Positive: At its highest, this symbol represents a positive outlook and a remarkable sense of timing, or a natural gift for being in the right place at the right time to catch the falling star or brass ring. Negative: Easy distraction and difficulty in paying attention or blind dependence on luck.

TODAY: The accent is on good fortune and prosperity. This could be your lucky day.

Opportunity: Your greatest advantage lies in expecting the best. There are no accidents. Look for unusual convergences or things that come together in time and space in significant ways.

Risk: Guard against missing your chance for happiness by telling yourself that you don't deserve it or by being too selective and picky.

STEPPING STONES: Good luck, prosperity, good fortune, reward, good omen, happiness, opportunity knocking.

SAGITTARIUS 25   A chubby boy on a hobbyhorse. KEYWORD:
Emulation

a chubby boy on a hobby horse

THEME: *Rehearsal.* This symbol speaks to imagination, ambition, and a desire for excitement and adventure. The playful image of a chubby boy on a hobby horse stresses the value of imitation, vicarious experience, pretense, and make-believe in helping individuals refine and achieve their goals. The emphasis here is on resourcefulness, or the ability to make creative use of whatever is at hand, to refine the skills needed to make a dream come true. Positive: At its highest, this symbol represents ingenuity, vision and a determination to elevate or dignify the little things of life. Negative: Self-pampering, false pretense, imposterism and delusions of grandeur.

TODAY: The accent is on ambition. Wannabes, look-alikes and other hopefuls may make their desires known today in a dramatic way.

Opportunity: Your greatest advantage lies in trying your hand at what you think you would like to do or be someday and see how you like it. If you don't have the resources you need, improvise or make do with whatever you can find at hand.

Risk: Guard against exaggerating your abilities or accomplishments. You will likely be found out. Take care not to get so involved in your work or hobbies that you neglect your family responsibilities.

STEPPING STONES: Make-believe, role-play, imitation, modeling, vicarious experience, copying, aspiration, ambition, rehearsal, practice, determination, desire, vision.

SAGITTARIUS 26   A flag-bearer. KEYWORD: *Nobility*

a flag bearer

THEME: *Honor.* This symbol speaks to the eclipse of common or everyday concerns by events of major significance, and to the personal sacrifice that individuals must be willing to make for the ultimate welfare of the group. The image of a flag-bearer alludes to allegiance, and pride in supporting higher values and ideals. The emphasis in this image is on collective or universal concerns rather than on individual objectives. Here at once is a rallying to a cause, the declaration of an allegiance, and the courage to fight or stand up for principles. At its highest, this symbol represents inspiration or spiritual upliftment through extraordinary acts of humanitarianism and altruism. Negative: Self-promoting tendency to take the credit for the accomplishments of others or promise what can't be delivered.

TODAY: The accent is on patriotism and pride. You may feel compelled to declare your loyalties today.

Opportunity: Your greatest advantage lies in being honest about who you are and what you believe. Act in the best interest of the group.

Risk: Guard against lowering your standards in order to fit in or avoid controversy. Don't compromise your integrity in an effort to achieve a surface harmony that won't last.

STEPPING STONES: Patriotism, allegiance, loyalty, standards, ideals, values, principles, dignity, honor, integrity, prestige, distinction, authority, representation, common cause.

SAGITTARIUS 27   A sculptor. KEYWORD: *Immortalization*

a sculptor

THEME: *Shaping Destiny*. This symbol speaks to vision, and to a desire to create and shape experience according to a particular design and purpose. The image of a sculptor alludes to the development of potential and the sharing of a personal vision or view of life with others. The emphasis here is on a mastery of mind over matter and the ability to inspire others through a dramatic articulation of the hidden beauty and meaning in all life forms. Positive: At its highest, this symbol represents self-fulfillment through creative expression. Negative: Self-serving manipulation or insensitivity and abrasiveness.

TODAY: The accent is on creativity. You may be feeling a strong desire to express your ideals and values in some concrete way such as writing a poem, painting a picture or composing a song.

Opportunity: Your greatest advantage lies in following your inner urgings. Use your talents to exalt a vision. Go with the flow.

Risk: Guard against trying to manipulate or pressure others into abandoning their own dreams to support yours. Even a good imposed on another is an evil.

STEPPING STONES: Creativity, vision, idealization, artistry, talent, development of potential, glorification, deification, exaltation, commemoration, preservation, perpetuation, immortalization.

SAGITTARIUS 28   An old bridge over a beautiful stream. KEY-
                   WORD: *Conservation*

THEME: *What Should Be Is*. This symbol speaks to balance, and to the preservation of those things of the world that are truly needed by man. The image of an old bridge over a beautiful stream dramatizes the principle that whatever has purpose and meaning will continue to exist. On a practical level, a bridge symbolizes transition, linkage, and the means for reaching some desired end. The suggestion here is that understanding can also be a bridge, and that individuals are inclined to stay where they are in any situation as long as some need is being met and not move on to new experience until the greater opportunity is perceived. Positive: At its highest, this symbol represents exceptional comprehension of higher purpose and meaning, and the ability to accomplish personal objectives by aligning them with universal patterns. Negative: Laziness and indifference or a failure to grasp the deeper significance in experience.

TODAY: The accent is on the survival of things that serve a purpose. A link to the past may be discovered or revealed today.

Opportunity: Your greatest advantage lies in understanding the reason some situation continues to exist.

Risk: Guard against trying to get rid of things that don't please you. Learn to use what you can't eliminate from your life.

STEPPING STONES: Endurance, continuance, stability, durability, dependability, preservation, purpose, linkage, means, pathway.

SAGITTARIUS 29   A fat boy mowing the lawn. KEYWORD: *Participation*

a fat boy mowing the lawn

THEME: *Effort.* This symbol speaks to self-improvement, and to social acceptance as it is gained through self-exertion, hard work, and participation in ordinary, everyday activities. The image of a fat boy mowing the lawn emphasizes the willingness to work, or give of self, that is the primary requirement for acceptance into any group. The actual giving of attention to the little or mundane details of life is evidence of a greater competency. The desire to belong, or for fellowship and friends, eventually triumphs over more primitive urges. Positive: At its highest, this symbol represents self-discipline, ambition and the willingness to work long and hard to achieve desired goals. Negative: Apathy and a deliberate avoidance of mental and social challenge.

TODAY: The accent is on acceptance and affiliation. You may be all caught up today in proving that you have what it takes to get where you want to be.

Opportunity: Your greatest advantage lies in getting yourself in shape. Decide what improvements you need to make in yourself in order to reach your goal. Develop a plan of action.

Risk: Guard against trying to make busy work for yourself in order to avoid social interactions with others in the give and take relationships of everyday life.

STEPPING STONES: Effort, exertion, work, ambition, self-expenditure, improvement, self-refinement, desire for social acceptance.

SAGITTARIUS 30   The Pope. KEYWORD: *Sanctity*

The Pope

THEME: *A Call to Higher Service.* This symbol speaks to the attainment by an individual of a high position of social or political merit based on personal excellence, an effective demonstration of high values, and the ability to both fulfill the requirements of the job and the needs of the people who put him there. The image of the Pope symbolizes spiritual power and leadership, and it alludes to the fact that any title or position of authority is meaningless if it doesn't provide the individual holding it with the opportunity to use his skills and perform a genuine service. It also stresses the importance of positive feedback and encouragement in strengthening and sustaining the individual who is trying to accomplish his goal. Positive: At its highest, this symbol represents self-immolation in some exalted role of special service and a willingness to sacrifice personal needs for a higher good. Negative: Pretentious self-exhibition or an obsession with power.

TODAY: The accent is on hierarchy and spiritual leadership. Religion could make the news today or you may hear about an important change in church structure or doctrine.

Opportunity: Your greatest advantage lies in living your ideals and ignoring criticism and ridicule. Do what you believe is right.

Risk: Guard against letting authority go to your head or getting carried away with power. Try not to confuse religious dogma with spiritual truth.

STEPPING STONES: Holiness, sacredness, Catholicism, religious leadership, service, dedication, devotion, self-sacrifice, piousness, righteousness, hierarchy.

Capricorn

♑

CAPRICORN 1   An Indian chief demanding recognition.
KEYWORD: *Inflexibility*

An Indian Chief demanding recognition

THEME: *Confrontation.* This symbol speaks to the fact that most individuals tend to honor and respect the established values, traditions, ranks and stations of their families and communities. The image of an Indian chief demanding recognition depicts bold self-assertion, a claim of special privilege and an insistence that some position of authority be acknowledged. On a practical level, this symbol is reflected in confrontations between parents and their children, managers and employees and other situations where authority is challenged. Positive: At its highest, this symbol represents dignity, strength of character and effective leadership. Negative: Authoritarianism and strong-arm tactics or pedantic fussing over trivial details.

TODAY: The accent is on self-assertion. You may feel a need to speak up or insist your voice be heard on some important issue.

Opportunity: Your greatest advantage lies in exercising your authority with dignity and letting the chips fall where they may. Be consistent and fair.

Risk: Guard against being a grandstander or monopolizing the conversation on topics that others have no interest in. Be willing to share the stage.

STEPPING STONES: Insistence, exaction, determination, resoluteness, inflexibility, standing on principle, authority, self-assertion, boldness, confrontation, authoritarianism, command.

CAPRICORN 2   **Three stained-glass windows, one damaged by bombardment.** KEYWORD: *Commemoration*

3 Stained glass windows, one
damaged by bombardment

THEME: *Reverence*. This symbol speaks to those objects and structures that commemorate the most meaningful experiences of our lives, and to the need to safeguard and protect these monuments from careless or superficial destruction by those who have no appreciation or understanding of higher values. The image of three stained-glass windows, one damaged by bombardment, is one of the reversed or negative symbols, and it alludes to strength and durability or survival. The emphasis in this degree is on the indestructibility of experience and spiritual reality. Windows symbolize vision, and here a beautiful vision has withstood an attack that damaged but didn't completely destroy it. The implication here is that visions and values are not always shared, and that there is also a need to protect these intangible treasures from attack by those who are indifferent or who see things differently and feel threatened. Positive: At its highest, this symbol represents integrity and inner strength or an ability to withstand criticism and personal assault. Negative: Overprotection and possessiveness.

TODAY: The accent is on stark reminders of painful periods of life that you have survived.

Opportunity: Your greatest advantage lies in protecting what you value from attack or loss. Also remember that experience can never be destroyed.

Risk: Guard against placing your values in things rather than in what they represent.

STEPPING STONES: Assault on values, survival, endurance, indestructibility, significance, memorial, historical record, chronicle, testimony.

CAPRICORN 3   The human soul receptive to growth and understanding. KEYWORD: *Avidity*

The human soul receptive to growth and understanding

THEME: *Readiness*. This symbol speaks to a simple and childlike openness to experience, and to each individual's need for the warm and caring support of friends who accept and understand him. The image of the human soul receptive to growth and understanding emphasizes the innocence, naïveté and optimism of the neophyte, novice or beginner. Here is joy in outreach and self-expression in normal, everyday living. Here also is eagerness and delight in the discovery that opportunities for experience are unlimited. Life is as full and rewarding as the individual will permit it to be. Positive: At its highest, this symbol represents friendliness, enthusiasm and an irrepressible zest for life. Negative: Dilettantism or indiscriminate dabbling.

TODAY: The accent is on eagerness for new experience. You could find yourself watching the clock or counting the days until the appointed time for some special event.

Opportunity: Your greatest advantage lies in knowing what you're getting yourself into. Make sure you have the support of those who matter before you get yourself out on a limb.

Risk: Guard against trying to do too many things at once or failing to stay with any one thing long enough to reap the benefit.

STEPPING STONES: Openness, receptivity, innocence, naïveté, gullibility, trust, friendliness, eagerness, desire for expansion.

CAPRICORN 4   A party entering a large canoe. KEYWORD: *Ordering*

[handwritten: a party entering a large canoe   canoe]

THEME: *Group Support.* This symbol speaks to preparation, and to the preliminary planning that precedes any special occasion or event. It also alludes to the fact that individuals often spend more time and energy getting ready to do something than actually doing it. The image of a party entering a large canoe emphasizes group effort and cooperation. The suggestion here is that individuals tend to be insecure or uncertain without the support of the group and inclined to seek the approval of their fellows before starting anything new. At its highest, this symbol represents a remarkable talent for organizing projects, marshaling resources and getting people focused on accomplishing objectives. Negative: Trouble-making or social insensitivity and a basic unfriendliness.

TODAY: The accent is on getting everything in order for some new undertaking. Maps or directions may be needed.

Opportunity: Your greatest advantage lies in making sure that all involved have their roles clearly defined and have everything they need at hand to complete a project. Cooperation and agreement is important.

Risk: Guard against insisting that everything be done your way or not trusting others to know how to do their jobs. Everyone needs a chance to learn.

STEPPING STONES: Planning, preparation, organization, cooperation, arrangements, group effort, new experience, trip, journey, travel.

CAPRICORN 5   Indians rowing a canoe and dancing a war
dance. KEYWORD: *Mobilization*

Indians rowing a canoe and dancing war dance

THEME: *Marshaling Resources*. This symbol speaks to impulsiveness, and to the tendency of individuals to leap into action when there is something personal to be gained, or when personal motives and incentives are involved. The emphasis in this symbol is on the need to restrain primitive impulses that threaten the ability to reason prudently and judiciously. The image of Indians rowing a canoe and dancing a war dance is highly aggressive, and it alludes to retaliation, retribution or revenge for subjectively perceived injuries. The suggestion here is that all practical alternatives and possible consequences should be considered before taking rash actions that may later be regretted. Positive: At its highest, this symbol represents strong leadership, a natural talent for mobilizing others through emotional appeals to deeply held values and the ability to prioritize things and get a job done. Negative: Anger, emotionalism and a tendency to harbor grudges.

TODAY: The accent is on grabbing the bull by the horns and taking more aggressive action to get things under control.

Opportunity: Your greatest advantage lies in not waiting until a situation gets completely out of hand before you step in and do something about it.

Risk: Guard against retaliating, or trying to even the score for every perceived wrong. Don't overreact or use more force than necessary to make your point.

STEPPING STONES: Mobilization, marshaling of resources, aggression, hostility, animosity, assault, offensive, attack, invasion, battle, combat, conflict.

CAPRICORN 6   A dark archway and ten logs at the bottom.
                   KEYWORD: *Thoroughness*

a dark archway and
ten logs at the bottom

THEME: *Piercing the Veil.* This symbol speaks to personal integrity and resourcefulness, or to the fact that each individual has everything within him that he needs to succeed in life. The image of a dark archway and ten logs at the bottom alludes to the unknown, the future, and that period of time between the completion of one cycle of experience and the beginning of the next when choices or decisions must be made as to what direction to take. The emphasis in this symbol is on personal growth and the exploration of individual potential. Positive: At its highest, this symbol represents a deep understanding of the meaning and purpose of life and a natural talent for capitalizing on the hidden opportunities in every situation. Negative: Bondage to superstition and a refusal to take risks or experiment with anything not fully understood.

TODAY: The accent is on completion. A new path of experience is now open. You have everything you need to succeed.

Opportunity: Your greatest advantage lies in having the courage to begin. All you have to do is take the first step.

Risk: Guard against allowing yourself be overcome by fear of the unknown. Don't turn back now. You may lose your opportunity.

STEPPING STONES: Readiness, resourcefulness, preparation for future needs, sensibility, carefulness, precision, completion, transition, new experience, the unknown.

CAPRICORN 7   A veiled prophet of power. KEYWORD: *Supremacy*

a veiled prophet of power

THEME: *Mastership*. This symbol speaks to adeptness, mastership, and the ability to command and control natural forces for practical, everyday problem-solving. The image of a veiled prophet of power also alludes to channelship and prophetic vision. The veil suggests that this skill or power may be hidden from view or is not being used. It can also imply power exercised from behind the scenes or anonymously. At its highest, this symbol represents uncanny psychological insight and a natural talent for motivating individuals and groups. Negative: Manipulation and exploitation or an improper use of power.

TODAY: The accent is on mastery and self-assurance. Your ability to bring about desired results is at its peak.

Opportunity: Your greatest advantage lies in taking stock of your present situation, and where you will eventually be if you do nothing to alter the natural progression of events. If you don't like where things seem to be headed, it may be wise to make changes.

Risk: Guard against losing your perspective or your sense of values. Try not to sacrifice time with loved ones in order to pursue what you merely hope might be a pot of gold at the end of a rainbow.

STEPPING STONES: Mastership, command, leadership, superiority, perception, insight, vision, seership, oracles, prophecies, clairvoyance, mediumship, divination, extrasensory perception, psychism, channelship.

CAPRICORN 8   Birds in the house singing happily. KEY-
WORD: *Establishment*

*Birds in the house
singing happily*

THEME: *Jubilation.* This symbol speaks to happiness and delight as the result of everything falling into place as planned or hoped for, and to an overall sense of everything being right with the world. The image of birds in the house singing happily suggests an unrestrained outpouring of spiritual fulfillment and joy. Implicit in this symbol is a healthy feeling of self-confidence and accomplishment as the result of being able to shape outer events according to inner desire and expectation. Positive: At its highest, this symbol represents optimism, light-heartedness, and a positive and enthusiastic attitude that inspires cooperation. Negative: Narcissism, or a total preoccupation with self.

TODAY: The accent is on cheerfulness and optimism. Entertaining at home could be on your agenda or you may feel content to just putter around the house and enjoy your own little world in peace. Everything's going your way.

Opportunity: Your greatest advantage lies in encouraging others by giving them positive feedback and appreciation for their efforts.

Risk: Guard against being self-centered, or falling into a habit of putting your own comfort and pleasure before the needs of others.

STEPPING STONES: Cheerfulness, happiness, jubilation, joy, harmony, self-fulfillment, self-sufficiency, competence, accomplishment, success.

CAPRICORN 9   An angel carrying a harp. KEYWORD: *Attunement*

An angel carrying a harp

THEME: *Inspiration*. This symbol speaks to the cosmic symphony behind all manifestation, and to the fact that the truly inspired individual recognizes no limitations. The image of an angel carrying a harp suggests a sympathetic attunement to spiritual source, a purity of heart and a natural inclination to seek the highest good in any situation. On a practical level, this image alludes to divine protection, a charmed life, and the ability to maintain a positive and optimistic attitude in even the most trying situations. Positive: At its highest, this symbol represents joy and self-fulfillment through inspiring others to achieve their hopes and dreams. Negative: Self-deception or delusions of power and omnipotence.

TODAY: The accent is on healing and harmony. You may feel serene, protected and safe from all harm today.

Opportunity: Your greatest advantage lies in tuning into what others need for encouragement and inspiring them to move forward. Make peace today.

Risk: Guard against developing a messiah complex or trying to save the world and everyone in it from the consequences of their own actions and the experiences they need in order to grow.

STEPPING STONES: Healing, harmony, accord, peace, composure, serenity, tranquility, inspiration, encouragement, facilitation, protection.

CAPRICORN 10   An albatross feeding from the hand. KEY-
WORD: *Nurture*

al batross

An albatross feeding from the hand

THEME: *The Golden Rule.* This symbol speaks to man's desire to make a place for himself in the world, and to the fact that he needs the cooperation of others in order to do this. Here is the principle of doing unto others as you would have them do unto you. The image of an albatross feeding from the hand symbolizes service and giving, and the basic premise here is that those who wish to receive must also be willing to give. The emphasis in this degree is on generosity, care, and concern for others. Positive: At its highest, this symbol represents the ability to live by example, or demonstrate kindness and draw out the best in others. Negative: Tendency to incapacitate others through over-helpfulness and indulgence or a failure to understand the critical issues in matters.

TODAY: The accent is on kindness. Activities center on helping those in need.

Opportunity: Your greatest advantage lies in casting your bread on the waters, or being generous with your time and resources.

Risk: Guard against disabling others by doing for them what they can do for themselves and encouraging them to depend on you for everything they need.

STEPPING STONES: Care, concern, nurturance, sustainment, help, assistance, service, giving, generosity, kindness, benevolence, thoughtfulness, consideration, compassion, charity, empathy.

CAPRICORN 11   A large group of pheasants. KEYWORD: *Illimitability*

(birds)

a large group of pheasants

THEME: *Variation*. This symbol speaks to the refinement of individuality and strengthening of self-confidence through social rituals. The colorful image of a large group of pheasants emphasizes the fact that there are many different ways to express the same idea or concept, and that the potential for variety is unlimited. The challenge here is to learn to make life interesting and be willing to experiment. On a practical level, this symbol encourages individuals to develop distinctiveness by finding their own unique ways of doing things and expressing themselves. Positive: At its highest, this symbol represents aspiration, versatility and a rich imagination. Negative: Fear of being perceived as different or rigid conformity to social conventions.

TODAY: The accent is on growth and expansion. Things could multiply or proliferate beyond expectation today. Group gatherings and celebrations are highlighted.

Opportunity: Your greatest advantage lies in making life interesting by finding ways to make each experience special. Experiment with color, taste and sound. Try a new setting and create atmosphere.

Risk: Guard against trying to gain success by imitating others. Don't be afraid to break pattern and try something different.

STEPPING STONES: Multiplication, expansion, increase, illimitability, proliferation, propagation, reproduction, social ritual, variety, diversity, distinctiveness.

CAPRICORN 12   A student of nature lecturing. **KEYWORD:**
Explanation

a student of nature lecturing

THEME: *Clarification*. This symbol speaks to education, and to the expansion of knowledge through the sharing of experience. The image of a student of nature lecturing emphasizes the use of reason and imagination to overcome limitations and build self-confidence. This symbol can characterize both the speaker and the listener. On the one hand it can indicate a talent for teaching and sharing experience in a meaningful way. On the other it suggests sympathetic understanding and the ability to see life clearly through the eyes of others. Positive: At its highest, this symbol represents keen analytical skills and the ability to profit from the experiences of others. Negative: Conceit and intellectual vanity.

TODAY: The accent is on expanding opportunities through education.

Opportunity: Your greatest advantage lies in gathering information on the options and choices available to you. Take a new class, surf the net, visit a library and listen to others who are willing to share their experiences.

Risk: Guard against being a know-it-all or giving the impression that you aren't interested in what others have to say.

STEPPING STONES: Teaching, education, enlightenment, instruction, tutoring, sharing experience, interpretation, exegesis, explanation, elucidation, clarification.

CAPRICORN 13   A fire worshiper. **KEYWORD:** *Magic*

a fire worshipper

THEME: *The Magician*. This symbol speaks to the strength and comfort an individual experiences when he realizes that he is not adrift or alone in the universe but is inseparably linked with his creator. It also speaks to the miracle of spiritual transformation that comes with this awareness. The image of a fire worshiper symbolizes devotion, and the offering or dedication of everything an individual has or is to a higher power. The emphasis in this dedication is on a release from material bondage and the limitations of the physical realm. On the one hand this image suggests a primitive and superstitious act of obeisance or supplication. On the other it dramatizes an act of faith, and therefore it alludes to inspiration and hope. It also alludes to a belief in magic and the supernatural. Positive: At its highest, this symbol represents mastery, and an extraordinary ability to make things happen according to personal will and desire through an effective alignment with the creative power of the universe. Negative: Delusions of adequacy.

TODAY: The accent is on self-empowerment. You could be feeling especially competent or that you can really make things happen today.

Opportunity: Your greatest advantage lies in tackling your most important projects. Your intuition will lead you to the people and resources you need to get the job done.

Risk: Guard against getting carried away with your enthusiasm and trying to do too much at once or taking on tasks and responsibilities that you aren't yet capable of handling.

STEPPING STONES: Devotion, dedication, aspiration, faith, belief, magic, enchantment, mysticism, supernaturalness, mystery, spiritual immolation.

CAPRICORN 14   An ancient bas-relief carved in granite. KEY-
WORD: *Foundation*

*An ancient bas relief
carved in granite*

THEME: *Enduringness.* This symbol speaks to the magic of any present
moment, and to its potential for expressing the greatest of all that ever has
been or will be. The image of an ancient bas-relief carved in granite
symbolizes enduringness, conviction, and the desire of a group to leave
a permanent record of their values and achievements for future generations. On a personal level, this image alludes to pride, confidence and
resoluteness. On a practical level, this symbol can indicate the survival of
some concrete object from the past that has great significance and meaning because of its ability to inspire men to even greater achievements.
Positive: At its highest, this symbol represents a special talent for
organization, or for systematically bringing together various elements
into a unified and functioning whole. Negative: Inflexibility and rigidity,
or a refusal to change or adapt.

TODAY: The accent is on formation and things coming into being. You
may suddenly recognize the direction things are taking or what a
situation is really all about at core.

Opportunity: Your greatest advantage lies in waiting until you are sure
before you make a decision or act. Make certain you're on solid ground.

Risk: Guard against being too rigid or unbending. Don't limit your
opportunities by demanding everything conform to your specifications
in every single way.

STEPPING STONES: Testimony, record, proof, achievement,
manifestation, absoluteness, conviction, certainty, definition, enduringness, organization, coming into being.

CAPRICORN 15   Many toys in the children's ward of a hospital.
KEYWORD: *Abundance*

Many toys in the children's ward of a hospital

THEME: *Coming Together*. This symbol speaks to a manifestation of wealth on the social and ideal side of life. The image of many toys in the children's ward of a hospital captures the essence of humanitarianism, or the process of reaching out to help and comfort those who suffer pain and tragedy. Thus it symbolizes charity, kindness, sympathy and love. This image also alludes to the fact that pain and suffering come alike to saint and sinner, and in ways that often seem unjust. The suggestion here is that such occasions are opportunities for fellowship at deeper and more meaningful levels. The emphasis in this symbol is on the end result of experience, or where experience leads, rather than on the experience itself. Positive: At its highest, this symbol represents the ability to get beyond the apparent inequities of life and bring out the best in self and others. Negative: False charity or sanctimonious giving.

TODAY: The accent is on sympathy and altruism. Activities center on reaching out, cushioning blows, and making the lives of others happier.

Opportunity: Your greatest advantage lies in changing your focus from accumulation to distribution, or from self-concern to compassion.

Risk: Guard against feeling sorry for yourself when misfortune strikes or you suffer, apparently due to no fault of your own.

STEPPING STONES: Charity, kindness, sympathy, altruism, benevolence, compassion, humanitarianism, philanthropy, generosity, abundance, thoughtfulness, consideration.

CAPRICORN 16   Boys and girls in gymnasium suits. KEY-
WORD: *Animation*

Boys & girls in gym suits

THEME: *Esprit de Corps*. This symbol speaks to self-development, and to the need to be flexible and willing to adjust as situations change and new opportunities arise. The image of boys and girls in gymnasium suits alludes to practice, challenge and the give-and-take cooperation required in all group effort. An individual is valued by his fellows as he becomes the source of their sustainment or as he is at least able to pull his own weight and make a contribution to the group. The emphasis in this symbol is on a genuine desire for self-improvement and a willingness to accept constructive criticism. Positive: At its highest, this symbol represents exceptional leadership, enthusiasm and a natural gift for motivating others and developing team spirit. Negative: Conventionality or herd mentality and an unwillingness to think independently.

TODAY: The accent is on physical fitness. Activities today center on getting in shape.

Opportunity: Your greatest advantage lies in getting involved in group activities that lead to self-improvement through cooperative effort.

Risk: Guard against following the crowd or doing what everyone else is doing because you're afraid to stand out or appear different. Don't sacrifice your individuality for the sake of avoiding controversy.

STEPPING STONES: Activity, exercise, exertion, vigor, health, physical fitness, athletics, development of competency, cooperation, group effort.

CAPRICORN 17   A girl surreptitiously bathing in the nude.
                  KEYWORD: *Immersion*

a girl surreptitiously bathing in the nude

THEME: *The Bare Essentials*. This symbol speaks to getting down to the bare essentials, and to spiritual renewal through a communion with nature or the divine creator. The image of a girl surreptitiously bathing in the nude alludes to modesty, shyness and inhibition. The human body symbolizes the temple of the living spirit, and bathing suggests purification and spiritual rebirth. On a practical level, this symbol can indicate psychological catharsis, or a shedding of defense mechanisms and a freeing of the self through psychotherapy or counseling. Positive: At its highest, this symbol represents directness and natural, unsophisticated self-expression. Negative: Secrecy and fear of public exposure or odd behavior.

TODAY: The accent is on overcoming shyness. You may decide to try something new today that you would prefer to do privately or without an audience.

Opportunity: Your greatest advantage lies in saturating yourself in anything you want to learn. Start with the basics and get comfortable at that level before going deeper.

Risk: Guard against dabbling in things, or only getting your toes wet. Don't be afraid to take a chance and dive right in.

STEPPING STONES: Modesty, shyness, inhibition, naturalness, covertness, furtiveness, secrecy, concealment, confidentiality, privacy, preoccupation, immersion.

CAPRICORN 18   The Union Jack. KEYWORD: *Supervision*

The Union Jack

THEME: *Sovereignty*. This symbol speaks to the broader protection offered by membership in large social or political organizations and to the greater gains to be achieved through well-organized group efforts. The image of The Union Jack, or the flag of Great Britain, symbolizes strength, power, unity and loyalty to a common ideal or principle. Positive: At its highest, this symbol represents an ever-increasing fulfillment of potentiality and special recognition for some outstanding achievement. Negative: Colonialism or a desire to control everything and everybody.

TODAY: The accent is on government. Group benefits and social services are emphasized. You may be concerned over your future security.

Opportunity: Your greatest advantage lies in group affiliations. Being part of a larger network may provide the protection and solutions you are looking for.

Risk: Guard against giving up your right to have a voice in your destiny in exchange for protection from the source that provides it. Don't be fooled into giving up present benefits by vague promises of greater future gain.

STEPPING STONES: Nationalism, patriotism, allegiance, loyalty, government, colonialism, dominance, strength, power, unity, protection.

CAPRICORN 19   A child of about five with a huge shopping
                   bag. KEYWORD: *Expectation*

*a child of about five
with a huge shopping bag*

THEME: *Great Expectations*. This symbol speaks to spiritual stewardship. The image of a child of about five with a huge shopping bag also
alludes to ambition and optimism. The emphasis in the 1953 commentary
is on an inherent sense of "responsibility for the welfare of others" and
a "desire to serve the community to the extreme of [the individual's]
particular range of skills." A willingness to try is suggested by the child
taking on a responsibility far beyond what ordinarily would be expected
for her age. This image also stresses a "special self-fulfillment" through a
"quickening to opportunity," or joy in the opportunity to be of service.
The implication here is that the chance for success is equal to the amount
of the effort put forth. Positive: At its highest, this symbol represents a
strong sense of responsibility, remarkable courage and a sincere desire to
be of help. Negative: Biting off more than can be chewed, or a tendency
to be a copycat.

TODAY: The accent is on responsibility. You may be tempted to
volunteer to take over some special project.

Opportunity: Your greatest advantage lies in asking the right questions
before you commit yourself.

Risk: Guard against taking on more than you can safely handle. Don't
overestimate your abilities and disappoint yourself and others by falling
short of what you promised to achieve.

STEPPING STONES: Ambition, aspiration, enterprise, enthusiasm,
effort, struggle, strain, responsibility, endeavor, undertaking, attempt,
courage, desire to help, willingness to try.

CAPRICORN 20   A hidden choir singing. KEYWORD: *Worship*

a hidden choir singing

THEME: *Resolution*. This symbol speaks to the symphony of cosmic reconciliation and the resolution of conflict. The image of a hidden choir singing alludes to the music of the spheres, or the universal harmony behind all manifestation. What may seem dissonant on the surface of things may only be the smaller and more distinguishable parts of a larger and unified whole. The emphasis in this symbol is on understanding the purpose behind difference and learning how to use it for a higher good. On a practical level, this symbol can indicate an anonymous or behind-the-scenes group of people exposing the truth, or "singing," about some situation that needs to be corrected. Positive: At its highest, this symbol represents a special talent for finding ways to bring people together to accomplish common goals. Negative: Timidity or indifference and withdrawal.

TODAY: The accent is on the restoration of harmony through bringing hidden situations to light, or exposing them so they can be dealt with and rectified.

Opportunity: Your greatest advantage lies in listening with a third ear and paying attention to subtle messages. If your personal differences become so great that you can't seem to get along with others, focus on what you have in common.

Risk: Guard against trying to solve your problems by running away from them or hiding your eyes from a truth that's staring you in the face.

STEPPING STONES: Harmony, oneness, peace, music of the spheres, cosmic reconciliation, inspiration, mood, background, celebration, whistle-blowing, exposing the truth, encouragement, praise.

CAPRICORN 21   A relay race. KEYWORD: *Fitness*

a relay race

THEME: *Teamwork.* This symbol speaks to the highest point of group opportunity, and to the importance of teamwork. It is through the group that the individual is given the greatest chance to sharpen his skills and develop his talents. The emphasis in this image of a relay race is on learning how to give and take, and on realizing that each individual's contribution is essential to the whole. By lightening the load on any one person, it thus becomes possible to achieve as a team what might be impossible to accomplish alone. On a practical level, this image suggests a race against time or competition between groups. Positive: At its highest, this symbol represents coordination, skill in getting people to work well together, and an outstanding sense of personal responsibility. Negative: Inability or unwillingness to think or act independently.

TODAY: The accent is on teamwork and efficiency. Others may be depending on you to do your part well.

Opportunity: Your greatest advantage lies in being as willing to give as to receive. Learn to be a good conductor of universal energy and keep the flow going.

Risk: Guard against becoming the broken link in a chain. Keep your skills and talents in shape and your knowledge up to date.

STEPPING STONES: Teamwork, coordination, give and take, cooperation, collaboration, interaction, effort, exertion, struggle, aspiration, competency, capability.

CAPRICORN 22   A general accepting defeat gracefully. KEY-
WORD: *Expediency*

THEME: *The Chess Player*. This symbol speaks to exploiting the
moment in order to gain a long-range advantage, or "striking while the
iron is hot." The image of a general accepting defeat gracefully suggests
a carefully considered and strategic surrender, and it illustrates the principle "lose a battle to win a war." Here is acquiescence, or compliance.
On a practical level, this symbol can indicate a simple giving in to the
inevitable, or facing the fact that there is no other choice than to yield to
group pressure. There is no chance of winning at this time. Implicit in
this symbol is the opportunity to save face by yielding with dignity.
Positive: At its highest, this symbol represents an extraordinary talent for
turning every loss to advantage and every short-term defeat to long-term
victory. Negative: Giving in too easily or refusal to admit error.

TODAY: The accent is on strategy. Life is sometimes like a game of
cards.

Opportunity: Your greatest advantage lies in knowing when to hold
them and when to fold them. Be willing to wait until you have a better
hand to play.

Risk: Guard against trying to bluff your way through. Someone might
call you on it.

STEPPING STONES: Strategy, long-range plans, temporary setback,
scheme, maneuver, design, method, tactic, exploitation, honor, surrender,
acquiescence, realism.

CAPRICORN 23   Two awards for bravery in war. KEYWORD: *Recognition*

2 awards for bravery in war

THEME: *Good Conduct*. This symbol speaks to practical resourcefulness, and to an ability to achieve tangible results in a way that inspires others to increase their own efforts. The image of two awards for bravery in war symbolizes appreciation and recognition for extraordinary risks taken to defend and preserve cherished values. It emphasizes personal vision and character, or the two qualities demanded of any leader who hopes to achieve social or political progress. Positive: At its highest, this symbol represents courage, integrity, and a willingness to honor commitments and defend principles. Negative: Bragging and boasting or reckless behavior.

TODAY: The accent is on heroism. You may receive recognition or praise for fighting or standing up for something you believe in.

Opportunity: Your greatest advantage lies in being true to yourself and defending those things that you value. Be willing to go the extra mile or act alone if you have to.

Risk: Guard against using more force than necessary to get your point across. Don't tempt fate by being foolhardy, or taking risks that aren't required to achieve your goals.

STEPPING STONES: Heroism, courage, appreciation, tribute, applause, acknowledgment, credit, commendation, recognition, character, honor, self-expenditure.

CAPRICORN 24   A woman entering a convent. KEYWORD: *Consecration*

a woman entering a convent

THEME: *The Retreat.* This symbol speaks to a stirring from within, and to the fact that individuals need challenge to move themselves forward. The image of a woman entering a convent symbolizes spiritual commitment, a search for meaning, and a desire for union with the All. It also indicates a turning point in life. On a practical level, this degree can indicate an attempt to gain release from stress, a desire for privacy, isolation, retreat or withdrawal from social activities. Positive: At its highest, this symbol represents cosmic insight, devotion and dedication to spiritual principles. Negative: Psychological escapism or cowardice.

TODAY: The accent is on withdrawal and solitude. You may be feeling like you need to get away from it all and take some time to think things over or get your life in order.

Opportunity: Your greatest advantage lies in learning when to slow down and take time for yourself. Schedule regular quiet time for rest, meditation or contemplation and keep the appointment.

Risk: Guard against being afraid to meet life on its own terms or trying to avoid all conflict and struggle by running for cover at the first sign of trouble. Try not to live your life sitting by the exit door.

STEPPING STONES: Withdrawal, seclusion, retreat, escapism, privacy, isolation, turning point, dedication, commitment, devotion, consecration, faithfulness, ordination, sanctification, responsibility.

CAPRICORN 25   An oriental-rug dealer. KEYWORD: *Consignment*

An oriental rug dealer

THEME: *Spiritual Materialism.* This symbol speaks to man's obligation to the reality in which he lives. The image of an oriental-rug dealer, or trader of exotic and expensive floor coverings, alludes to the fact that higher values have no substance unless they are woven into the tapestry and made the foundation of an individual's everyday transactions with his fellows. It is in meeting the practical challenges of everyday living that man develops his competency. And it is only when an individual begins to develop his potential and use his skills and talents that he is able to be of service to others. On a practical level, this symbol addresses the difficulties of living a spiritual life in a material world. Positive: At its highest, this symbol represents a remarkable combination of spiritual integrity and sharp business skills. Negative: Shrewd opportunism or a psychological compartmentalizing of the spiritual and material aspects of life.

TODAY: The accent is on business. The message today is to learn to function effectively in the practical and everyday world. Render unto Caesar that which is Caesar's.

Opportunity: Your greatest advantage lies in making your spiritual values tangible by living them. Do unto others as you would have them do unto you.

Risk: Guard against living a double life or compromising your integrity by saying one thing and doing another.

STEPPING STONES: Business, commerce, economics, trade, enterprise, industry, finance, transactions, materialism.

CAPRICORN 26   A water sprite. KEYWORD: *Restlessness*

a water sprite

THEME: *The Light Touch*. This symbol speaks to a spiritual mastery of experience. The image of a water sprite alludes to the magic of spontaneity and naturalness, and to the fact that being yourself is the best course of action in any situation. This degree also symbolizes intuition, imagination and delicacy or the use of a light touch. Positive: At its highest, this symbol represents psychic sensitivity, insight and effervescence. Negative: Avoidance of commitments or flightiness and instability.

TODAY: The accent is on spontaneity and unpredictability. Be prepared to change gears at a moment's notice. Things aren't likely to stay the same for long. Expect the unexpected.

Opportunity: Your greatest advantage lies in following your intuition and being flexible. Move quickly to seize any opportunities that present themselves.

Risk: Guard against trying to use pressure or force issues. Avoid tasks that require sustained concentration or monotonous repetition until things settle down.

STEPPING STONES: Spontaneity, effervescence, excitability, bubbliness, sparkle, liveliness, high-spirit, vivaciousness, impatience, energy, exuberance, enthusiasm, exhilaration, gaiety, animation, restlessness, sensitivity.

CAPRICORN 27   A mountain pilgrimage. KEYWORD: *Perseverance*

a mountain pilgrimage

THEME: *The High Road*. This symbol speaks to vision, and to the perception of a higher reality. The image of a mountain pilgrimage symbolizes a spiritual journey, or a quest for understanding and enlightenment, and it dramatizes the determination of man to comprehend the ultimate purpose or meaning of life. The emphasis here is on the importance of not giving up before a goal is reached or a dream fulfilled. Positive: At its highest, this symbol represents aspiration and devotion to high and noble goals. Negative: Hypocrisy and pretense to spiritual superiority.

TODAY: The accent is on endurance and staying power. Getting to the finish line may seem particularly difficult today.

Opportunity: Your greatest advantage lies in taking it one step at a time and keeping your eye on the goal until you get there.

Risk: Guard against quitting because you think your aspirations were set too high. Don't give up until the dream is realized.

STEPPING STONES: Mission, purpose, calling, intention, vision, spiritual journey, quest, inspiration, determination, perseverence, aspiration, devotion, dedication.

CAPRICORN 28   A large aviary. KEYWORD: *Community*

THEME: *Networking.* This symbol speaks to a broad variety of interests, and to a need to coordinate efforts so that each activity facilitates and supports the others. The image of a large aviary, or a place for keeping many birds confined, symbolizes harmony, fellowship and aspiration. The implication of diversity suggests the availability of many resources, or talents and skills that can be utilized for problem solving. In simple terms, what one individual doesn't know or have another usually will. On a practical level, the fact that the birds are confined to an aviary suggests restraint, or a taming of wild or frivolous impulses. This image also alludes to the expression "birds of a feather flock together," implying a community of interest or common bond. Positive: At its highest, this symbol represents a dedication of personal resources to the accomplishment of group objectives. Negative: Tendency to meddle or force unwanted attentions on others.

TODAY: The accent is on social activities. Things could get a little hectic trying to coordinate people and resources for some special event.

Opportunity: Your greatest advantage lies in getting organized. Make lists and create a schedule. Do what you can to help others find their niche in the scheme of things.

Risk: Guard against interfering in matters that aren't your concern. Avoid being a meddlesome busybody.

STEPPING STONES: Society, colony, commune, fellowship, group, aspiration, harmony, happiness, community interest, common bond, variety, confusion of thoughts.

CAPRICORN 29   A woman reading tea leaves. KEYWORD: *Signature*

a woman reading tea leaves

THEME: *The Screen of Prophecy.* This symbol speaks to divination and prophecy or a desire to pierce the veil between the visible and invisible worlds. The image of a woman reading tea leaves emphasizes psychic insight, intuition, and the interpretation of symbolic imagery. The keyword is signature, a Sabian concept defined by Marc Edmund Jones in his book *Occult Philosophy* as "the indication of ramifying sequence in cause and effect; the potential convenience or the varying correspondence in any given situation revealed by an object or event at the forefront of attention; the symbol or its significance in logical alertness, rational creativity or intellectual psychometry." Sabian "signature" is similar to Jungian synchronicity, "a coincidence in time of two or more causally unrelated events which have the same or a similar meaning" or "the simultaneous occurrence of a certain psychic state with one or more external events which appear as meaningful parallels to the momentary subjective state."* At its highest, this symbol represents exceptional intuition and an understanding of the deeper significance of events and situations. Negative: Superstitiousness or an obsession with cheap fortunetelling.

*Jung, C.G., *Synchronicity An Acausal Connecting Principle*, Bollingen Foundation, New York (1960), p. 25.

TODAY: The accent is on divination and seeing into the future. Trying to predict the outcome of events or get a handle on what you should be focusing on may occupy your time today.

Opportunity: Your greatest advantage lies in paying attention to patterns and looking at things symbolically. Look for unusual convergences and be alert to the timing of things.

Risk: Guard against superstitious thinking or abandoning your common sense. Don't look for supernatural explanations when a simple answer will do.

STEPPING STONES: Insight, intuition, divination, psychism, augury, prophecy, discernment, forecasting, prediction, vision, prognostication, revelation, omens, significance, encouragement, potentiality.

CAPRICORN 30   A secret business conference. KEYWORD: *Opportunity*

A Secret Business Conference

THEME: *Executive Session*. This symbol speaks to politics, and to the determination of individuals to control the course of events and resolve important issues through political alliances. The image of a secret business conference, or a behind-the-scenes meeting, alludes to a power play, or an attempt to determine the outcome of some situation by quietly and cleverly manipulating the personal resources at hand. The emphasis here is on psychological insight, a keen understanding of human behavior and tactical maneuvering. Positive: At its highest, this symbol represents strategic planning and extraordinary administrative skills. Negative: Abuse of power, hidden agendas, or taking unfair advantage of others.

TODAY: The accent is on things going on behind the scenes. Secret or private alliances may be involved.

Opportunity: Your greatest advantage lies in keeping your plan to yourself until you're ready to put it into action. Line up support before you begin.

Risk: Guard against placing your personal desires above the best interest of the group. Don't try to manipulate others to achieve your own ends.

STEPPING STONES: Meeting, conference, consultation, association, allegiances, conversation, parlay, deliberation, colloquy, congress, assembly, discussion, forum, administration, politics, strategizing, planning, maneuvering, hidden agendas, power plays, background.

Aquarius

≋

AQUARIUS 1   An old adobe mission. KEYWORD: *Durability*

An old adobe mission

THEME: *Spiritual Foundations*. This symbol speaks to reassurance, sustainment, anchorage and durability. The image of an old adobe mission alludes to the ability of everything rooted in the spiritual to flourish and survive. In the 1800s, Spanish missionaries sprinkled the coast of California with missions in an attempt to establish religious roots as an adjunct to territorial expansion. These historic missions have survived to the present day. The emphasis in this symbol is on psychological as well as physical survival, and on the necessity for maintaining meaningful ties to the enduring values that sustain all men. Positive: At its highest, this symbol represents spiritual integrity, strength of character and endurance. Negative: Apathy and indifference or an inability to grasp the deeper meaning of things.

TODAY: The accent is on sustainment. You may find it important to surround yourself with things or people that help you feel anchored and secure.

Opportunity: Your greatest advantage lies in giving time and attention to the relationships that are most important to you. Write that letter or make that call to someone who hasn't heard from you in a long time.

Risk: Guard against getting overinvolved in superficial and time-consuming activities. Don't neglect the things and people who really matter.

STEPPING STONES: Reassurance, sustainment, certainty, endurance, stability, anchorage, lastingness, survival, continuity, indestructibility, spiritual integrity, incorruptibility, service, hope.

AQUARIUS 2   **An unexpected thunderstorm. KEYWORD:** *Accident*

An unexpected thunder storm

THEME: *The Probability of the Improbable.* This symbol speaks to potential, and to the fact that there are some things in life that individuals simply can't control. It also speaks to the natural inclination of all situations to eventually climax in one form or another. The image of an unexpected thunderstorm emphasizes the necessity that each individual develop a sensitivity to changing conditions and be consciously aware of and responsible for his own role in the scheme of things. There are no accidents. Implicit in this symbol is the inclination of people in crisis to come together for mutual support. On a practical level, this symbol can indicate a build-up of tension that results in an unexpected drama or plans washing out. It can also indicate a crisis in some situation or relationship that results in a catharsis or cleansing. Positive: At its highest, this symbol represents the ability to take charge in confusing or highly-charged situations and bring things to an orderly and profitable conclusion. Negative: Emotional outbursts, temper tantrums or trouble-making.

TODAY: The accent is on surprises and unexpected events. Things may not turn out the way you planned today. Situations could reach a boiling point with emotions running high.

Opportunity: Your greatest advantage lies in making the best of it. Remind yourself that "this too shall pass." Work with others and do what needs to be done.

Risk: Guard against allowing yourself to get carried away by your sentiment or feelings. Be careful not to let someone get your goat and prod you into losing your temper.

STEPPING STONES: Surprise, chance, unanticipated happenings, plans washing out, tension release, quickening, catharsis, cleansing, emotional outbursts, instability, misadventure, crisis, emergency, happenstance, drama.

AQUARIUS 3   A deserter from the navy. KEYWORD: *Defiance*

a deserter from the navy

THEME: *Endings are Beginnings*. This symbol speaks to rebellion, or a refusal to cooperate any further in some situation or relationship, regardless of the consequences. The image of a deserter from the navy is one of the negative or reversed symbols and it alludes to the repudiation of a commitment, or a desire to break free from a relationship of perceived bondage. The emphasis in this symbol is on responsibility, faithfulness, and the need to make the best of situations or capitalize on the challenges they present. On a practical level, this symbol can indicate escape, or running away from problems. The inference here is that the way a relationship is ended can create more problems than it solves. Positive: At its highest, this symbol represents a refusal to make promises and commitments against better judgment, and the courage to end all unprofitable relationships responsibly and with dignity. Negative: Cowardice or incorrigibility.

TODAY: The accent is on rebellion. Expect resistance to rules and regulations. People are inclined to want to do their own thing. Job walk-outs and resignations are possible.

Opportunity: Your greatest advantage lies in reevaluating commitments that have proven to be detrimental to your physical or psychological well-being. Find responsible ways to end destructive relationships with full cooperation.

Risk: Guard against the temptation to quit or abruptly abandon your responsibilities when things don't go the way you like. Take care not to disappoint those who put their trust in you.

STEPPING STONES: Independence, betrayal, neglect of duty, repudiation, insubordination, rebellion, resistance, misbehavior, disobedience, disrespect, insolence, boldness, opposition, recalcitrance, misconduct.

AQUARIUS 4   **A Hindu healer. KEYWORD:** *Therapy*

a Hindu healer

THEME: *Realignment*. This symbol speaks to impact, or the ability to make a difference in the world, and to healing, or the corrective realignment of body, mind and circumstance. The image of a Hindu healer alludes to an ability to touch all things in a unifying magic. The emphasis in this degree is on dedication, spiritual self-discipline and the perfection of skill and method. Positive: At its highest, this symbol represents physical and mental mastery and a natural gift for bringing out the best in others. Negative: Fraud and fakery.

TODAY: The accent is on realignment. Efforts today center on spiritual as well as physical healing. Unusual or unorthodox methods may be used to treat particularly difficult situations.

Opportunity: Your greatest advantage lies in focusing on the situation as you would like it to be and holding that image in consciousness.

Risk: Guard against wasting your time and energy on trying to get rid of or destroy what you don't like. Do your best to understand the reasons for your experience. Be careful not to fall victim to frauds and quacks who promise to cure you of all your ills for the right price.

STEPPING STONES: Treatment, care, remedial measures, rehabilitation, restoration, rejuvenation, cure, unification, recuperation, amelioration, alleviation, improvement, assuagement, elixir, panacea, therapy, magic, healing.

AQUARIUS 5   A council of ancestors. KEYWORD: *Antecedence*

a council of ancestors

THEME: *Standing on Principle*. This symbol speaks to the values and ideals that survive from generation to generation. The image of a council of ancestors symbolizes inspiration and guidance from the past, and the implication here is that background guides and influences men's choices. On a practical level, this degree alludes to overshadowing, bias, persuasion and advice. Positive: At its highest, this symbol represents a strong sense of tradition, historical perspective and firm convictions. Negative: Inflexibility and resistance to change or a tendency to live in the past.

TODAY: The accent is on traditions that have proven their value. You could find answers you are looking for from older members of your family or community.

Opportunity: Your greatest advantage lies in staying with those practices or rituals that have survived for many generations. Follow precedent.

Risk: Guard against thinking that everything modern is necessarily better because it is newer. Don't be too quick to try to change what's already working well or try to fix what's not broken.

STEPPING STONES: Advisement, counseling, inspiration, wisdom, guidance, instruction, experience, training, direction, recommendation, background, tradition, roots, historical perspective.

AQUARIUS 6   A performer of a mystery play. KEYWORD: *Subtlety*

a performance of a mystery play

THEME: *The Drama of Life*. This symbol speaks to revelation, and to the role of mind as translator and mediator between man and his world. The image of a performer of a mystery play highlights allegory and drama as universally understood mediums of expression. The emphasis here is on man's desire for spiritual truth and his attempts to comprehend the secrets or meaning and purpose of life. On a practical level, this degree can indicate a baffling or perplexing message or situation or behavior that is difficult to understand. Positive: At its highest, this symbol represents a keen sensitivity to symbolism and the underlying significance of things, and the ability to articulate that meaning to others. Negative: Inability to communicate clearly or a tendency to exaggerate.

TODAY: The accent is on interpretation. You may see or hear something today that won't be fully understood until later.

Opportunity: Your greatest advantage lies in paying attention to unusual happenings. Write down what you observe and see if you can make any connection to a change that might be coming in your life.

Risk: Guard against dismissing what you don't understand as irrelevant or nonsense. Try not to be too practical. You may miss your cue to seize an important opportunity.

STEPPING STONES: Interpretation, translation, revelation, communication, expression, mediation, messenger, nuance, diplomacy, drama, secrets unveiled, symbolism.

AQUARIUS 7   A child born of an eggshell. KEYWORD: *Essentiality*

A child born of an eggshell

THEME: *Creative Self-renewal*. This symbol speaks to new beginnings. The image of a child born of an eggshell symbolizes rebirth, or the process of creating the self anew. Everyone has within himself an infinite source of potential, and it is only as this potential is recognized and put to use in a present moment that an individual truly is reborn. The emphasis in this symbol is on self-realization, enlightenment and regeneration. The practical implication of this degree is that limitations are never an obstacle to achievement but the means for calling forth inherent potential for greater accomplishment. Positive: At its highest, this symbol represents ingenuity, creativity and unlimited resourcefulness. Negative: Tendency to give up too easily or a belief that individuals are simply pawns of circumstance.

TODAY: The accent is on rebirth and self-realization. You may discover a talent or aptitude you didn't know you had that inspires you to focus in some new direction.

Opportunity: Your greatest advantage lies in refusing to accept limitations, and in viewing each day as a new beginning with its own special promise.

Risk: Guard against failing to capitalize on your prior experiences in new situations. Avoid burning your bridges behind you when you decide to make a change or move on to something new.

STEPPING STONES: Creation, rebirth, regeneration, new beginnings, potential, self-realization, self-renewal, resourcefulness, individualism, infinite regression or progression, anomaly.

AQUARIUS 8　　　　Beautifully gowned wax figures. KEYWORD:
　　　　　　　　　　　Impact

Beautifully gowned wax figures

THEME: *Imitation of Life.* This symbol speaks to vanity, public display
and the expression of personal ideals. The image of beautifully gowned
wax figures dramatizes man's need to have his values appreciated and
confirmed by others. The wax figures allude to the tendency of individuals to focus on the appearance of things. Implicit in this image is the
concept of window-shopping, or looking for inspiration, ideas and
something worth emulating or owning. On a practical level, this degree
can refer to setting examples for others to follow. Positive: At its highest,
this symbol represents positive role modeling, or an effective demonstration of the highest virtues in practical, everyday living. Negative:
Psychological regression, or loss of all opportunity through futile
attempts to recapture the past.

TODAY: The accent is on emulation. You could be feeling less than
satisfied with your life right now and decide to do a little window-
shopping in an effort to change your image or create new opportunities
for yourself.

Opportunity: Your greatest advantage lies in enhancing who you already
are by dramatizing your finest qualities. Take a fresh look at yourself and
be willing to experiment.

Risk: Guard against trying to become like someone else rather than
improving on who you are. Don't be misled by superficial appearances.

STEPPING STONES: Vanity, superficiality, artificiality, parody,
simulation, fabrication, impersonation, emulation, role modeling,
imitation, dramatization, aspiration, ideals.

AQUARIUS 9   A flag turned into an eagle. KEYWORD: *Dramatization*

a flag turned into an eagle

THEME: *A Pledge of Allegiance.* This symbol speaks to loyalty, and to a willingness to defend principles. The image of a flag turned into an eagle symbolizes vision, aspiration, and a growing awareness of values worth fighting for. The emphasis in this symbol is on imagination and the ability to see beyond superficial appearances to the higher purpose and possibility of things. On a practical level, this symbol indicates patriotism valor and transformation. Positive: At its highest, this symbol represents determination and success through an ability to capitalize on the self's highest potential. Negative: Retaliation, vindictiveness, and a tendency to react aggressively to perceived threats or criticism.

TODAY: The accent is on assertiveness. You may find yourself taking action to protect what you believe in or belong to.

Opportunity: Your greatest advantage lies in dramatizing your point. Use your imagination. Speak up and let people know where you stand.

Risk: Guard against overreacting to criticism or being too defensive. Avoid the temptation to try and get even if someone offends you.

STEPPING STONES: Assertiveness, action, ascendancy, rise to power, success, defense, loyalty, patriotism, transformation, imagination, vision.

AQUARIUS 10   A popularity that proves ephemeral. KEY-
WORD: *Approbation*

A popularity that proves ephemeral

THEME: *The Swing of the Pendulum*. This symbol speaks to having the courage to keep moving forward even when the going gets rough or when there seems to be no appreciation of effort or accomplishment. The image of a popularity that proves ephemeral alludes to the inevitable downfall or personal rejection that every individual will experience at some time in his life. The implication is that success is actually the greatest point of challenge in any experience. The average person is inclined to rest on his laurels when he hears applause, while the individual with foresight knows that eventually the pendulum will swing in the other direction. The suggestion here is to learn to use the praise and approval of others as an incentive to higher achievement, while looking within for any ultimate source of strength or sustainment. Positive: At its highest, this symbol represents imperturbability, self-confidence and fortitude in the face of discouragement and criticism. Negative: Using others or going along with the crowd in the hope of gaining personal advantage.

TODAY: The accent is on rejection and disappointment. You could be criticized or ignored by those who previously patted you on the back and praised your efforts or performance.

Opportunity: Your greatest advantage lies in being yourself. If you aren't appreciated where you are, find a friendlier environment. Do your best and let the chips fall where they may.

Risk: Guard against trying to please everyone. It can't be done.

STEPPING STONES: Trendiness, transientness, elusiveness, evanescence, change, instability, impermanence, momentary, passing, mutable, perishable, short-lived, temporary, brief, disappearing.

AQUARIUS 11   Man tête-à-tête with his inspiration. KEY-
                     WORD: *Ecstasy*

Man tête à tête with his inspiration

THEME: *The Cosmic Connection*. This symbol speaks to spiritual guidance, vision and inner communion with the higher self. The image of man tête-à-tête with his inspiration describes a creative interlude from outer activities and relationships, and a turning instead to a private enjoyment of mental and emotional stimulation. The emphasis in this symbol is on the need to serve the self's best interests by putting ideas to work in the practical and everyday world. Positive: At its highest, this symbol represents intuition, imagination, and cosmic overshadowing. Negative: Complete self-involvement or a tendency to live in a dream world.

TODAY: The accent is on enthusiasm and excitement. Ideas you get today could encourage you to try something new and inspiring.

Opportunity: Your greatest advantage lies in scheduling yourself a break from work and responsibilities. Spend some quiet time alone and let your imagination flow where it may.

Risk: Guard against escaping into a fantasy world every time things get rough or difficult. Don't lose touch with reality.

STEPPING STONES: Bliss, joy, delirium, delight, euphoria, elation, excitement, exaltation, exhilaration, devotion, elation, rapture, jubilation, vision, enthusiasm, idealism, happiness, enchantment.

AQUARIUS 12   People on stairs graduated upwards. KEY-
                     WORD: *Progression*

People on stairs
graduated upwards

THEME: *Stairway to the Stars*. This symbol speaks to the fact that life
is a journey of continual growth, onward and upward. The image of
people on stairs graduated upwards depicts individuals at various stages or
levels of competency, and it symbolizes aspiration, ambition and struggle.
But the suggestion here is that any single attainment is merely a resting
place where progress can be evaluated and future goals set. As such, it can
bring only temporary satisfaction. The emphasis in this degree is on the
differences between people that create genuine fellowship and make it
possible for individuals to share their struggles by offering or asking for
a helping hand when needed. Positive: At its highest, this symbol
represents optimism, and the ability to learn from experience, think
ahead and plan wisely. Negative: Unfriendly competition and envy.

TODAY: The accent is on varying levels of skills and experience.

Opportunity: Your greatest advantage lies in cooperating with others
and being willing to take advice as well as give it. Be as eager to share
your expertise as you are to solicit it from others.

Risk: Guard against turning every group endeavor into a one-upmanship
opportunity, or focusing more on competition than cooperation. Try not
to look for opportunities in every conversation to brag about yourself.

STEPPING STONES: Aspiration, accomplishment, betterment,
improvement, progress, succession, capitalization, advancement,
attainment, development, growth, maturation, evolution, sequence,
transition, difference.

AQUARIUS 13   A barometer. KEYWORD: *Indication*

a Barometer

THEME: *Forecasting*. This symbol speaks to prophetic insight and to the anticipation of experience. The image of a barometer refers to measurement, or the forecasting and reflection of change. As such, it alludes to man's desire to know what contingencies he needs to prepare for, or what skills and knowledge will be required to deal effectively with coming situations and events. The implication in this degree is that the ability to predict the future is dependent on understanding the basic order or patterning of the universe, and that the signs are there for those who have eyes to see. Positive: At its highest, this symbol represents keen observation, uncommon analytical skills, insight, vision, and superior judgment. Negative: Vacillation and lack of self-confidence or a tendency to avoid struggle by retreating or laying low with every change in events, in the hope that things will soon blow over.

TODAY: The accent is on forecasting, or trying to determine what to prepare for. You may be unusually concerned over some future possibility and how you can best handle it.

Opportunity: Your greatest advantage lies in gathering information and analyzing it in terms of how it best fits patterns you are familiar with. If you can't find the answers you're looking for, consult an expert.

Risk: Guard against being afraid to make a move without knowing exactly what to expect. There are times that require a leap of faith.

STEPPING STONES: Forecast, prophecy, augury, omen, harbinger, clue, portent, sign, forewarning, allusion, hint, reference, index, evidence, measure, indication, meaning.

AQUARIUS 14   A train entering a tunnel. KEYWORD: *Courtesy*

a train entering a tunnel

THEME: *Pulling Together.* This symbol speaks to an expectation that things will be there when needed, and to an impersonal but effective division of labor. The image of a train entering a tunnel reflects a situation where everyone has done his job independently of the others. The railroad tracks have been laid, the train carries its load, and the tunnel that will shorten the distance and ease the strain of an upward climb has been built. On a practical level, this symbol indicates the overcoming of obstacles, breakthroughs and determination. It can also imply self-analysis or a journey inward, penetration, insight, or even invasive surgery. Positive: At its highest, this symbol represents leadership, tremendous inner strength and the ability to stay on track until a goal is reached. Negative: Dull plodding, self-limitation and narrow-mindedness.

TODAY: The accent is on overcoming obstacles. It may be necessary to operate in the dark or play it by ear for awhile in order to break through an impasse and reach your goal.

Opportunity: Your greatest advantage lies in being willing to help others achieve their goals or get where they want to go. At the same time, be willing to ask for help when you need it.

Risk: Guard against refusing to cooperate with others, or insisting on doing things your way or not at all. Don't make things difficult for yourself by trying to do it all alone.

STEPPING STONES: Directness, penetration, breakthrough, determination, focus, work, labor, overcoming obstacles, journey.

AQUARIUS 15   Two lovebirds sitting on a fence. KEYWORD:
                   Affirmation

Two love birds singing on a fence

THEME: *The Magic of Romance.* This symbol speaks to the infectious nature of romance, and to the magic it brings, not only to lovers but to those who in any moment of vicarious sharing are lifted in beauty above the practical routine of everyday living. Here is the lightness of heart and brightness of spirit that result when a thoughtful added touch transforms an ordinary moment into a special occasion. The image of two lovebirds sitting on a fence speaks to love, happiness and at-onement. Positive: At its highest, this symbol represents psychological wholeness and a self-integration that stimulates others to see themselves and their fellows in terms of their similarities and common needs rather than their differences. Negative: Possessiveness and a tendency to form symbiotic or co-dependent relationships with others.

TODAY: The accent is on romance. This should be a time of contentment and self-fulfillment. You may hear of a marriage or engagement between two people who have been trying to make up their minds about whether to commit to each other or go their separate ways.

Opportunity: Your greatest advantage lies in forming alliances and coming to an agreement or decision in some important matter. Now is a good time to reach out and heal a strained relationship.

Risk: Guard against being overly protective or possessive. Give others room to grow and be themselves.

STEPPING STONES: Happiness, self-fulfillment, contentment, consummation, tenderness, completeness, romance, courtship, cooperation, sharing, loyalty, approval.

AQUARIUS 16   **A big-business man at his desk. KEYWORD:** *Accomplishment*

a big business man at his desk

THEME: *The Executive.* This symbol speaks to organization, management and efficiency as the foundation of personal stability. The ability of any individual to maintain his poise and balance in the midst of crisis or change is dependent upon his ability to remain calm and centered and keep his priorities in order. The image of a big-business man at his desk suggests a effective decision-maker and project-minded individual who finds his greatest fulfillment in his accomplishments. Here is the individual who is able to hold his place at the top, through every unforeseen emergency or calamity, by staying focused on the goal at hand and keeping his head when all about him are losing theirs. Positive: At its highest, this symbol represents exceptional executive skills and a highly developed ability to meet the challenges of life with ever-increasing mastery. Negative: Stuffed-shirt pompousness or workaholic.

TODAY: The accent is on efficiency. Business affairs and management take top priority.

Opportunity: Your greatest advantage lies in getting organized. Document all actions taken and anything important that happens. Double-check your appointment book and pay attention to detail.

Risk: Guard against getting yourself overscheduled, or trying to accomplish too much in too little time. Try not to confuse your priorities or neglect your family and friends.

STEPPING STONES: Management, achievement, success, work, proficiency, organization, regulation, supervision, administration, executive skill, competency, expertise, mastery, power, decision-making, effectiveness.

AQUARIUS 17   A watchdog standing guard. KEYWORD: *Probity*

a watch dog standing guard

THEME: *Guardian and Defender.* This symbol speaks to guardianship, and to the personal protections guaranteed each individual by law and social sanction. The image of a watchdog standing guard symbolizes loyalty, faithfulness and a readiness to defend and safeguard whatever is most highly valued. In a large sense, this symbol stands for the "liberty and justice for all" philosophy that encourages each individual to be his brother's keeper and protects the weak or disenfranchised from being taken advantage of by the strong and privileged. The implication in this degree is that the survival of any community is dependent on the strength of its individual members. On a practical level, this symbol can stand for regulatory or social service agencies, human rights groups, and all entities that oversee the welfare or protect the rights of each member of society. Positive: At its highest, this symbol represents integrity, vigilance, high principles and courage. Negative: Hostility and pervasive distrust of others.

TODAY: The accent is on vigilance. You may sense that things are not quite right today or that you need to be particularly on guard about something.

Opportunity: Your greatest advantage lies in knowing your rights and being sensitive to when they are in jeopardy. Be prepared to defend what you value.

Risk: Guard against being overly suspicious in your relationships with others. On the other hand, don't borrow trouble by inviting the fox into the hen house.

STEPPING STONES: Guardianship, protection, defense, preservation, safeguarding, vigilance, watchfulness, attentiveness, faithfulness, loyalty, fidelity, devotion, allegiance, dedication.

AQUARIUS 18   A man unmasked. **KEYWORD:** *Analysis*

a man unmasked

THEME: *Investigation.* This symbol speaks to curiosity, psychological insight, analysis, and penetrating beneath surface appearances to get to the truth of things. The image of a man unmasked alludes to the stripping away of defenses and outer facades and the uncovering of hidden motivations. Implicit in this symbol is a suggestion that something has been kept secret and suspicions are aroused. This degree also implies a rejection of individualism, or an insistence on conformity. The emphasis in this symbol is on revelation and public exposure or disclosure when it is in the best interest of a group. On a practical level, this image applies to media exposés, SEC investigations, detective work, and scientific or medical research. It can also indicate the end of a masquerade, the solving of a mystery, or an individual being recognized for who he really is. Positive: At its highest, this symbol represents keen analytical skills and a natural gift for seeing through things. Negative: Inability to keep a secret or relentless probing and prying into the personal affairs of others.

TODAY: The accent is on disclosure. Hidden motivations and other secrets may be revealed today.

Opportunity: Your greatest advantage lies in analyzing all the facts at hand. Remain objective and be prepared to accept the fact that things aren't always what they appear to be. Pay more attention to actions than words.

Risk: Guard against deception and deceit but avoid snap judgments. Don't base your decisions on how things look on the surface. Take the time to investigate.

STEPPING STONES: Revelation, announcement, clarification, declaration, explanation, disclosure, uncovering, exposure, accounting, divulgence, publication, curiosity, unveiling the truth.

AQUARIUS 19   A forest fire quenched. KEYWORD: *Concern*

a forest fire quenched

THEME: *Rising to the Occasion.* This symbol speaks to the successful resolution of an emergency or crisis, and to satisfaction in a job well done. The image of a forest fire quenched symbolizes the suppression or quelling of a dangerous and destructive force. The emphasis in this degree is on the opportunity in every group experience for discovering personal skills and abilities previously unrecognized, and on turning every ordeal into a productive adventure in social responsibility. On a practical level, this symbol alludes to defusing explosive situations, calming tempers, and bringing potentially volatile or dangerous situations under control. Positive: At its highest, this symbol represents the ability to function efficiently and effectively under pressure. Negative: Lack of enthusiasm and a tendency to avoid getting involved in anything out of the ordinary or private enjoyment of the misfortunes of others.

TODAY: The accent is on getting things under control. An emergency situation could be resolved today, much to everyone's relief.

Opportunity: Your greatest advantage lies in recognizing the skills and abilities that a crisis reveals and making the effort to refine them.

Risk: Guard against being a coward or telling yourself that you are ill-equipped to deal competently with the problems of life. Don't make a habit of depending on others to get you out of situations that you created.

STEPPING STONES: Success, conquest, triumph, achievement, accomplishment, mastery, self-expenditure, victory, resolution, relief, suppression, arrest, cancellation.

AQUARIUS 20   A big white dove, a message bearer. KEY-
WORD: *Conviction*

O big white dove

A message bearer

THEME: *The Hidden Messages in All Things.* This symbol speaks to
higher wisdom and inspiration. The image of a big white dove, a message
bearer, speaks to the symbolic or hidden messages in things that will
always be found by those who have the faith that they will be there. The
dove is a symbol of peace, hope, divinity and spiritual guidance. The
emphasis in this degree is on keeping a positive attitude and learning to
trust intuitive perceptions. Positive: At its highest, this symbol represents
sensitivity and discernment, or a special gift for knowing the right time
to act and the right thing to do. Negative: Holier-than-thou attitude or a
tendency to be a know-it-all who refuses to admit error, even to the self.

TODAY: The accent is on certainty. The emphasis today is on recognizing a higher power than yourself. You may receive a message that eases
your mind or reassures you.

Opportunity: Your greatest advantage lies in listening with the ears of
your heart. Keep a positive outlook and pay attention to things going on
around you. The information or answer you need may come from an
unexpected source.

Risk: Guard against being myopic, or deluding yourself with the idea that
there is only one way to solve a problem. Avoid cosmic dissonance.

STEPPING STONES: Faith, assurance, inspiration, divine favor, help,
holy spirit, hope, spiritual guidance, enlightenment, wisdom, certainty,
peace.

AQUARIUS 21   A woman disappointed and disillusioned.
KEYWORD: *Clearance*

[handwritten] A woman disappointed and disillusioned

THEME: *The Long and Winding Road.* This symbol speaks to the consequences of relying totally on things outside the self or believing that physical and material possessions are the ultimate source of happiness. The image of a woman disappointed and disillusioned is one of the negative or reversed symbols, and it symbolizes grief, emotional distress, loss and discouragement. The implication here is that when individuals are anchored within themselves, rather than in the outer world in which they live, they learn that frustration and limitations are merely challenges for developing potential and the means for a genuine fulfillment through the never-ending process of self-discovery. Positive: At its highest, this symbol represents resilience and a determination to succeed, or the ability to bounce back after disappointment and defeat and try again. Negative: Pessimism, or a tendency to give up too easily.

TODAY: The accent is on regret. You may realize too late that you relied on the wrong thing to get what you wanted.

Opportunity: Your greatest advantage lies in applying what you learn through experience to achieving new goals. Pick yourself up and keep moving forward.

Risk: Guard against giving up on everything when things go wrong in one area of your life. Never lose hope. Small failures are stepping stones to success.

STEPPING STONES: Distress, disappointment, frustration, defeat, disillusionment, grief, loss, discouragement, sadness, despondency, discontent, dejection, letdown, regret, anguish, misplaced values.

AQUARIUS 22   **A rug placed on a floor for children to play.**
                   KEYWORD: *Refinement*

a rug placed on a floor for children to play

THEME: *The Game of Life.* This symbol speaks to the comforts and conveniences that life provides for man's development. The image of a rug placed on a floor for children to play alludes to caretaking and thoughtfulness, and it illustrates the natural tendency of the experienced and strong to try to protect the innocent and weak. The emphasis in this degree is on self-discovery through creative experimentation and recreation. On a practical level this symbol speaks to guardianship and nurturance, or the kinds of relationships that exist between a parent and child, minister and parishioner or teacher and student. Positive: At its highest, this symbol represents a natural gift for making a game of life and using whatever lies at hand to accomplish immediate objectives. Negative: Immaturity and avoidance of responsibility, or childish self-pampering.

TODAY: The accent is on facilitation. You may receive a helping hand or assistance from someone who cares about you.

Opportunity: Your greatest advantage lies in making the best possible use of what life gives you to work with. If you find yourself in a difficult situation, there is a something for you to gain from it.

Risk: Guard against taking things for granted, or failing to appreciate what you have. Remember the adage "if you don't use it you lose it."

STEPPING STONES: Accommodation, facilitation, care, assistance, assuagement, aid, concern, helpfulness, empathy, sensitivity, service, comfort, improvement, amelioration, civility.

AQUARIUS 23   A big bear sitting down and waving all its
                     paws. KEYWORD: *Aptitude*

*a big bear sitting down
and waving all its paws*

THEME: *Achievement.* This symbol speaks to the mastery of primitive impulses, and to progressive self-refinement. The image of a big bear sitting down and waving all its paws reflects pride in personal improvement and accomplishment, and delight in the ability to participate in life at higher levels. Here is the effective demonstration of skills and know-how that will be demanded of every individual who seeks certification of his competency in some special area. Every man must prove himself before he will be fully accepted by his fellows. On a practical level, this image says quite boldly, "Look what I can do!" Positive: At its highest, this symbol represents a remarkable talent for making experience meaningful, and a willingness to stand up to scrutiny and prove the self or endure whatever tests are necessary to accomplish objectives. Negative: Exhibitionism or crude self-display.

TODAY: The accent is on mastery. You may be feeling proud of yourself today for something you've accomplished.

Opportunity: Your greatest advantage lies in demonstrating your abilities. Welcome all challenges as an opportunity to prove what you can do.

Risk: Guard against being a show-off or an attention-grabber. Don't make a fool of yourself by trying to bend over backwards to pat yourself on the back.

STEPPING STONES: Pride, mastery, accomplishment, achievement, performance, dramatics, display, exhibition, realization, success, self-discovery, capability, talent, skill, exhibition.

AQUARIUS 24:   A man turning his back on his passions and teaching from his experience. KEYWORD: *Serenity*

[handwritten: A man Turning his back on his passions and teaching from his experience]

THEME: *Enlightenment.* This symbol speaks to conversion, or the type of sudden change that occurs when an individual becomes aware that his lifestyle is causing him unpleasant and unwanted consequences. It also speaks to proselytizing and the tendency of the newly reformed and enlightened to want to share the fruits of their experiences with others. The image of a man turning his back on his passions and teaching from his experience emphasizes self-mastery and control over physical and emotional compulsions. On a practical level, this symbol can apply to the recovering alcoholic, the "born again" Christian, or others who have had a transcendental experience. Positive: At its highest, this symbol represents wisdom gained through first-hand experience. Negative: Discouragement and disappointment with the self and life in general.

TODAY: The accent is on enlightenment. You could be thinking about how you can give up one of your vices as a result of realizing it is taking you in the opposite direction from where you want to be.

Opportunity: Your greatest advantage lies in sharing the fruits of your experiences with those who show an interest in hearing about your journey.

Risk: Guard against trying to convert others who see things differently from you or trying to convince them that their beliefs and values are somehow inferior or wrong.

STEPPING STONES: Wisdom, sharing, understanding, self-discipline, self-mastery, enlightenment, metamorphosis, transformation, reformation, conversion, contentment, peace of mind, tranquility.

AQUARIUS 25   A butterfly with the right wing more perfectly formed. KEYWORD: *Uniqueness*

a butterfly with the right wing more perfectly formed

THEME: *The Process of Becoming*. This symbol speaks to individual difference, and to man's ability to overcome handicaps through the use of will power and determination. The image of a butterfly with the right wing more perfectly formed does not imply that the left or unconscious and subjective side is defective, but rather that there is a fuller development of the right or conscious and objective side. The emphasis in this degree is on using anomaly or difference to advantage. The butterfly is a universal symbol of metamorphosis, immortality and spirit. Thus this image is also poetic illustration of the never-ending process of spiritual growth and transformation. Positive: At its highest, this symbol represents ingenuity and a talent for creatively capitalizing on inadequacies and imperfections. Negative: Exploitation of personal handicaps or a refusal to conform or cooperate as the result of believing that some self-perceived superiority entitles the individual to special privilege and exemption.

TODAY: The accent is on difference. Things and people could seem more peculiar or odd today.

Opportunity: Your greatest advantage lies in capitalizing on what makes you unique. Take some time to think about what makes you distinct from others and how you can use it to your greatest benefit.

Risk: Guard against being arbitrary or difficult to get along with. At the same time, don't sacrifice your individuality in an attempt to fit in with everyone else.

STEPPING STONES: Uniqueness, individuality, rarity, novelty, distinction, originality, style, peculiarity, abnormality, distinctiveness, prominence, variation, difference, consciousness.

AQUARIUS 26   A hydrometer. KEYWORD: *Efficiency*

a hydrometer

THEME: *Controlling the Variables.* This symbol speaks to an ability to instantly size up or assess a situation and know just what has to be done to achieve a goal. The image of a hydrometer, a device for determining the specific gravities of liquids, emphasizes the scientific approach. It indicates an ability to understand how all things interrelate, predict how a change in one thing will affect another, and use the inherent properties and forces of things to accomplish specific objectives. Implicit in this symbol is the idea that when an individual assumes responsibility over any project he also controls the right to decide when and how things will be done. Positive: At its highest, this symbol represents keen analytical skills and an exceptional ability to manage complex projects. Negative: Insecurity and a tendency to obsessively check and recheck the reliability of everything he encounters.

TODAY: The accent is on assessment. Analyzing a situation that you are trying to get under control could occupy your time today.

Opportunity: Your greatest advantage lies in being objective and using a scientific approach to problem solving. Take advantage of natural conditions and resources in your immediate environment.

Risk: Guard against confusing yourself with irrelevant details or worrying about every little thing that goes wrong. Concentrate on the overall objective and eliminate those time-consuming procedures or steps that aren't necessary to achieving your goal.

STEPPING STONES: Assessment, prediction, analysis, scientific approach, research, scrutiny, measurement, appraisal, estimation, evaluation, diagnosis, examination, calculation.

AQUARIUS 27   An ancient pottery bowl filled with violets.
                 KEYWORD: *Tradition*

THEME: *Anchorage.* This symbol speaks to man's need for roots or security in his life, and to those things that represent stability and permanence. The image of an ancient pottery bowl filled with violets symbolizes the ability of all things that hold great meaning and significance to last or survive. The delicate violets symbolize sensitivity, refinement, faithfulness, the soul, and spiritual or aesthetic values. The pottery bowl or container symbolizes structure and cultural values. The suggestion here is that although on the surface of things life constantly changes, men will continue to comfort and sustain themselves in the traditions and rituals that celebrate all they hold dear. Positive: At its highest, this symbol represents a special talent for inspiring others by effectively living their highest ideals. Negative: Compulsive adherence to established rules and procedures, or an unimaginative preference for living life in a safe and predictable rut.

TODAY: The accent is on sentiment and assurance. You may find yourself reminiscing over little mementos or treasured keepsakes from the past.

Opportunity: Your greatest advantage lies in focusing on the meaning of things rather than on the things themselves. Look for the unexpected and special opportunities created when things don't go as planned.

Risk: Guard against trying to control everything in your life by insisting that everything be done exactly the same way every time. Learn to go with the flow and enjoy yourself.

STEPPING STONES: Inspiration, assurance, tradition, legacy, custom, culture, aesthetic values, stability, continuance, anchorage, significance, nostalgia, faithfulness, beauty, memory, reincarnation.

AQUARIUS 28   **A tree felled and sawed.** KEYWORD: *Immediacy*

a tree felled and sawed

THEME: *Doing What Needs to Be Done*. This symbol speaks to foresight, preparation, and an ability to quickly grasp what needs to be done in a crisis and do it. The image of a tree felled and sawed symbolizes practicality and a sacrifice of the lesser for the good of the greater. The emphasis here is on common sense, initiative, and the wisdom of not waiting until the last minute to get things done. Positive: At its highest, this symbol represents industriousness and efficiency or the type of individual who is prepared for any unforeseen emergency or event. Negative: Lack of imagination and creativity and a tendency to do things the hard way.

TODAY: The accent is on being practical. You may find it necessary to sacrifice or use up one thing in order to create something better or fill a higher need.

Opportunity: Your greatest advantage lies in using your common sense. Look for ways to create what you need from other things that you don't need.

Risk: Guard against being shortsighted or overconfident about the availability of resources. Try not to get caught unprepared for an emergency. Plan ahead.

STEPPING STONES: Practicality, utilitarianism, functionalism, resourcefulness, skillfulness, constructiveness, fundamentalism, pragmatism, realism, productiveness, sensibility.

AQUARIUS 29   Butterfly emerging from chrysalis. KEY-
WORD: *Emanation*

Butterfly emerging from chrysalis

THEME: *Metamorphosis*. This symbol speaks to curiosity, and to man's quest for knowledge. The image of butterfly emerging from chrysalis symbolizes transformation and self-renewal, or rebirth in a new form. As such it alludes to reincarnation, the forgetting of past experience and a lack of intellectual sophistication. The emphasis in this degree is on innocence and vulnerability. Positive: At its highest, this symbol represents a delightful sense of wonderment and a childlike faith in the ultimate goodness of the world. Negative: Difficulty in understanding the simplest things and a complete failure to comprehend the relationship between cause and effect.

TODAY: The accent is on unfoldment. Change is in the air. Things are likely to start moving to the next level or stage in a situation.

Opportunity: Your greatest advantage lies in being willing to let go of the safe and familiar and allow yourself to enjoy the freedom to create and experiment with new ways of living or doing things.

Risk: Guard against failing to pay attention to what is going on around you, or missing obvious cues that things have changed. Don't wake up too late to be able to do something about a situation or miss your chance to capitalize on a new opportunity.

STEPPING STONES: Creativity, desire for experience, curiosity, self-assurance, self-renewal, rebirth, aspiration, commencement, evolution, transformation, maturation, unfoldment, freedom.

AQUARIUS 30   The field of Ardath in bloom. KEYWORD:
                   Continuity

The field of Ardath in bloom

THEME: *Ancient Mysteries.* This symbol speaks to spiritual integrity, and to the basic friendliness of the universe. The image of the field of Ardath in bloom, or Marie Corelli's mystic meadow of ancient Babylon, is poetic testimony to the ability of seeds and ideas sown far in the past to maintain their identity and purpose, and to survive and flourish through many lifetimes. Implicit in this image of blossoms in an ancient field is an allusion to group consciousness and the sustainment of the invisible brotherhood. On a practical level, this image symbolizes loveliness, inspiration and those soul-refreshing moments that renew hope and remind an individual of the good in the world and himself. Positive: At its highest, this symbol represents mysticism, growth in consciousness, and spiritual illumination through the fulfillment of a commitment to higher service. Negative: Psychic delusions or looking at the world through rose-colored glasses and a refusal to face reality when it doesn't square with expectation.

TODAY: The accent is on survival and endurance. You may feel especially thankful or relieved that a difficult challenge or situation was successfully resolved.

Opportunity: Your greatest advantage lies in expecting that your prayers will be heard and answered. Think positive.

Risk: Guard against losing faith, or refusing to recognize that there is a higher power behind all material manifestation. Don't be too proud to ask for help when you need it.

STEPPING STONES: Spiritual integrity, agelessness, mysticism, endurance, survival, continuance, group consciousness, invisible brotherhood, loveliness, inspiration, renewal, rebirth, soul.

Pisces

♓

PISCES 1   A public market. KEYWORD: *Commerce*

a public market

THEME: *Interchange*. This symbol speaks to the role of groups in helping each member grow and refine his own unique potential. The image of a public market symbolizes interchange of every kind, whether this takes the form of trade and barter or social communication. Every group has its own special genius and purpose, and the ability of a group to fulfill its mission is largely dependent on the willingness of each member to carry his share of the load and perform his individual task to the best of his ability. The emphasis here is on the necessary give and take at the heart of any collective effort, and on being careful not to neglect personal needs and responsibilities in the process of trying to help others. Positive: At its highest, this symbol represents an exceptional talent for mediating and resolving disputes, and for getting people to work together cooperatively for the mutual benefit of all. Negative: Solipsism or complete self-centeredness and an inability to comprehend or appreciate the needs and desires of others.

TODAY: The accent is on interchange. Today could be marked by network disruptions or some kind of breakdown in a system.

Opportunity: Your greatest advantage lies in keeping the lines of communication open. Make sure you are holding up your end of things. Focus on equal distribution and fairness to all concerned.

Risk: Guard against putting your own interests above the welfare of the group. Avoid the "every man for himself" approach.

STEPPING STONES: Shopping, interchange, communication, trade, barter, exchange, business, buying and selling, give and take, finance, transactions, enterprise, industry, commerce.

PISCES 2   A squirrel hiding from hunters. KEYWORD: *Caution*

A squirrel hiding from hunters

THEME: *Danger Signs*. This symbol speaks to self-preservation, and to the avoidance of unnecessary risk. The image of a squirrel hiding from hunters is one of the negative or reversed symbols and it symbolizes danger and a need to exercise caution. The emphasis in this degree is on being conservative, or playing it safe, thinking things through carefully before acting, and having the courage to say no when the risks outweigh the benefits. Positive: At its highest, this symbol represents independent thinking, good judgment and a keen sense of timing, or a natural instinct for knowing when and how to take chances. Negative: Lack of self-confidence and low self-esteem or inhibition and fearfulness.

TODAY: The accent is on self-preservation. Discretion is advised. Open enemies are easier to deal with than hidden ones.

Opportunity: Your greatest advantage lies in paying attention to signs that indicate all is not well. Take precautions to protect yourself. Use your discrimination.

Risk: Guard against taking unnecessary risks. Keep a low profile and wait for more favorable conditions. This is not the time to draw attention to yourself.

STEPPING STONES: Danger, fear, threat, forewarning, exigency, hazard, jeopardy, peril, risk, trouble, pursuit, self-preservation, discretion, prudence, alertness, carefulness, wariness, circumspection, discretion, prudence, sensibility, caution.

PISCES 3   A petrified forest. KEYWORD: *Survival*

a petrified forest

THEME: *Conviction.* This symbol speaks to intellectual certainty, strength of character, and to the ability of concepts and ideas to survive long after the mind that formed them is gone. The image of a petrified forest symbolizes endurance, permanence and stability. At the same time it alludes to crystallization, and it cautions the individual against relying on any thing or idea that has outlived its usefulness or to which he cannot contribute and be a part of. The suggestion here is that what looks like a stepping stone may instead be a stumbling block. The emphasis in this degree is on continuance. Positive: At its highest, this symbol represents unswerving faithfulness to the highest principles and ideals and a courage born of conviction. Negative: Inability to adapt to change, or inflexibility, stubbornness and resistance.

TODAY: The accent is on stumbling blocks to progress. You may find yourself having to deal with the problems of what to do with things and ideas you held onto that have outworn their usefulness.

Opportunity: Your greatest advantage lies in cleaning up your life. Get rid of what you don't need and polish up what you do need and want to keep. Create a little space in your life for something new.

Risk: Guard against holding on to, or taking and keeping, more than you need. Avoid the compulsion to save everything for a rainy day. Don't let things rule your life.

STEPPING STONES: Preservation, certainty, stability, endurance, continuance, lastingness, survival, strength, durability, perseverance, persistence, resilience, toughness, stamina, rigidity, inflexibility, stubbornness, testimony, evidence.

PISCES 4   Heavy traffic on a narrow isthmus. KEYWORD: *Convergence*

Heavy traffic on a narrow isthmus

THEME: *Relieving Pressure*. This symbol speaks to overcrowding, or congestion, and to the frustrations that arise in everyday living when time and space are at a premium and a large number of people are all trying to accomplish their individual objectives at once. The image of heavy traffic on a narrow isthmus alludes to irritation, stress and confusion. On a practical level, this image can describe rush hour traffic, the frenzy of holiday shopping or any overwhelming social situation that pushes an individual to his limits. The emphasis here is on the need for cooperation and self-discipline, and the importance of balancing short-term personal goals against the greater needs of the self and the community. Positive: At its highest, this symbol represents a natural talent for soothing ruffled feathers and coming up with creative ideas for resolving group conflicts. Negative: Self-centeredness and a complete disregard of the rights and needs of others.

TODAY: The accent is on congestion. You might be feeling pressured or crowded by too many activities and long for more space or a little peace and quiet.

Opportunity: Your greatest advantage lies in getting organized. Learn to say "no."

Risk: Guard against failing to pay attention to the welfare of the whole, or insisting on having your desires met at the expense of others. On the other hand, don't be afraid to let others know that you have your own priorities to be met when they are intruding or interfering.

STEPPING STONES: Congestion, convergence, overpopulation, overcrowding, inundation, blocking, choking, compression, saturation, consolidation, constriction, condensation, aggregation, centralization, limitation, confusion, conflict, obstruction, impediments, hindrance.

PISCES 5   A church bazaar. KEYWORD: *Benefit*

a church bazaar

THEME: *Cheerful Giving.* This symbol speaks to affiliation and commitment, and to man's ability to capitalize on his social connections and friendships. The image of a church bazaar alludes to community involvement, fellowship and camaraderie. The emphasis in this degree is on charity, benevolence, good will and kindness. Positive: At its highest, this symbol represents philanthropy, humanitarianism and an exceptional talent for inspiring people to support those institutions and organizations that benefit society as a whole. Negative: Snobbery, elitism, cliquishness and social prejudice or bigotry.

TODAY: The accent is on charitable giving, fund raising, and finding ways to support those institutions and organizations that benefit society as a whole.

Opportunity: Your greatest advantage lies in focusing on what is in the best interest of all concerned. Think long range.

Risk: Guard against self-serving generosity. Avoid conflicts of interest and self-dealing. Don't take advantage of a position of trust.

STEPPING STONES: Social activity, charity, philanthropy, humanitarianism, benevolence, good will, community involvement, fellowship, camaraderie, service, welfare, aid, assistance, altruism, contribution, generosity, kindness, benefit.

PISCES 6   Officers on dress parade. KEYWORD: *Discipline*

Offices on dress parade

THEME: *Practice and Drill.* This symbol speaks to respect for tradition, and to pride in personal responsibility. The image of officers on dress parade alludes to ritual, protocol, formality, rehearsal, and an attempt to live up to an ideal. The emphasis in this degree is on self-discipline, commitment and an investment of time and energy in personal self-improvement. On a practical level, this symbol can apply to any public demonstration of skill and competency. Positive: At its highest, this symbol represents accountability, self-confidence, composure and pride in accomplishment. Negative: Feelings of entitlement, or attempts to get one's way by pulling rank and demanding special treatment.

TODAY: The accent is on self-discipline and protocol. The possibility of being inspected or having your work looked into makes it important to put your best foot forward and follow the rules.

Opportunity: Your greatest advantage lies in acting with dignity. Brush up on the rules of etiquette and make sure you know how to do what you committed to do.

Risk: Guard against getting out of step with your fellows or insisting on doing your own thing. This is not a good time to act on impulse or fly by the seat of your pants.

STEPPING STONES: Ritual, discipline, rules, rehearsal, dignity, protocol, decorum, formality, propriety, etiquette, convention, custom, display, show, drama, ceremony, competency, responsibility.

PISCES 7   A cross lying on rocks. KEYWORD: *Conscience*

A cross lying on rocks

THEME: *Slippage*. This symbol speaks to fear of personal rejection, and to blindly following the crowd in order to gain acceptance. The image of a cross lying on rocks alludes to desolation, disillusionment, a loss of faith, and the abandonment of spiritual values. The emphasis in this degree is on the importance of being true to self, listening to the voice of conscience, thinking independently and standing up for what is believed in, even when it isn't popular. Positive: At its highest, this symbol represents moral integrity, courage and a refusal to compromise the self or lower personal standards in order to please others. Negative: Spinelessness and giving in to the demands of others, or a tendency to be easily intimidated.

TODAY: The accent is on letting your conscience be your guide. You could decide to make a clean break of it or sever ties of some sort.

Opportunity: Your greatest advantage lies in refusing to compromise your integrity. Release whatever has brought no welcoming response.

Risk: Guard against hanging on to what may be detrimental to your own best interests in the foolish belief that "something is better than nothing" or "no one can do the job as well as I can." Don't be afraid to let go and let God.

STEPPING STONES: Abandonment, withdrawal, repudiation, rejection, renunciation, retraction, defection, neglect, denial, annulment, cancellation, disavowal, disapproval, disowning, negation, nullification, objection, protest, dissent, refutation.

PISCES 8   A girl blowing a bugle. KEYWORD: *Summons*

a girl blowing a bugle

THEME: *A Call to Action*. This symbol speaks to self-refinement, and to the development of special expertise and skill. The image of a girl blowing a bugle emphasizes personal responsibility and pride in accomplishment. The suggestion here is that individuals find their ultimate happiness through being of genuine service to others and finding a special niche for themselves among their fellows. On a practical level, this degree can indicate a wake-up call, bragging, or tooting one's own horn. Positive: At its highest, this symbol represents directness and a special gift for finding opportunities to demonstrate competency and talent. Negative: Intrusiveness or loud attention-getting behavior.

TODAY: The accent is on a wake up call. This day could present a special challenge. It's definitely a time to pay attention to what you hear.

Opportunity: Your greatest advantage lies in being prepared to take action. Keep your wits about you and do what has to be done. Be responsible.

Risk: Guard against dismissing some signal you get as a false alarm. Try not to have everything in your life so ordered and controlled that you can't handle the unexpected emergency or take advantage of that opportunity you've been waiting for.

STEPPING STONES: Summons, call, invitation, solicitation, signal, challenge, command, directive, citation, evocation, proclamation, achievement, responsibility, announcement, self-expression, alert, warning, cue, prompt.

PISCES 9   A jockey. KEYWORD: *Practice*

THEME: *Going for Broke.* This symbol speaks to the requirement that an individual throw himself into life, hone his skills and talents, and make every effort his best one if he wishes to stand in the winner's circle. The image of a jockey emphasizes competition and maneuvering for position or advantage. The implication here is that the individual who sloughs off, or fails to give life his best shot, will lose out in the long run. Positive: At its highest, this symbol represents persistence, tenacity and a remarkable gift for coming from behind to win the games of life. Negative: Foolish risk-taking and a love of gambling.

TODAY: The accent is on competition and skill in being able to maneuver yourself into the best position to get what you want.

Opportunity: Your greatest advantage lies in practicing what you would like to be good at. Be willing to sacrifice immediate pleasure for long-term gain.

Risk: Guard against being over-confident or trusting your luck to bring you success. Don't take things for granted or exhaust your resources before they can be replaced.

STEPPING STONES: Competition, contest, match, rivalry, race, game, skill, maneuvering, coordination, orchestration, dexterity, agility, equilibrium, litheness, lightness, smallness, gambling.

PISCES 10   An aviator in the clouds. KEYWORD: *Observation*

An aviator in the clouds

THEME: *Global Perspective.* This symbol speaks to rising above the limitations of eye-to-eye problem solving and viewing things from a higher and more holistic point of view. The image of an aviator in the clouds emphasizes imagination, exploration and curiosity. The implication here is that this degree refers to creative or abstract thinking and the development and testing of new ideas. Positive: At its highest, this symbol represents broad-mindedness, exceptional scope of vision, and the ability to foresee and plan effectively for future needs. Negative: Head-in-the-clouds impracticality or aloofness and rejection of social responsibility.

TODAY: The accent is on perspective. What seems to be true at first glance may not be, when all the factors are taken into consideration.

Opportunity: Your greatest advantage lies in distancing yourself from a difficult problem or situation in order to take a more objective view. Look at the whole picture. Find the patterns in things and events.

Risk: Guard against losing touch with what's going on by isolating yourself or living in a dream world. Don't get trapped in your own mindset and blind yourself to the obvious.

STEPPING STONES: Transcendence, exploration, perspective, overview, circumspection, observation, vision, long-range planning, domination, surmounting, going beyond, rising above, viewpoint, outlook, abstract thinking.

PISCES 11   Men seeking illumination. **KEYWORD:** *Dedication*

men seeking illumination

THEME: *Seekers on the Path.* This symbol speaks to initiation, discipleship and apostolic succession, or the transmission of spiritual authority and a specific mission in one long and unbroken line. The image of men seeking illumination refers to all seekers on the spiritual path, and it alludes to a willingness to assume responsibility and endure the hardships and discipline demanded of those who wish to achieve a conscious immortality. Just as the Divine Spirit is dependent upon Itself to sustain Its existence in the hearts of men, individuals must nurture and develop their own potential if they hope to survive. Positive: At its highest, this symbol represents mystical awakening, devotion, and a commitment to preserving the spiritual integrity of life in whatever form it is found. Negative: Pretense or false claims of spiritual merit and enlightenment.

TODAY: The accent is on aspiration. It becomes obvious that accomplishing higher goals requires hard work and self-discipline. The focus is on the desire to know.

Opportunity: Your greatest advantage lies in keeping your eye on your goal and your shoulder to the wheel. Keep your motives pure and your hands clean.

Risk: Guard against false prophets and others who claim to have the inside track with higher powers.

STEPPING STONES: Aspiration, initiation, aspirants, seekers, candidates, postulants, nominees, mission, quest, goal, devotion, commitment, consecration, invocation, fidelity.

PISCES 12   An examination of initiates. KEYWORD: *Qualification*

an examination of initiates

THEME: *Initiation.* This symbol speaks to ethics, and to a time of spiritual evaluation or testing. The image of an examination of initiates portrays a rite of passage that demands proof of knowledge, skills and progress after a period of rigorous training. The emphasis here is on the ability to effectively demonstrate the highest ideals and principles, even in the face of criticism. It also suggests the possibility of misunderstanding or rejection by those whose values lie more in material realms. This degree can also indicate a group ordeal or personal challenge that compels an answer to the question, "Are you who you say you are?" Positive: At its highest, this symbol represents integrity, moral courage, strength of character, and achievement through self-discipline. Negative: Apprehensiveness, self-protection and fear of failure.

TODAY: The accent is on testing. You may be subjected to scrutiny or have to provide evidence or proof that you're qualified in some area or can do what you say you can do.

Opportunity: Your greatest advantage lies in being prepared. Find out what is required to achieve your objective and sharpen your skills and knowledge.

Risk: Guard against making claims you can't back up. Avoid exaggerating your credentials or experience.

STEPPING STONES: Testing, proving, trial, inquest, investigation, analysis, assessment, inspection, review, scrutiny, observation, inquiry, interrogation, qualification, diagnosis, certification, ordination, confirmation, accreditation, affirmation, authorization, validation.

PISCES 13   A sword in a museum. KEYWORD: *Example*

A sword in a museum

THEME: *The Power of Precedent.* This symbol speaks to the far-reaching effect of the lives and deeds of historic figures of the past. The image of a sword in a museum emphasizes courage, honor and willpower. But the sword here is also a weapon laid to rest, and as such it can symbolize prior hostilities, bitterness and conflict. At every critical turn of events in recorded history, some one or more individuals rise to glory and shape the destiny of the race, and down through the years, their courage and achievements continue to influence the thinking and decisions of new leaders in similar situations. Positive: At its highest, this symbol represents personal power, decisiveness, and the ability to inspire others by living collective ideals in practical, everyday ways. Negative: Gross exaggeration of the difficulty and magnitude of achievements.

TODAY: The accent is on influence from the past. You may find yourself trying to discover how immediate predicaments were successfully resolved in similar situations.

Opportunity: Your greatest advantage lies in following precedent or tradition. Do your research. Look at the background or history of the immediate situation.

Risk: Guard against making mountains out of molehills. Don't blow things out of proportion or exaggerate the magnitude of a problem you solved.

STEPPING STONES: Prior achievement, battles won, archetype, paradigm, paragon, representation, exemplar, ideal, hero, paladin, peace, courage, honor, valor, bravery, power, decisiveness, inspiration.

PISCES 14   A lady in fox fur. KEYWORD: *Tastefulness*

a lady in fox fur

THEME: *Seduction*. This symbol speaks to personal charm and charisma. The image of a lady in fox fur emphasizes elegance, sophistication, and a desire to make an impact on others or be regarded as special. It also alludes to a need to be socially accepted and admired. The challenge in this symbol is on learning how to fit in and be considered part of a group without sacrificing individuality and personal freedom. Positive: At its highest, this symbol represents a fascinating talent for captivating a crowd and creating special effects. Negative: Taking unfair advantage through clever manipulation, or an uncanny ability and inclination to capitalize on the weaknesses of others.

TODAY: The accent is on sophistication. You may be concerned about appearances and making a good impression.

Opportunity: Your greatest advantage lies in developing your own unique style. Be distinctive but not outrageous. Express yourself creatively.

Risk: Guard against misrepresenting the facts in order to gain an unfair advantage or avoid embarrassment. Don't promise more than you can deliver.

STEPPING STONES: Elegance, charm, charisma, glamour, panache, polish, grace, gentility, sophistication, style, refinement, taste, class, luxury, affluence, breeding, cultivation, dignity, seduction, shrewdness.

PISCES 15   An officer preparing to drill his men. KEYWORD: *Preciseness*

an officer preparing to drill his men

THEME: *Making the Best of It.* This symbol speaks to a desire to avoid consequences by shifting responsibility or blame upward or downward in a hierarchy of authority. The image of an officer preparing to drill his men describes one of life's predicaments that is difficult if not impossible to get out of easily, and it stresses the importance of making the best of those situations that can't be avoided or immediately resolved by finding some higher value or purpose in the experience. Every individual gets out of life what he is willing to put into it. Positive: At its highest, this symbol represents a "can-do" attitude and a knack for making every experience a profitable adventure. Negative: Lack of enthusiasm and constant complaining about one's lot, or how life is so unfair.

TODAY: The accent is on ingenuity and self-discipline. You could resent being where you are, or trying to find a place for yourself that holds a greater potential for growth.

Opportunity: Your greatest advantage lies in creating your own opportunities. Think positive about a situation you might be stuck in. When life gives you lemons, get out the sugar and water.

Risk: Guard against looking at the dark side of things. Don't whine and complain that you are being taken advantage of against your wishes. Life is what you make it.

STEPPING STONES: Rehearsal, practice, instruction, exercise, lesson, correctness, efficiency, rigor, system, precision, organization, discipline, preparation, planning, maneuver, work-out.

PISCES 16   The flow of inspiration. KEYWORD: *Ingenuity*

The flow of inspiration

THEME: *Creative Solutions*. This symbol speaks to the practical application of spiritual power. The image of the flow of inspiration alludes to a divine outpouring of creative energy that can be used for everyday problem solving, but the greater implication is that inspiration can be found everywhere by the individual who has trained himself to be sensitive to the illimitable potential waiting to be discovered in everything that exists. The suggestion here is that every challenge is an opportunity for stretching the imagination and developing resourcefulness. Positive: At its highest, this symbol represents inventiveness, originality, and a special gift for seeing unique possibilities in the most unpromising things and situations. Negative: Self-deception, or a tendency to live in a fool's paradise and a preference for taking the easy way out.

TODAY: The accent is on inventiveness. You may be struck by a novel idea that helps you solve a problem or inspires you to try something new.

Opportunity: Your greatest advantage lies in creating enough time and space in your life to get in touch with your higher self. Use your imagination and listen to your intuition.

Risk: Guard against falling victim to the delusion that thinking is the same as doing. Put your ideas to work in the practical and everyday world.

STEPPING STONES: Creativity, spiritual power, stimulation, encouragement, imagination, inventiveness, ingenuity, originality, resourcefulness, idea, innovation, talent, brilliance, cleverness, vision, insight, intuition, foresight, prescience, revelation, prophecy.

PISCES 17   An Easter promenade. KEYWORD: *Celebration*

an Easter promenade

THEME: *Standing Out.* This symbol speaks to the magnification of self in a very conspicuous and highly individualistic way. The image of an Easter promenade is an especially dramatic representation of individual self-expression as it alludes to vanity and the extremes an individual will go to in order to draw attention to himself. Easter symbolizes a time of rebirth and regeneration, and here it signifies self-renewal and an attempt to present the self in a new light or share new or heretofore unrevealed facets of the self with others. On a practical level, this symbol refers to those situations in which there is an urge to demonstrate some newly acquired skill or progress made and win the admiration of others, perhaps in a music recital, a craft, flower or art show or a public contest. Positive: At its highest, this symbol represents an admirable and inspiring dedication to self-improvement. Negative: Ostentatious self-display or attention-getting behavior.

TODAY: The accent is on individuality. People may take unusual steps to gain attention today.

Opportunity: Your greatest advantage lies in knowing how best to showcase your talents. Make sure you're prepared for all contingencies. Appearances will count.

Risk: Guard against making a fool of yourself in your efforts to stand out from the crowd. Avoid extremes in dress and behavior.

STEPPING STONES: Exhibition, show, display, vanity, exaltation, self-expression, ritual, ceremony, festival, holiday, celebration, commemoration, drama, fashion, style.

PISCES 18   A gigantic tent. KEYWORD: *Apportionment*

a gigantic tent

THEME: *Revival*. This symbol speaks to the gaining of a gestalt or holistic understanding of life through a dramatic intensification of experience. Thus, the image of a gigantic tent alludes to integration and the process of pulling various pieces together into a unified and organized whole. The 1931 mimeograph version of this symbol referred to a revivalist's tent and a "revision of ideas back to source," or a renewal of faith. In the 1953 version, the image was described as a circus tent. The focus there was on excitement, and a "sharing of skills and risks" that brings an individual "renewed insight into his capacity for putting his world in order ... as well as for his immediate entertainment." Viewed from a modern perspective, this commentary appropriately describes the effects of an emotional high that results in a quickening of spirit, or a sudden rebirth of self-confidence and self-esteem. On a practical level, this symbol can refer to any gathering where the participants are inspired or stirred to action through an appeal to the emotions. Positive: At its highest, this symbol represents a special talent for getting things done by motivating or stimulating others to rally to some cause at hand. Negative: Psychic manipulation or grandstanding, rebel rousing and instigation.

TODAY: The accent is on getting it all together. You could be involved in some community affair that requires you to juggle your priorities.

Opportunity: Your greatest advantage lies in getting organized. Put first things first and the rest will fall into place. Grouping things will help.

Risk: Guard against getting carried away with a false sense of self-importance. Avoid being too loud or monopolizing the conversation. Give others a chance to express themselves. Be willing to share the stage.

STEPPING STONES: Intensification, excitement, self-renewal, quickening, motivation, inspiration, entertainment, gestalt understanding, insight, completeness, integration, unification, shelter.

PISCES 19   A master instructing his pupil. KEYWORD: *Elucidation*

a master instructing his pupil

THEME: *Training*. This symbol speaks to learning, and to man's desire to take charge of his life and enhance his opportunities for meaningful experiences through higher education and the acquisition of greater knowledge and expertise. The image of a master instructing his pupil suggests an openness to new ideas, a desire for self-improvement, and an eagerness to gain proficiency in some special area. Implicit in this symbol is the concept of self-discipline, or the willingness to give up lesser freedoms in order to gain higher ones. On a practical level, this degree governs all educational situations, and it emphasizes listening to the voice of higher reason. Positive: At its highest, this symbol represents a special gift for explaining difficult concepts in simple terms, a talent for motivating others to want to learn, and the ability to command respect from others. Negative: Self-defeat through rule-driven behavior or a reputation for being a self-deluded know-it-all.

TODAY: The accent is on improvement. Training and education are the keys to success.

Opportunity: Your greatest advantage lies in being willing to admit that you don't have all the answers. Ask for help when you need it and be patient with those who are learning.

Risk: Guard against thinking you're smarter than the rest of your fellows. It's surprising what you can learn when you take the time to listen.

STEPPING STONES: Education, teaching, scholarship, indoctrination, preparation, training, orientation, clarification, interpretation, articulation, discourse, explanation, definition, description, refinement, illumination.

PISCES 20   A table set for an evening meal. KEYWORD: *Familiarity*

a Table set for an evening meal

THEME: *Indulgence.* This symbol speaks to abundance, and to the fact that everything an individual needs is readily available in the world about him if he will only recognize it. The image of a table set for an evening meal suggests nurturance and caretaking. It also alludes to the fact that man is free to accept or reject whatever life offers him; however, it is usually the case that an individual will not move to claim anything for his own until he recognizes the value or potential usefulness of a thing to himself. On a practical level, this degree symbolizes prosperity and gift giving with no strings attached. Positive: At its highest, this symbol represents a special sensitivity to the needs of others and a sincere desire to be of service. Negative: Inability to recognize the needs of others or witless optimism and a refusal to face reality.

TODAY: The accent is on being provided for. You may discover that things appear today just when you need them.

Opportunity: Your greatest advantage lies in anticipating what others will need. Be observant. As you give, so shall you receive. Be generous.

Risk: Guard against taking unfair advantage of others' kindness. Don't forget to say thank you or express your appreciation when someone does you a favor or goes out of their way to make your life more comfortable.

STEPPING STONES: Abundance, nurturing, caretaking, sensitivity, service, aid, assistance, prosperity, comfort, ease, solace, contentment, gratification, fulfillment, pleasure, satisfaction.

PISCES 21   A little white lamb, a child and a Chinese servant.
KEYWORD: *Talent*

a little white lamb, a child & a Chinese servant

THEME: *Perceiving the Beauty in Difference.* This symbol speaks to the importance of finding the meaning and opportunity in diversity. The image of a little white lamb, a child and a Chinese servant alludes to the value of respecting individual differences and finding creative ways to motivate individuals with unique or special gifts to work together toward common goals. The figures in this image have no apparent relationship to each other. They are unique and complete within themselves and yet they appear together as a *tableau vivant*—separate, yet together. The emphasis here is on integration and synthesis. The Chinese servant looks to the past, the lamb to the present and the child to the future, yet time is an illusion and each is a part of the eternal now. Positive: At its highest, this symbol represents extraordinary versatility and imagination, a preference for the unusual, and a natural gift for spotting and developing talent in others. Negative: Confusion, lack of organization and inability to understand or make sense of life.

TODAY: The accent is on diversity and specialization. You may be challenged to find ways to help people work together on some group project.

Opportunity: Your greatest advantage lies in being able to bring diverse or seemingly heterogeneous elements together into a unified and well-functioning whole. Capitalize on the unique talents of the individuals in any group endeavor. Find the opportunities that difference creates.

Risk: Guard against trying to force everyone into the same mold or expecting them to think and act alike. Don't resent or ignore what doesn't seem to fit. There is a use or niche for everything and everyone.

STEPPING STONES: Diversity, difference, dissimilarity, heterogeneity, variation, contrast, diffusion, versatility, eclecticism, specialty, division of labor, amalgamation, mélange, potentiality, promise, aptitude, skill.

PISCES 22   **A man bringing down the new law from Sinai.**
              KEYWORD: *Mandate*

A man bringing down
the new law from Sinai

THEME: *Higher Authority.* This symbol speaks to revelation, and to the transcendental experience that brings insight and awareness of a higher authority. The image of a man bringing down the new law from Sinai, or the mountain, emphasizes spiritual or ethical rules of conduct. Although this image alludes to Moses and the Ten Commandments, it can also refer to a mystical experience or spiritual quickening that transforms the way an individual lives his life. On a practical level, this degree can indicate a change in church doctrine, new public policies or laws, or a modernization of codes and procedures. Positive: At its highest, this symbol represents moral integrity, a willingness to make personal sacrifices for the good of the whole, and a personal commitment to making a positive difference in people's lives. Negative: Arrogance and conceit or taking unfair advantage of others through position and privilege.

TODAY: The accent is on ethics and moral integrity. You could experience internal conflict when considering your options today.

Opportunity: Your greatest advantage lies in making sure that the means you take justifies the end result. Be honest. Be truthful. Be fair.

Risk: Guard against thinking you can get away with misrepresenting the facts or taking unfair advantage of a situation or person. Taking the easy way out by breaking the rules or ignoring your responsibilities and obligations could result in unexpected consequences.

STEPPING STONES: Authority, decree, directive, order, ordinance, commandment, dictum, edict, law, policy, legislation, proclamation, regulation, statute, spiritual experience, religious doctrine, moral integrity, inspiration.

PISCES 23   Spiritist phenomena. KEYWORD: *Sensitivity*

5 piritist phenomena

THEME: *Strange Things Happening*. This symbol speaks to the materialization of a higher reality, or the ability of man to tap into a potential that he can make manifest according to his particular will and desire. The image of spiritist phenomena emphasizes the power of the mind and the importance of focus and mental discipline. The challenge in this degree is on learning how to break through the conditioning effects of experience and develop a greater sensitivity to the possibilities of what yet can be achieved. The key is in not allowing the self to become distracted by the allure of every passing whim and fancy or the trivial problems of everyday living. On a practical level, this image alludes to psychic phenomena and the oftentimes entertaining activities of the invisible world. It also suggests cosmic comedies, practical jokes and "gremlins," or the mysterious causes of those things that inexplicably go wrong, break, disappear, or change in some way. Positive: At its highest, this symbol represents psychic sensitivity, a highly refined attunement to the higher potential of all things and a powerful depth of focus that leads to significant achievements. Negative: Confusion, nervousness and instability or a tendency to easy distraction.

TODAY: The accent is on strange events that disrupt business as usual. Things could go wrong or turn out unexpectedly today.

Opportunity: Your greatest advantage lies in understanding the greater significance being revealed when things don't go as planned or when patterns and habits are suddenly broken. Be sensitive to the opportunities created by change and confusion.

Risk: Guard against creating your own chaos by refusing to discipline yourself or establish order in your life. Avoid trying to be everywhere at once in a frantic attempt to not miss everything that's going on. Learn to sit still and listen.

STEPPING STONES: Telekinesis, psychokinesis, psychic phenomena, caprice, confusion, practical jokes, gremlins, aberrations, peculiarities, quirks, unexplained happenings.

PISCES 24   An inhabited island. KEYWORD: *Cultivation*

an inhabited island

THEME: *Adaptability*. This symbol speaks to self-containment, self-sufficiency, and having everything needed to function independently ready and available at hand. It also speaks to skill in organizing resources for their maximum or most profitable use. The image of an inhabited island emphasizes ingenuity, and it stresses the importance of thoroughly analyzing the potential usefulness of everything that can be found at hand in any situation of need. In practical terms, this degree is about learning how to adapt and look at things in new and different ways, and being willing to "make do." Positive: At its highest, this symbol represents inventiveness, creativity, and the ability to find clever or novel ways to get a job done. Negative: Selfishness, self-indulgence and egocentric isolation.

TODAY: The accent is on self-sufficiency. You may find that this is a "do-it-yourself" day.

Opportunity: Your greatest advantage lies in using your ingenuity to create what you need from things you already have. Get rid of presumptions. A thing is what it does.

Risk: Guard against trying to be too independent or telling yourself that you don't need help from anyone. Avoid cutting yourself off from people who won't let you have it all your own way. Learn to cooperate.

STEPPING STONES: Development, civilization, culture, resourcefulness, organization, refinement, adaptation, self-sufficiency, self-containment, ingenuity, making do, establishment, advancement, progress, growth.

PISCES 25   The purging of the priesthood. KEYWORD: *Reformation*

The purging of the priesthood

THEME: *Purification.* This symbol speaks to integrity, and to the consequences of violating a sacred trust. The image of the purging of the priesthood refers to holding individuals in high places to equally high standards, and to the fact that those who set standards for others will also be judged by them. Man finds hope and inspiration for his own ongoing in those who live his ideals, and he will not abide betrayal. On a practical level, this symbol points to a separation of the wheat from the chaff, or a weeding out of whatever has lost its value and usefulness. Positive: At its highest, this symbol represents high standards, ethical behavior, and a rejection of hypocrisy and pretense. Negative: Prejudice and bigotry or retaliation and vindictiveness.

TODAY: The accent is on dismissal. Higher authorities could be removed from office or exposed for wrongdoing.

Opportunity: Your greatest advantage lies in getting rid of things in your life that no longer serve any purpose. Be willing to release and let go. It's time for a good housecleaning.

Risk: Guard against trying to destroy what you don't understand. Avoid making accusations that have no proven basis in fact.

STEPPING STONES: Purification, cleansing, rehabilitation, amelioration, refinement, elimination, dismissal, censoring, eradication, expiation, expungement, expurgation, extermination, removal, riddance, banishment, abolishment, deletion, discharge, disqualification, divestment, ejection.

PISCES 26   A new moon that divides its influences. KEYWORD: *Finesse*

A new moon that divides its influences

THEME: *The Stirring From Within*. This symbol speaks to initiative, or the stirring from within that leads to outreach and new beginnings. The image of a new moon that divides its influences refers to the different impact that the same event can have on various individuals, depending on the reality that each is a part of. The earliest description of this image contrasted the romantic significance of the new moon for lovers with the intimation of eternity that the philosopher perceives. The emphasis in this degree is on experimentalism, and on man's instinctive need to move outside himself and become an active participant in life, even if he is uncertain about how to do this. But the greater suggestion here is that an individual should avoid making permanent commitments until he clearly knows what he wants and needs. Positive: At its highest, this symbol represents the ability to take full advantage of the opportunities that arise in any changing situation and capitalize on every newly-discovered aptitude and talent in self. Negative: Indecisiveness, ambivalence and self-defeating fence-straddling.

TODAY: The accent is on uncertainty. You may be unsure about how to begin some new project or wavering back and forth on a decision you have to make.

Opportunity: Your greatest advantage lies in choosing one of your options and going with it on a trial basis.

Risk: Guard against vacillating until it's too late and you lose your opportunity to have a say in the matter.

STEPPING STONES: Uncertainty, tentativeness, irresolution, qualm, apprehension, insecurity, reluctance, ambiguity, ambivalence, doubt, hesitation, questioning, reservation, timidity, vacillation, indecision, misgivings, mistrust.

PISCES 27   A harvest moon. KEYWORD: *Benediction*

a harvest moon

THEME: *Climax.* This symbol speaks to fullness, ripeness and maturity, or the highest point in any cycle that immediately precedes achievement and carries within itself the seeds of new beginnings. The image of a harvest moon alludes to a time for reaping what has been sown, and so it also symbolizes the concept of karma. But the deeper significance of this symbol is discovered in that crowning moment when potentiality is transformed into actuality. The emphasis in this symbol is on effort, and the implication here is that an individual gets out of a thing what he puts into it. On a practical level, this symbol dramatizes the breath-holding moment that anticipates immediate success. Positive: At its highest, this symbol represents self-fulfillment and accomplishment through creative visualization and hard work. Negative: Immaturity and ineptitude as the result of an unfortunate lack of opportunity for struggle or any real necessity to have to work hard for a living.

TODAY: The accent is on completion. Events are heading toward a climax and you should see the results of your efforts soon.

Opportunity: Your greatest advantage lies in looking toward the future. Review what you've learned. Count your blessings.

Risk: Guard against agonizing over past mistakes or dwelling on what has been lost. Don't worry about what you don't have. The universe is generous when you're willing to use what you've been given.

STEPPING STONES: Culmination, climax, consummation, completion, conclusion, realization, accomplishment, actualization, fruition, fulfillment, ripeness, maturity, achievement, productivity, blessing.

PISCES 28 **A fertile garden under the full moon. KEYWORD:** *Ultimacy*

A fertile garden under the full moon

THEME: *Culmination.* This symbol speaks to an appreciation of the simple things in life. The image of a fertile garden under the full moon also alludes to reflection, expansion of consciousness and a deeper understanding of the importance of traditional accomplishments, or those achievements that are commonly recognized and valued by the average individual. There is also a melancholy or wistful undertone in this symbol. In his 1953 commentary, Marc Jones referred to the "lonely genius," comparing him to the average individual who is blessed by virtue of his being the collective embodiment of those features that ensure the survival of the race. There is no archetype for the individual genius, and thus whatever he creates of enduring worth is given over to the world and he goes his way alone. The creation of the Sabian symbols and commentary by Marc Edmund Jones is an example of such an immortal contribution. Positive: At its highest, this symbol represents material wealth, wisely administered. Negative: Greed, materialism and tasteless show.

TODAY: The accent is on reward and accomplishment. The fruits of your labor may manifest now in a tangible and satisfying way.

Opportunity: Your greatest advantage lies in sharing what you have with others. Use your gifts wisely.

Risk: Guard against boasting about your skills and possessions. Be sensitive to the possibility that you could make others feel deficient or somehow less worthy.

STEPPING STONES: Satisfaction, manifestation, accomplishment, prosperity, profusion, abundance, fruitfulness, productiveness, affluence, outpouring, fortune, plenty, success, victory, wealth, reward, riches, bounty.

PISCES 29   A prism. KEYWORD: *Validation*

a prism

THEME: *Analysis.* This symbol speaks to the delicate interplay between the parts and the whole of a thing, and it alludes to the fact that changing or altering a part can affect the ability of the whole to function effectively and maintain its stability. The image of a prism suggests looking at things and events from different angles, and it illustrates the process of analysis, or the attempt to understand how things work and what they can do. The implication here is that any whole can be interpreted through its parts, or that every part can be used as a tool to accurately measure the potential of the whole. In many ways this degree refers to the scientific process and its goal of being able to understand, predict and control. Positive: At its highest, this symbol represents keen judgment and highly developed analytical skills. Negative: Intellectual vanity and psychological manipulation.

TODAY: The accent is on analysis. You could find yourself perplexed about some condition or situation or wondering how to validate a hunch you have.

Opportunity: Your greatest advantage lies in being objective and using your reason. Break things down into small parts that are easy to analyze. Look at how each thing affects the other and how the parts reflect the whole. Pay attention to detail.

Risk: Guard against the temptation to use your knowledge to take unfair advantage or manipulate others for personal gain.

STEPPING STONES: Analysis of the whole through the parts, perspective, measurement, scientific process, verification, certification, confirmation, substantiation, validation, insight, intelligence, vision, comprehension, discernment, acumen, cognition, perception, discrimination, discretion, spectrum.

PISCES 30   **The Great Stone Face. KEYWORD:** *Discernment*

The great stone face

THEME: *A Tower of Strength*. This symbol speaks to the achievement of immortality through a consistent demonstration of responsibility that becomes a hallmark of personal distinction. It also speaks to self-transformation through the process of living an ideal. The image of The Great Stone Face refers to Nathaniel Hawthorne's story about a young boy named Ernest who grew up in the shadow of a majestic natural rock formation that resembled the head of a man. Day after day, and throughout the years, the boy naively projected his own benevolent nature and wisdom onto the granite head. He shaped his own destiny by developing in himself what he saw reflected in his beloved Great Stone Face. On a practical level, this symbol symbolizes stoicism, strength of character and reliability. It can also indicate the ability to mask emotions or resist emotional appeals. Positive: At its highest, this symbol represents keen judgment, self-discipline, integrity, and the ability to inspire others through monumental achievements. Negative: Emotional coldness or an inability to express the self effectively.

TODAY: The accent is on integrity and character. You may find yourself admiring someone and wishing you could be more like them.

Opportunity: Your greatest advantage lies in choosing your heroes and role models wisely. Have the courage to live your ideals.

Risk: Guard against compromising your values. Don't give in to pressure to relax your standards or go along with something you feel is wrong or immoral in order to avoid an unpleasant confrontation. Stand up for what you believe in.

STEPPING STONES: Immortality, character, personal distinction, integrity, responsibility, self-discipline, reliability, wisdom, dramatization of ideals, inspiration, self-realization, achievement.

NOTES

Notes

INTRODUCTION

1.   Marc Edmund Jones, *Blue Letter 1212*, "The Screen of Prophecy" (Stanwood, WA, 1/25/71).

2.   Jones, *Symbolical Astrology* (1931).

3.   Dane Rudhyar, *The Astrology of Personality* (Lucis Publishing Company, 1936)

4.   Jones, *The Sabian Symbols in Astrology* (New York: The Sabian Publishing Society, 1953), pp. 135-36.

5.   Rudhyar, *An Astrological Mandala: The Cycle of Transformations and Its 360 Symbolic Phases* (New York: Random House, 1973).

6.   Jones, *Sabian Symbols*, p. 140.

1. THE ORIGIN AND HISTORY OF THE SABIAN SYMBOLS

1.   Marc Edmund Jones, "The Dynamic Focus of Personality," *Dell Horoscope*, 1941.

2.   Jones, *Sabian Typescript Series*, Philosophy XXXII-7, [private issue for students of the Sabian Assembly] 10/22/79, p. 1.

3.   Jones, *Dell Horoscope*.

4.   Jones, *The Sabian Symbols in Astrology*. (New York: *The Sabian Publishing Society*, 1953), p. 135.

5.   Jones, *Sabian Typescript Series*, Philosophy XXXII-13, [private issue for students of the Sabian Assembly] 1/14/80, p. 2.

6.   Jones, *Fortnightly Field Notes* 889, (Stanwood, Washington, 4/28/73).

7.   Jones, *Sabian Typescript Series*, Philosophy XXXII-13, [private issue for students of the Sabian Assembly] 1/14/80, p. 2.

8.   Jones, *Fortnightly Field Notes* 274, (New York, New York, 10/8/49).

9.   Jones, *The Sabian Symbols in Astrology*, p. 333.

10.   Ibid., p. 334.

11.   Jones, *Sabian Typescript Series*, Astrology XXIX-4, [private issue for students of the Sabian Assembly] September 20, 1976, p. 8.

12.   Jones, *The Sabian Symbols in Astrology*, p. 334.

13.   Jones, *Sabian Typescript Series*, Philosophy XXXII-13, [private issue for students of the Sabian Assembly] 1/14/80, p. 2.

14.   Jones, *Sabian Typescript Series*, Astrology XXIX-6, [private issue for students of the Sabian Assembly] October 18, 1976, pp. 1-2.

15.   Jones, *The Sabian Symbols in Astrology*, p. 334.

16.   Dane Rudhyar, *An Astrological Mandala: The Cycle of Transformations and Its 360 Symbolic Phases* (New York: Random House, 1973), p. 391.

17.   Jones, *Sabian Typescript Series*, Philosophy XXXII-13, [private issue for students of the Sabian Assembly] 1/14/80, p. 2.

18.   Jones, *Fortnightly Field Notes* 889, (Stanwood, Washington, 4/28/73).

19.   Jones, *The Sabian Symbols in Astrology*, p. 135.

20.   Ibid., p. v.

21.   Ibid., pp. v-vi.

22.   Jones, *Fortnightly Field Notes* 889, (Stanwood, Washington, 4/28/73).

23.   Jones, *The Sabian Symbols in Astrology*, p. 330.

2. METHODS AND TECHNIQUES

1.   Marc Edmund Jones, *The Sabian Symbols in Astrology* (New York: The Sabian Publishing Society, 1953), p. 139.

2.   Dane Rudhyar, *An Astrological Mandala: The Cycle of Transformations and Its 360 Symbolic Phases* (New York: Random House, 1973), p. 356ff.

3.   Jones, *Sabian Symbols*, p. 102.

4.   Ibid., p. 103.

5.   Ibid., p. 126.

6.   Ibid., p. 124.

7.   Ibid., p. 141 ff.

8.   Ibid., p. 146 ff.

INDEX TO SABIAN SYMBOLS

Key to Astrological Glyphs

♈	ARIES	♎	LIBRA
♉	TAURUS	♏	SCORPIO
♊	GEMINI	♐	SAGITTARIUS
♋	CANCER	♑	CAPRICORN
♌	LEO	♒	AQUARIUS
♍	VIRGO	♓	PISCES

---

dog ♐ 21
domain ♏ 28
door ♐ 7, ♐ 24
double ♈ 25
dove ♉ 22, ♎ 26, ♒ 20
down ♏ 24, ♒ 23, ♓ 22
drawing ♍ 9, ♏ 20
dreaming ♍ 5
dress ♓ 6
dress parade ♓ 6
dressed ♋ 8, ♌ 4
drill ♓ 15
drilling ♊ 6
drink ♎ 22
drowning ♏ 11
duck ♈ 30
ducks ♏ 22
Dutch ♊ 15
duty ♏ 21

E

eagle ♎ 26, ♐ 12, ♒ 9
early ♌ 10
east ♈ 8
Easter ♐ 17, ♓ 17
edge ♌ 5
eggshell ♒ 7
electrical ♉ 2
embassy ♏ 12
embraces ♈ 1
emerging ♎ 12, ♒ 29
empty ♈ 18
enjoyed ♋ 15
enlightenment ♌ 22, ♐ 11
entering ♈ 21, ♐ 23, ♑ 4,
♑ 24, ♒ 14
entertaining ♈ 2
ephemeral ♒ 10
epidemic ♌ 2
eruption ♍ 17
evening ♌ 12, ♓ 20
everything ♎ 3
examination ♐ 21, ♓ 12
experience ♊ 11, ♒ 24
experimenting ♏ 13
explosion ♈ 13, ♍ 17

expressing ♈ 7
expression ♌ 14, ♍ 21
eyeglasses ♐ 21

F

face ♏ 16, ♓ 30
facing ♈ 8, ♋ 14, ♋ 24
fairies ♋ 7, ♍ 5, ♏ 28
fairy ♏ 23
falling ♊ 10
false ♍ 30
false call ♍ 30
family ♍ 14
fat ♐ 29
father ♏ 17
feathering ♋ 6
feeding ♈ 20, ♎ 7, ♑ 10
felled ♒ 28
fellowship ♏ 10
fence ♒ 15
fertile ♓ 28
field ♒ 30
figures ♒ 8
filled ♊ 9, ♒ 27
filling ♊ 2
finger ♉ 21
fire ♑ 13, ♒ 19
fireplace ♎ 8
first ♊ 29, ♍ 8
fish ♋ 9
five ♏ 15, ♑ 19
flag ♋ 1, ♍ 25, ♐ 12,
♐ 26, ♒ 9
flag-bearer ♐ 26
fledglings ♊ 23
flexed ♋ 13
flock ♈ 12
floor ♒ 22
flow ♓ 16
flowers ♉ 11
flying ♈ 8
folded ♌ 4
forest ♊ 27, ♒ 19, ♓ 3
formally ♌ 4
formations ♌ 5
formed ♉ 19, ♒ 25

N

narrow	♓ 4
nature	♑ 12
navy	♒ 3
nest	♊ 23
nests	♋ 6
net	♈ 24
new	♈ 10, ♊ 11, ♎ 3, ♓ 22, ♓ 26
new moon	♓ 26
newly	♉ 19
night	♋ 7
nonvested	♌ 17
noon	♎ 14
northeast	♋ 14
nude	♋ 9, ♑ 17
nurse	♉ 10
nursing	♋ 12

O

oak	♌ 11
ocean	♐ 2
officer	♓ 15
officers	♓ 6
oil	♊ 6
old	♈ 10, ♉ 16, ♊ 7, ♋ 14, ♌ 6, ♌ 13, ♎ 9, ♐ 5, ♐ 28, ♒ 1
old-fashioned	♊ 7, ♌ 6
once	♈ 7
one	♈ 6, ♋ 13, ♎ 26, ♏ 24, ♑ 2
open	♈ 24, ♉ 5, ♉ 21
opportunity	♈ 27, ♌ 14, ♐ 10, ♑ 30
orangutan	♍ 16
ornamental	♍ 15
other	♎ 26
ouija	♍ 18
out	♈ 1, ♉ 18, ♊ 27, ♍ 10, ♏ 22
outline	♈ 3
over	♉ 22, ♋ 2, ♋ 25, ♎ 11, ♐ 28

overeaten	♋ 15
overhead	♎ 27
owl	♐ 5
own	♏ 17

P

pageant	♌ 15
palms	♊ 25
paper	♍ 29
parade	♋ 8, ♓ 6
parading	♉ 30
park	♉ 25
parrot	♏ 19
party	♌ 12, ♌ 19, ♑ 4
passions	♒ 24
past	♐ 13
pastel	♈ 23
path	♊ 11
paths	♎ 15
paws	♒ 23
peacock	♉ 30
peering	♎ 11
pelicans	♐ 19
people	♋ 15, ♋ 26, ♒ 12
perfect	♎ 1
perfectly	♒ 25
perfectly formed	♒ 25
performer	♒ 6
performing	♋ 19
perfume	♏ 2
petrified	♓ 3
pheasants	♑ 11
phenomena	♓ 23
physical	♐ 11
piano	♊ 13
pigeon	♌ 22
pilgrimage	♑ 27
place	♋ 2
placed	♎ 18, ♒ 22
play	♒ 6, ♒ 22
playing	♉ 14, ♍ 4, ♏ 15, ♐ 3
pleading	♏ 29
Pocahontas	♋ 28
pointing	♉ 21
political	♍ 13

pond	♈ 30
Pope	♐ 30
popularity	♒ 10
possessed	♈ 26
pot	♉ 4
pottery	♒ 27
power	♍ 13, ♑ 7
precipice	♌ 5
preparing	♓ 15
president	♈ 11
priest	♋ 19
priesthood	♓ 25
prim	♈ 17
prima donna	♋ 21
prism	♓ 29
professor	♎ 11
profile	♈ 3
promenade	♓ 17
prominent	♋ 13
promise	♈ 25
propagandist	♌ 8
prophet	♑ 7
protecting	♎ 7
protection	♍ 3
proves	♒ 10
public	♉ 25, ♓ 1
pugilist	♈ 21
pupil	♓ 19
purging	♓ 25
pursued	♉ 28
Pyramids	♐ 14

Q

quenched	♒ 19
quiver	♊ 9

R

rabbi	♎ 20
rabbits	♋ 8
race	♍ 19, ♎ 2, ♑ 21
radical	♊ 5
rainbow	♉ 4, ♌ 26
rakish	♉ 15
reaching	♋ 9
reading	♋ 26, ♍ 29, ♑ 29

realism	♊ 11
realms	♈ 7
receptive	♑ 3
recognition	♑ 1, ♑ 23
Red Cross	♉ 10
regained	♈ 27
relay	♑ 21
relay race	♑ 21
republic	♐ 1
rescued	♏ 11
retired	♎ 17
reveal	♉ 16
Revolution	♋ 30
rich	♏ 18
rider	♌ 23
right	♋ 25, ♒ 25
ring	♈ 21
rises	♈ 1
robbers	♎ 19
rock	♌ 5
rocking	♌ 13
rocks	♐ 8, ♓ 7
rocky	♏ 5
romance	♉ 28
rowing	♑ 5
royal	♍ 22
rug	♑ 25, ♒ 22
rush	♏ 6

S

safety	♎ 10, ♏ 11
sailboat	♋ 22
Samaria	♉ 7
sand	♏ 15
Santa Claus	♊ 2
saucily	♊ 12
sawed	♒ 28
scalp	♉ 24
scratching	♋ 18
scroll	♋ 16
sculptor	♐ 27
sea	♌ 13, ♎ 17, ♏ 7, ♐ 16
sea captain	♌ 13, ♎ 17
sea gulls	♐ 16
seal	♈ 1

INDEX TO KEYWORDS

INDEX TO THEMES

Aries to Pisces

Taurus 9	The magic of sharing	Gemini 2	The magic of giving
Taurus 10	The magic of service	Gemini 3	The fruits of privilege
Taurus 11	The green thumb	Gemini 4	The magic of anticipation
Taurus 12	Looking at options	Gemini 5	Personal statements
Taurus 13	Putting forth the effort	Gemini 6	Taking a risk
Taurus 14	Respect for personality	Gemini 7	Regeneration
		Gemini 8	A call for change
Taurus 15	Nonchalance	Gemini 9	Survival
Taurus 16	Finding the right way to get the message across	Gemini 10	Free fall
		Gemini 11	Practical involvement
		Gemini 12	Self-assertion
Taurus 17	Competing factors	Gemini 13	Creative fulfillment
Taurus 18	Making things better	Gemini 14	Invisible ties
		Gemini 15	Common interests
Taurus 19	Fresh opportunity	Gemini 16	Liberty and justice for all
Taurus 20	Holding to center	Gemini 17	Maturation
Taurus 21	Reconsideration	Gemini 18	Specialization
Taurus 22	A higher call	Gemini 19	History lessons
Taurus 23	All that glitters	Gemini 20	A full supply for here and now
Taurus 24	The conqueror		
Taurus 25	Group work	Gemini 21	Protest
Taurus 26	Romance	Gemini 22	A good time
Taurus 27	Intrinsic value	Gemini 23	Give it a try
Taurus 28	No time like the present	Gemini 24	Adventures in experience
Taurus 29	Different points of view	Gemini 25	Dedication
		Gemini 26	Temporary setback
Taurus 30	Pride		
		Gemini 27	In search of success
GEMINI			
		Gemini 28	Starting over
Gemini 1	Window of opportunity	Gemini 29	Awakening
		Gemini 30	The appearance of things

Leo 25	Endurance	Virgo 21	Team spirit
Leo 26	Hope	Virgo 22	The rights of privilege
Leo 27	New beginnings		
Leo 28	Rising above the petty	Virgo 23	Achieving mastery
Leo 29	Doing what comes naturally	Virgo 24	Eternal spring
		Virgo 25	Reputation
Leo 30	Trust	Virgo 26	Wonderment
		Virgo 27	The conclave
VIRGO		Virgo 28	The power of personality
Virgo 1	Integrity	Virgo 29	Discovering deeper meaning
Virgo 2	Testimony		
Virgo 3	Invisible assistance	Virgo 30	A higher call to duty
Virgo 4	Integration		
Virgo 5	The magic of vision	**LIBRA**	
Virgo 6	Cycles of experience	Libra 1	Emergence
		Libra 2	Light on the path
Virgo 7	Retreat and regroup		
		Libra 3	Fresh start
Virgo 8	Learning how to do it	Libra 4	Fellowship
		Libra 5	Congruency
Virgo 9	Personal distinction	Libra 6	Manifesting the ideal
Virgo 10	Objectivity	Libra 7	Balancing opposite forces
Virgo 11	Shaping the future		
Virgo 12	A moment of truth	Libra 8	Matters of the heart
		Libra 9	Self-integration
Virgo 13	Taking the reins	Libra 10	Proficiency
Virgo 14	Background as influence	Libra 11	Scholarship
		Libra 12	Plumbing the depths
Virgo 15	Noblesse oblige		
Virgo 16	Primitive urges	Libra 13	The art of play
Virgo 17	A dramatic outburst	Libra 14	Taking it easy
		Libra 15	Wheel of life
Virgo 18	Extrasensory perception	Libra 16	The opportunity in loss
Virgo 19	Competition	Libra 17	The melody lingers on
Virgo 20	Group adventure		

Sagittarius 7	The glory of love	Capricorn 4	Group support
Sagittarius 8	Building on firm foundations	Capricorn 5	Marshaling resources
Sagittarius 9	The teacher	Capricorn 6	Piercing the veil
Sagittarius 10	Looking beyond surface appearances	Capricorn 7	Mastership
		Capricorn 8	Jubilation
		Capricorn 9	Inspiration
		Capricorn 10	The golden rule
Sagittarius 11	Approximation	Capricorn 11	Variation
Sagittarius 12	Transformation	Capricorn 12	Clarification
Sagittarius 13	Forgiveness	Capricorn 13	The magician
Sagittarius 14	Building on the past	Capricorn 14	Enduringness
		Capricorn 15	Coming together
Sagittarius 15	Checking things out	Capricorn 16	Esprit de corps
		Capricorn 17	The bare essentials
Sagittarius 16	Staying alert to opportunity	Capricorn 18	Sovereignty
Sagittarius 17	Upliftment	Capricorn 19	Great expectations
Sagittarius 18	Health and well-being	Capricorn 20	Resolution
Sagittarius 19	Migration	Capricorn 21	Teamwork
Sagittarius 20	The grasshopper and the ants	Capricorn 22	The chess player
		Capricorn 23	Good conduct
Sagittarius 21	Scrutiny	Capricorn 24	The retreat
Sagittarius 22	Self-sufficiency	Capricorn 25	Spiritual materialism
Sagittarius 23	Trying something new	Capricorn 26	The light touch
Sagittarius 24	Providence	Capricorn 27	The high road
Sagittarius 25	Rehearsal	Capricorn 28	Networking
Sagittarius 26	Honor	Capricorn 29	The screen of prophecy
Sagittarius 27	Shaping destiny		
Sagittarius 28	What should be is	Capricorn 30	Executive session
Sagittarius 29	Effort		

AQUARIUS

Sagittarius 30	A call to higher service	Aquarius 1	Spiritual foundations
		Aquarius 2	The probability of the improbable

CAPRICORN

Capricorn 1	Confrontation	Aquarius 3	Endings are beginnings
Capricorn 2	Reverence		
Capricorn 3	Readiness		

GENERAL INDEX

Better books make better astrologers.
Here are some of our other titles:

AstroAmerica's Daily Ephemeris, 2010-2020
AstroAmerica's Daily Ephemeris, 2000-2020
  - both for Midnight. Compiled & formatted by David R. Roell

Al Biruni
The Book of Instructions in the Elements of the Art of Astrology, *1029 AD,*
  translated by R. Ramsay Wright

Derek Appleby
Horary Astrology: The Art of Astrological Divination

E. H. Bailey
The Prenatal Epoch

Joseph Blagrave
Astrological Practice of Physick

C.E.O. Carter
The Astrology of Accidents
An Encyclopaedia of Psychological Astrology
Essays on the Foundations of Astrology
The Principles of Astrology, *Intermediate no. 1*
Some Principles of Horoscopic Delineation, *Intermediate no. 2*
Symbolic Directions in Modern Astrology
The Zodiac and the Soul

Charubel & Sepharial
Degrees of the Zodiac Symbolized, *1898*

Nicholas Culpeper
Astrological Judgement of Diseases from the Decumbiture of the Sick, *1655,*
  and, **Urinalia,** *1658*

Dorotheus of Sidon
Carmen Astrologicum, *c. 50 AD, translated by David Pingree*

Nicholas deVore
Encyclopedia of Astrology

Firmicus Maternus
Ancient Astrology Theory & Practice: Matheseos Libri VIII,
c. 350 AD, translated by Jean Rhys Bram

William Lilly
Christian Astrology, *books 1 & 2, 1647*
  The Introduction to Astrology, Resolution of all manner of questions.
Christian Astrology, *book 3, 1647*
  Easie and plaine method teaching how to judge upon nativities.

Alan Leo
The Progressed Horoscope, *1905*

Jean-Baptiste Morin
The Cabal of the Twelve Houses Astrological, *translated by George Wharton,*
  edited by D.R. Roell

Claudius Ptolemy
Tetrabiblos, *c. 140 AD, translated by J.M. Ashmand*
  The great book, in the classic translation.

Vivian Robson
Astrology and Sex
Electional Astrology
Fixed Stars & Constellations in Astrology

Richard Saunders
The Astrological Judgement and Practice of Physick, *1677*
  By the Richard who inspired Ben Franklin's famous Almanac.

Sepharial
Primary Directions, a definitive study
  A complete, detailed guide.

Sepharial On Money. *For the first time in one volume, complete texts:*
  • **Law of Values**
  • **Silver Key**
  • **Arcana, or Stock and Share Key** — *first time in print!*

James Wilson, Esq.
Dictionary of Astrology
  From 1820. Quirky, opinionated, a fascinating read.

H.S. Green, Raphael & C.E.O. Carter
Mundane Astrology: *3 Books, complete in one volume.*
  A comprehensive guide to political astrology

If not available from your local bookseller, order directly from:
The Astrology Center of America
207 Victory Lane
Bel Air, MD 21014

on the web at:
http://www.astroamerica.com

Milton Keynes UK
Ingram Content Group UK Ltd.
UKHW020656010824
1115UKWH00011B/94